IN THE SHADOW OF
THE DOME

ALSO BY MARK BISNOW

DIARY OF A DARK HORSE:
The 1980 Anderson Presidential Campaign

IN THE SHADOW

OF THE

DOME

CHRONICLES OF A CAPITOL HILL AIDE

Mark Bisnow

WILLIAM MORROW AND COMPANY, INC.

New York

Copyright © 1990 by Mark Bisnow

Recognizing the importance of preserving what has been written, it is the policy of William Morrow and Company, Inc., and its imprints and affiliates to have the books it publishes printed on acid-free paper, and we exert our best efforts to that end.

Library of Congress Cataloging-in-Publication Data

Bisnow, Mark, 1952–
In the shadow of the dome : chronicles of a Capitol Hill aide /
Mark Bisnow.
p.   cm.
ISBN 0-688-08719-1
1. United States.   Congress—Officials and employees.   I. Title.
JK1083.B57   1990
328.73'0761—dc20   89-13674
                                                       CIP

Printed in the United States of America

First Edition

1 2 3 4 5 6 7 8 9 10

BOOK DESIGN BY RICHARD ORIOLO

*To my parents
with love*

CONTENTS

III. THE SENATE

IV. CAMPAIGN

V. JOINT COMMITTEE

VI. MAJORITY LEADER

FOREWORD

At a recent conference committee on appropriations, Democrat Edward Roybal of California, the leader of the House conferees, objected to the Senate's refusal to broaden the authority of the Treasury Department's inspector general.

Roybal told Democrat Dennis DeConcini of Arizona, the leader of the Senate conferees:

"The language is not acceptable to the staff and I can't work with a staff that's not happy."

Staff? Not happy? Language not acceptable?

What does the staff being happy or unhappy have to do with public policy?

The answer, in short, is everything.

Roybal's comment was a startling admission that his staff knew more and felt more strongly about the issue than he did. The fact is, to be effective, members of Congress must surrender almost unconditionally to their staffs. They simply cannot do it all.

Gone, of course, are the days when Harley M. Dirks, Senator Warren Magnuson's staff man of the Appropriations Committee, inserted faked testimony into the printed hearings to make it appear the absent Magnuson had been present.

Gone also are the days when Martin Sweig, Speaker John McCormack's aide, was riding high and would pick up the telephone and, in a voice that matched his boss's in timber, accent, and pitch, announce: "This is the Speaker calling."

Today it is frequently the reverse. That is, the power of the congressional staff is such that they don't have to imitate anybody. They call on their own recognizance, so to speak.

The Capitol's staff now forms a second, separate layer of government.

If proof is needed, go down to Glynn County, near Brunswick, in southeast Georgia to the Federal Law Enforcement Training Center. One of its buildings is the Aubrey A. Gunnels Dormitory Complex.

Who is Aubrey A. Gunnels? A famous G-man? A DEA agent shot to death in Central America? A Texas Ranger?

No. None of the above. Aubrey A. Gunnels is the staff director of the House Appropriations Subcommittee on Treasury, Postal Service, and General Government, a thirty-year veteran of the Hill with what the *Washington Post* called "ancient connections into every nook and cranny . . . from the Secret Service to the Treasury's Bureau of Alcohol, Tobacco and Firearms."

In the old days on Capitol Hill, you had to have a vote to get a building named in your honor.

Over the years, the standard way of measuring (and decrying) the influence of the congressional staff has been by head count—"20,000 congressional staffers . . . three times the number in the mid-1970s . . . grown six times faster than the population . . . etc., etc."

But numbers do not take into account quality, dedication, professionalism, idealism, and camaraderie.

Washington lawyer Harry McPherson, who worked for both Lyndon Johnson and Mike Mansfield in the Senate, wrote in his autobiography, *A Political Education:*

"There was an esprit de corps among us, something of the irreverence of valets toward great masters, something of their pride in reflected glory."

Now comes another valuable and perceptive addition to the growing body of literature about congressional staffs. Mark Bisnow's account is a personal one, not a numerical one; it is real, not theoretical; and it comes from a participant wise beyond his years who has seen Congress from both houses and both sides of the aisle.

The national legislature could not have a finer guide.

ROGER MUDD

ACKNOWLEDGMENTS

I am deeply indebted to friends who read the manuscript in various stages and offered immensely constructive criticism: journalists Alan Murray, Evan Thomas, and Bernard Weinraub; Congressional scholars Alan Ehrenhalt, Alton Frye, Norman Ornstein, and Stephen Wayne; and critics-at-large Jeff Baker, Richard Danzig, Peter Galbraith, Abigail McCarthy, and Robert Machol. Their collective comments gave cause for much rewriting, but of course they bear no responsibility for the failings that remain. My agent, Raphael Sagalyn, lent me his renowned knowledge of the publishing world. My editor, Adrian Zackheim at Morrow, assisted by Pamela Altschul, masterfully brought the project to fruition.

The original idea for this book came from John Kenneth Galbraith. He is known to most of the world as the eminent economist and social critic, but better known to me as the father of two close friends described herein and the kindly gentleman who (together with his wife, Catherine) gave me residence in his home during my return to law school after several years on the Hill. One day, as we raked leaves in the backyard, he asked me whether I had ever considered writing a memoir of my years as a congressional staffer. No, I laughed: "Why would I?" Because people ought to see Congress the way it really works, he said. Yes, he repeated with charming certitude, that's what you must do. I thanked him politely for the idea, but put it out of mind; at the moment I was thinking mainly of impending exams. Only years later, as I was again leaving the Hill, this time fresh from participation in Byzantine staff maneuvers on the trade bill, did I remember our conversation.

By far my largest debt is to my wife, Margot, who was not only flexible in trading hours of baby duty as required but who sustained me through a largely weekend and nocturnal project with unceasing wisdom and love; and to my young children, Elliott and Austin, who did what they could to prevent the completion of my task—but whose affection put everything in perspective. They have also made me understand better what I owe my own parents, to whom I dedicate this book.

1

LIFE IN THE SHADOW: INTRODUCTION AND PURPOSES

The hour hand edged toward midnight on the clock above, but Senator John Danforth had settled at my desk on the second floor of the Capitol, propped up his feet, and asked if I had any interesting memos he could read. Danforth was an impressively intellectual legislator, but his unusual request at this late hour, I knew, had less to do with an inquisitive mind than with sheer political horse sense. All evening I (as an aide to Senate Republican Leader Bob Dole) had been cloistered in negotiations on the 1987 trade bill with Danforth's aide, Sue Schwab—a young, knowledgeable, and above all savvy adviser who had brought her boss to my office at just the right moment. Our discussion had foundered on a key word, and Danforth, one of the Senate's most influential players on trade issues, firmly urged us to find a middle ground. No doubt Sue expected that his hovering presence would quickly bring me around.

She was almost right. Senator Danforth himself did not participate in our continuing talks—he knew that Sue was better versed in the details and had utmost confidence in her judgment—but with tactical adroitness he wandered into the adjoining conference room regularly to see how we were doing and to remind us that he was waiting. Meanwhile Senator Dole, who as party leader juggled many simultaneous obligations, had departed the office to other activities, delegating me to reach a compromise in his behalf. Under normal circumstances it might have been hard to resist Danforth's entreaties; he was, after all, a United States senator, and not least a friendly and important member of my boss's party. But earlier in the day I had recommended to Dole what I thought our position ought to be, and he had, in his clear if laconic way, nodded and told me to "work it out." Now I felt an obligation to protect his interests.

Fortunately I was not left holding the fort alone: I had invited an ex-Dole aide and one-time Reagan trade adviser, Claud Gingrich, to stop by and lend a second opinion; and current Reagan trade officials Alan Holmer and Judy Bello had agreed to station themselves in the Senate Reception Room, a hundred yards away, to supply needed detail, for which purpose I shuttled through darkened corridors once or twice during the evening. Sheila Burke, Dole's hardworking chief-of-staff, remained on the scene, as she often did, late into the night, and aides from other offices continually passed through. The Leader's suite functioned as a nerve center for the Senate, and in these gilded and high-ceilinged rooms, crystal chandeliers gazing over our work, it was easy indeed to feel powerful. Claud, Alan, and Judy agreed strongly with the position I had staked out, and Sheila offered her traditional encouragement. Ultimately I persuaded myself that our position was no less than critical to U.S. trade policy—and that Senator Danforth's presence, if anything, signified his eagerness for a result, giving us the upper hand if we could simply hold out.

Suddenly Dole phoned in for a status report. Sheila took the call, explaining that we were stalled on one word and describing Danforth's exasperation. It happened that the word was pivotal; we were drafting what would be enacted as the "Super 301" provision of the trade law, requiring retaliation against foreign markets hostile to American exports, and the language we chose would determine how many specific countries and practices an administration would be mandated to target. But the idea that one word could divide us admittedly sounded trivial, and Dole, who deservedly possessed a reputation as the Senate's most effective legislator, instructed us to give Danforth what he wanted. To Dole it was not worth the fight that I had supposed; he calculated that in return for a concession Danforth would give us something on another occasion when it mattered more. The negotiation was quickly adjourned.

Moments like this captured the delight and frustration of an aide. I had helped draft a major initiative—most of which would survive the intervention of my boss, become law, and have real impact. And yet I had latitude only as he gave it to me. I gladly accepted the arrangement. No one had elected me; it was exciting enough to operate in the shadow of public figures and satisfying enough to be able to invest public policy with as much of my own viewpoint as I did.

Usually the implication of a memoir is that the writer's life has had historical significance that deserves to be commemorated for posterity. I harbor no such illusion. Thousands of Capitol Hill aides have had experiences similar to my own, and some far more consequential. Rather, I have written what follows because I believe that there is value in telling the story of an *ordinary* staffer privileged to work in the Congress of the United States.

In the last twenty years the legislative branch has become far more staff-driven than many recognize. Americans still elect 535 men and women to the House and Senate, of course, but the Congress now includes, by various counts, between 16,000 and 40,000 aides. More than simply a large city hall, it has come to resemble an entire city. Yet countless otherwise well-informed citizens maintain touchingly antiquated notions about it. They seem to think, for example, that when their congressman sends them a letter, he has personally dictated and signed it; that when he gives a speech or publishes an op-ed column, he has personally conceived and written it; that when he submits legislation, he has researched and labored over its many details. Sometimes, of course, these assumptions are valid; most congressmen are smart and diligent. But more often, as Hill staffers can tell you, much of a legislator's daily work has been delegated. It may well be that the country is too large, the issues too numerous and complex, to do otherwise. It may also be that Congress tries to do more than it should.

The absence of public knowledge about congressional staff is startling. One would be hard-pressed to find elsewhere a group so bright, energetic, and civic-spirited—or one that exercises so much influence under other people's names. Although it is logical to think that aides are simply an extension of the members of Congress who employ them, in a sense they lead a highly independent existence. Many have no initial connection to the offices where they find work and over the years freely move about among them. They may arrive in the Congress much sooner than their employers and inhabit its halls much longer. Or they may move on and off the Hill with virtual abandon. The matters they work on are often unrelated to a member's constituency, and if pressed, some would be unable to define their district's basic geographical or demographic characteristics. Their loyalty, in short, may be as much to the Congress as a whole, or to their own personal careers, as to the individual members who hired them. Not surprisingly staffers have developed their own culture and values, which ultimately give Congress much of its day-to-day personality.

For all this, Congress is often explained either through scholarly works that impart no real flavor of everyday life or through those that focus on elected officials, the celebrities of Capitol Hill who live in a more rarefied political stratosphere. Surprisingly there are few works on Congress written by staff, and those that exist tend to be circumscribed in their portrayal of staff life, describing (in one case) a week in the life of the Senate or (in another) the year-long journey of a single bill. My purpose has been broader. I have sought to give a sense of the challenging if often undramatic routine of a modern congressional aide who works in numerous roles over many years and in so doing to address topical aspects of career staff life: how and why young people go to the Hill, what jobs and responsibilities they perform there, the customs and colleagues they encounter, the thrills and satisfactions they find in their work, the frustrations that may cause them to leave.

In part therefore this book is meant to be a primer for young people—perhaps still in college or working on political campaigns—who may have contemplated a job in Congress or in a state or local legislative environment. In addition it is intended to help illuminate the internal workings of Congress for the many Washingtonians—executive branch and foreign-embassy personnel, lawyers and lobbyists— who deal professionally with the institution. Most of all it is an effort to update average citizens on the much-changed contemporary character of the American democratic process.

Inevitably this has been a book about my own generation, the story of someone who came to political consciousness in the heady days of Vietnam and Watergate and wanted to go to Washington to see for himself what it was all about. In recent years, when so many college graduates have dreamed instead of going to Wall Street, the idea of seeking fulfillment on Capitol Hill might have seemed far-fetched. Yet as current scandals bring the cult of money into disrepute, it may be that Washington will gain new appeal as a destination for those who want to sublimate their energies into public-spirited activities. To me the city still holds the promise of excitement and opportunity that I first glimpsed nearly twenty years ago.

A word about my own career and political paths. For better or worse I have always valued (at least in my youth) professional adventure and new experience; as such, I was eager to sample Hill life in its many facets and willing to move around to do so. Such spontaneity is not for everyone, but I feel greatly enriched for the unusual variety of my jobs and wiser for the broad vantage point they gave me. Off and on I spent a total of ten years there, during which time I worked in the House and the Senate; on personal staffs, committee staffs, and a leadership staff; for junior members and senior members; for Republicans and Democrats; and even in a presidential campaign. The bulk of this experience occurred during my twenties. As the reader will learn, I took several years out toward the end (to study and practice law) and then returned one last time with a nostalgic but perhaps more critical perspective. Now I am back to lawyering, but still one of those people who look forward every day to consuming the news columns in the morning papers and care with some passion about the outcome of events. As for my politics, I have tended in recent years to support "moderate" Republicans (for example, I was a Dole, then Bush, supporter in 1988), but remain registered as an independent. This latter status is rare in official Washington, but I value the intellectual freedom it gives me to vote or work for the particular men or women I choose.

I must also acknowledge an ambivalence in my perspectives on staff. In one sense they are the Hill's unsung heroes; it might well be said that behind every successful congressman is a good aide (or, more accurately, many). Congress has required sizable resources to redress historical accretions of executive power and to reassert the proper legislative role in lawmaking; staff is essential in helping Congress to master increasingly complex issues and shoulder ever-wider responsibilities. And personally I enjoyed my years as a staffer—so much so that I have wanted to write about and relive them.

Yet over the years I have come to wonder whether a good thing has been carried too far. A larger congressional bureaucracy sometimes generates, as well as alleviates, demands on members' time; it sometimes heightens, rather than relieves, tensions with the executive branch. This should come as no surprise; it would not be the only line of work in which too many cooks can spoil a broth. Staff also provide questionable election advantages to incumbents. And there is, finally, the central question of whether, even if everything staff did was a good thing, it is right to invest so much power in those who are neither elected nor confirmed. Perhaps in the end what one thinks about the power of staff is determined by what one thinks about the power of Congress. The more you believe legislators should be encouraged to review and possibly reverse presidential actions, the more you ought to like staff—for they are the ones that help them do it.

Personally I favor an activist, powerful Congress—on the big issues. The concern I have is that Congress has become at least equally involved in the small issues, where I think it often does not belong. At turns in this book, therefore, I express my doubts about staff proliferation. But I know that readers examining the same evidence can arrive at different conclusions. Whatever our prescriptions, I hope we can acknowledge sharing the same objective: to strengthen the Congress as a thoughtful and effective institution of government.

2

EVOLUTION OF THE SPECIES

Until the end, it never occurred to me how my own experience might parallel that of the man I saw first on Little League opening day of 1961. The dugouts at Franklin Field No. 6 in Van Nuys, California, were beribboned in patriotic colors, and the bleachers spilled over with legions of proud parents. The winning raffle tickets had been announced, and the starting lineups were ready to take the field. Suddenly from out of the sky a helicopter appeared and moments later, with deafening noise and a swirl of infield dust, landed to cap off the official ceremonies. The aircraft was ferrying an important visitor— local U.S. Congressman James C. Corman—who would bid the players good luck and throw out the first ball.

I was almost nine years old, my team's first baseman, and until that moment had been daydreaming about double plays, center-field homers, and a season of Sno-Kones yet to come. Indeed my proudest possession was a large mitt that showcased the autographs of local baseball stars, such as Bo Belinsky of the Los Angeles Angels. Now came a politician into my life, alighting from his vehicle as the rotor still spun and looking nearly as heroic as a winning pitcher. When the dust settled, I had added his scrawl, too, and for many seasons more would remember him whenever I looked down at my glove moments after I had put a runner out at first.

The events of that day must have stirred my subconscious, for I made contact with Corman again. I was fourteen years old and had written his office to request help in obtaining a pen used by the president. It seemed to me that average citizens, not just VIPs, deserved such things; of course I hoped that having a presidential pen would make me a VIP myself. In a few months I was summoned to the congressman's local office to receive a pen used by Lyndon Johnson to sign into law a Corman-sponsored bill creating the new Federal Judicial Center (which only years later did I learn anything about—it trains judges). Knowing little of politics, I imagined that Corman had complied with the request solely out of an interest in advancing the aspirations of young people. That may have been part of it, but the presence at his office of a photographer from the *Valley News and Green Sheet*, a much read local advertiser, should have tipped me off to a more compelling motive: another useful press notice in a representative's never-ending quest for reelection.

Still more years passed and I began seeing Corman frequently in the halls of Congress once I started working there. He was by now quite influential, focusing on important tax policy issues, and I was proud to think he represented my hometown. But although he was also known as a gentle and approachable politician, I did not actually talk to him again until early 1977, when President Gerald Ford came to Congress to deliver his farewell address. Ford was not especially revered in those waning days of power, and ushers in the House of Representatives chamber, where he would speak, were having trouble filling it with congressmen. To avoid photographs of an embarrassingly low turnout, they decided at the last minute to allow staff members standing in the back of the hall to claim empty seats. I found myself by coincidence next to Corman and, as the diplomatic corps and others ceremonially filed in, reminded him that we had met before. He said he remembered and suggested that we try to get together some time, but I assumed he was a busy man merely rendering a polite gesture.

Only in the spring of 1985, eight years later, did I take him up on it. He had been defeated in the election of 1980 in rather notorious circumstances. Jimmy Carter made an early concession speech before the polls had closed on the West Coast, and many disappointed Democrats there did not bother to cast votes; Corman lost by a thin margin, and commentators blamed the president for Corman's unexpected political demise. When I saw the ex-congressman now, he was sitting anonymously in the back of the cavernous and crowded hearing room of the House Ways and Means Committee, on which he had once served as a senior member. He had since become a Washington-based lawyer specializing in lobbying the Hill. In his sixties, he had remarried and even started a new family. He seemed to enjoy being recognized, and now when he suggested getting together, it occurred to me that he might really have time to do so.

Shortly afterward we had breakfast, and I recalled to him the first occasion we had met, at the very beginning of his congressional career. He had a vivid recollection: "I thought that damn helicopter was going to crash in the middle of your Little League field." Corman's new status was poignant, faintly like that of a deposed monarch. No longer at the height of his power, he was now an ordinary citizen consigned to taking his breakfast at a nondescript diner near his office rather than the elegant Members' Dining Room, a workaday Washingtonian rather than an exotic Californian ambassador. And yet there was something revivifying about him as well: He had been relieved of the demanding existence of minute-by-minute schedules and unrelenting pressures to tailor a public image. Instead he was permitted at last to lead a leisurely and private personal life. He seemed at once nostalgic yet liberated.

Corman's political career, I see now, is a paradigm of the congressional life cycle, not only for congressmen but also for the staffers who walk in their shadows. As the pages that follow suggest, denizens of Capitol Hill typically start out with high ideals and large ambitions, become absorbed in the alternately glamorous and grating aspects of their jobs, and finally leave, however reluctantly, with an audible sigh of relief. But they also take with them the gratification that they have contributed to the larger causes of their country and done something interesting with their lives. Compared with Corman, I was only a bit player; but in our own ways we traveled the same path—and, for my part, I believe would do it all again.

PART I

STARTING OUT

Sacramento, 1970. Governor Ronald Reagan invited Senator William Coombs
to bring his whole staff to the office—even the seventeen-year-old intern.
CHARLES (JACK) GIBBS

3

THE MAKING OF
A POLITICAL JUNKIE

In the late summer of 1988 my wife and I took to the back roads of France for a week-long vacation. The Republican convention was poised to nominate George Bush for president, but the identity of his running mate was as yet unknown. By now I had left the Hill, but old fascinations die hard, and the suspense of not knowing who would be chosen plagued us even in the tranquillity of the rolling Burgundian countryside. Every hour we tuned our car radio to the crackling sounds of the BBC's news summary, the only English-language station we could locate. (We deemed our ability in the French language to be unreliable for such important matters.)

At last, through the static, we heard the stunning report that it would be Dan Quayle. Although the Indiana senator was well known on Capitol Hill, his name had not figured in serious speculation, and when we arrived shortly in the medieval town of Beaune for lunch, we were still discussing the news breathlessly. We took a table in an outdoor café and heard some American voices nearby; they were among the first we had encountered in several days. Anxious to share our discovery with out-of-touch compatriots, we ran up and shouted, "It's Quayle! It's Quayle!"

"Who's Quayle?" they answered. "What's Quayle?"

It turned out these travelers were barely aware a convention was being held, and they certainly had never heard of Senator Quayle. Nor did they seem to share our intensity of interest in the matter. In fact we could tell from the look on their faces that they thought we were pretty much off our rockers.

I guess you could say that over the years I had become somewhat more obsessed with politics than the rest of the world. Yet I think back fondly on how it happened.

A portly figure with finely combed-back white hair rose from his chair in the California state senate chamber and turned in my direction. He squinted to make me out, laid aside a sheaf of letters he had been signing, and, with the gait of a man much older than his sixty years, edged slowly past several colleagues and toward the back of the chamber where I waited.

It was June 1970, and I had come nervously to Sacramento for the first job interview of my life. The prospect was only that of a summer position before my sophomore year of college, but conservative state senator William Coombs, the man now approaching me, had conditioned my employment on his meeting me first. So I stood rehearsing answers to a hundred imagined questions and, luggage at my side, worrying that I would be told to return to the airport from which I had just hauled much of my personal wardrobe.

"Good morning, Senator Coombs," I said in my most polite voice. Coombs looked me over a moment. "They let you in college with such short hair?" he asked. He turned to an aide and broke into a relieved smile; I was not the hippie he had feared. "A fine young man," he said. "We'll take him." In fact I possessed no strongly developed political philosophy—I had been assigned to Coombs randomly—but I evidently compensated for this by an elementary sense of job-interview techniques. Given the era's common suspicion of long-haired youths, I had arrived at the capital with my hair uncharacteristically trimmed for the occasion.

His arm now around me, Coombs lost no time administering my induction into the local political fraternity. We went across the street to a luncheon buffet sponsored by the state railroad lobby, where for added effect he seated me next to the president of the state senate,

Hugh Burns, then a venerable figure in Sacramento. Burns was retiring from office at the end of the term and joked during much of the meal about the letters he was intending to write constituents now that he was safe from their electoral disapprobation. To one woman in particular who had been persistent over the years in her inquiries, requests, and complaints, he planned to dictate a valedictory note that afternoon: "Dear Madam," he chuckled, "Fuck you." All at once I felt transported to the fabled backrooms of politics to hear such invigorating talk my very first day on the job.

It was a startling transition. I had signed up for this summer stint with only a tentative interest in politics. Two years before, I had seen Robert Kennedy at a presidential campaign rally in my hometown but, while supporting his antiwar message, lacked the passion of many in the chanting crowd around me. Of course as a fifteen-year-old I would have had trouble identifying Vietnam on a map. Although young people of the time were expressing themselves in regular spasms of political activity, I had yet to march, join a sit-in, or otherwise protest the actions of my elders.

My passivity did not much change throughout the first year of college—I was perhaps too studious—and if I had come now to Sacramento, it was as much to see the sights and have an adventure away from home as to make a political statement. During twelve weeks there I served as something called an intern, in theory a brief apprenticeship in politics designed to provide an inside glimpse of government and elicit a sympathetic view in return. But the title glorified the humbler character of the job, and it was a more telling fact that as a birthday present at the end of the summer my office awarded me the metal letter opener that I had used so effectively during my tenure.

The experience, however, galvanized my interest in politics—and upset some of my most treasured stereotypes. Senator Coombs, for example, turned out not to be the entrenched and grasping officeholder I assumed to populate state capitals, even if his courtly qualities placed him on the far side of a deep generational divide. He was a certified public accountant from a small community who had sought elective office only late in life, apparently inspired by a concern about student rebellion and the rising challenge to traditional values. In manner he was mild and soft-spoken, and thus it was to my surprise, laboring under student images of the day, that he was not only a Republican but one pronounced to be among the state's "best" legislators by the local chapter of the ultrarightist John Birch Society.

His principal aide, Dick Reddick, who acted as my affable supervisor, subsequently became publisher of *Human Events*, a newspaper renowned for similar leanings. Yet he commented to me once that the best thing about politicians was the way they could talk to each other even if they disagreed. I thought of this years later when I observed the friendship of California congressmen John Burton and John Rousselot. Burton was an irreverent Bay Area liberal who had been a legislator in Sacramento during my time there; he was famous for wearing red-white-and-blue socks onto the assembly floor in displays of mock patriotism. Rousselot, from Orange County, was known as a card-carrying Bircher. There was not much on which these two could have seen eye-to-eye, but they kidded each other and helped keep their differing opinions in perspective.

So my impressions of government turned on the personalities I encountered in scores of similar informal contacts that summer. At a welcoming picnic for interns on the capitol lawn, Senator Walter Stern, chairman of the powerful Revenue and Taxation Committee, challenged me to guess his original profession. "A lawyer," I said confidently. "Nope," he grinned. "A teacher," said a friend. "An accountant," surmised another. By this time our inquisitor was beaming with the delight he had no doubt shown on countless identical occasions before. "A veterinarian!" he announced triumphantly. We marveled at the revelation, and our views about politicians would never be quite the same.

Cocktail receptions were similarly educational. (Although they were intended as a convenient place for the mingling of lobbyists and legislators, we interns—who wangled invitations in whatever way possible—valued them more for their collateral benefit: free food.) At one a fellow intern rushed over to those of us congregated at the buffet table. "You see that guy," he said, pointing to a prominent Republican assemblyman who had just entered the room. We listened expectantly. "He drove his car onto the Capitol steps one night." "Was he . . . ?" I hesitated. My friend finished the sentence: "Drunker than all outdoors." "Wow!" I said, another stereotype shattered. "Awright!" said one of my colleagues from a faster crowd, approvingly.

After a while the highest officials had descended the pedestals in our minds, and we began to treat them on our own terms. One evening Willie Brown, a hip young assemblyman, in later years to become Speaker of the assembly, came to meet with us at our summer quarters in a dormitory of Sacramento State University. After a stirring speech about the need to broaden participation in the political system, a young woman arose to ask the first question: "Where do you buy those *fabulous* clothes?" (Brown gave a detailed explanation.) Those were not our only concerns. Following an otherwise solemn discussion with the head of the state's public health service, several of us gathered around him—to ask for personal advice on acne.

Eventually we entered even lions' dens with abandon. One day a friend and I met with Ed Meese, executive secretary to then governor Ronald Reagan. Meese had been instrumental in persuading Reagan to call out the National Guard in response to recent student demonstrations, and we were prepared for a hostile reception. But he turned out to be perfectly amiable, welcoming us into his office and leaning back to talk at length about his experiences. (At one point our conversation was interrupted as Meese took a call from Lyn Nofziger, even then well known as another Reagan adviser, startling us further by his openness in letting us overhear a candid exchange of political intelligence.) On another occasion we met Max Rafferty, the controversial superintendent of public instruction, whose salty conservative views and smug manner of argument had earned him vast unpopularity among students. Yet his willingness to see us and his obvious convictions made us wonder.

Our frequent glimpses of Governor Reagan himself gave us the most pause in our attitudes. Although he had virtually become the Antichrist in student lore of the day—he had been quoted recently, for example, as suggesting that a "bloodbath" would be necessary to curb college demonstrations—we were disarmed by his avuncular nature. At first I could not decide whether his perennial cheerfulness was artificial or genuine. One day I accompanied Senator Coombs to a picture-taking session in the governor's office. An aide seated the governor at an ornate desk, instructed the photographer on the proper angle at which to catch the plaques and framed certificates on the wall behind, and finally brought him an official document and ceremonial pen.

Reagan signed his name and looked up, smiling broadly. The photographer clicked away, but the aide rushed back and waved at him to stop. "Governor," the aide said, "I don't think you should be smiling. Remember, this legislation gives the death penalty to political bombers." Reagan reflected a moment. "Why shouldn't I be happy about that?" "But Governor . . ." the aide began. "Oh, I suppose you're right," Reagan said compliantly, putting on a more serious look. "But hurry up and take the picture so I can smile again."

It turned out that Reagan had a sunny disposition about everything. I attended his press conferences regularly—they were just an elevator's ride away within the compact Capitol Building—and one day I even interrupted his exit to ask whether he would be willing to meet with the summer interns. Reporters swarmed around us, and flashbulbs popped from all directions, but visions of an angry confrontation between the governor and a college student were quickly dispelled. "Why, of course," Reagan said, without hesitating, "I'd love to."

The interns were defused several days later with equal ease. Reagan opened his remarks by informing us that, contrary to reports, he did not begin each morning by eating his own children for breakfast. During the next two hours he tamed an audience of initially belligerent questioners through a combination of humor, Hollywood war stories, and passionately stated political philosophy. The congeniality of these officials was, of course, not to be confused with their policies. But it went a long way toward convincing us that up close, and seen as the collection of individuals it is, government was not entirely the nefarious activity of which campus leaflets warned. It was, in fact, both a serious business and quite a lot of fun.

4

SUMMERING
IN WASHINGTON

Another legislative internship beckoned the following summer, and there was no resisting. It would be in Washington, D.C., the mother capital itself and pure ether to a burgeoning political junkie. I would be working for a congressman, and of course I knew that, like my Sacramento experience, it would consist in large measure of mundane office-boy chores. But I was equally confident that any workaday regimen would again be flexible enough to permit the celebrity watching and reception hopping necessary to satisfy the social drive of a college sophomore. I concluded that calloused fingertips from excessive use of a letter opener would be a small price to pay for replenishing my store of political gossip to relate when I returned to school the following September.

The trip to Washington was my first east of the Mississippi, and the long flight from Los Angeles evoked the sense of an exotic foreign journey. On that day in June 1971 nothing could have seemed as exciting as touching down at Dulles Airport with the prospect that I would soon be working in the halls of Congress. I had been engrossed during the plane ride in the best-seller of the time, *Future Shock,* and on the bus drive along the scenic edge of the Potomac River into town, I mused upon the importance of Washington in guiding modern economic and social change. Already the city had begun to take on mythological proportions in my mind, so it was inevitable that realities would prove at once tantalizing and disappointing.

Each morning I rode the bus in from Chevy Chase, transferring twice and peering through the windows at the massive subway construction that was tearing the downtown area asunder. The seats were jammed with white-collar bureaucrats who commuted from outlying areas in Maryland and were serially deposited at the departments of Commerce, Agriculture, Justice, and other federal agencies. Their professional lives were oriented to the details of national policy, interests that spilled into their personal realms. I regularly overheard animated conversations concerning stories from the morning newspaper that few other Americans would have debated; I was delighted to find an entire city absorbed in interests like my own. Still, these were not politicians but career government workers. Only when I arrived at the Capitol Building did authentic political life begin.

I had come for the summer to work in the office of freshman Democrat George Danielson of Los Angeles. Fortuitously I had made his acquaintance at cocktail receptions the summer before when he had been serving as a state senator in Sacramento. I teamed up with an old friend whose father had been a prominent Danielson supporter, and we presented ourselves as a unit. The office generously accommodated us, dipping into its clerk-hire allowance when the special internship kitty proved insufficient to pay our combined subsistence wages. In return for my friend's political clout, I arranged Spartan quarters in the home of a college classmate. More than once my folding cot collapsed in the middle of the night, and our lack of kitchen privileges made sustenance continually uncertain. But all of this was part of the hand-to-mouth existence that interns have romanticized to be an integral part of their summer experience.

In these and other respects we typified the army of collegians who descend each year upon Washington. Today over five thousand students serve short periods on Capitol Hill in the course of a year, mostly during the summer. (Interns are not to be confused with pages, who are in their early teens and spend much of their day fetching water glasses on the House and Senate floors; nor with "patronage" appointees, who are older, on the permanent payroll, and perhaps best exemplified as the superfluous operators of the Capitol's automatic elevators—although even these positions can launch political careers. Jimmy Carter's top aide, Hamilton Jordan, came to Washington the first time to run not the White House but an elevator assigned him by Georgia senator Richard Russell.) Interns find their positions through persistent letter writing, the intervention of school placement offices, or the timely use of political contacts. Arriving in Washington, their creative abilities are tested again as they scramble to find shelter in dormitories, group houses, or spare rooms. For this they are paid modestly, if at all, but their assignments are expected to be commensurately lenient. It is for many a first job, and the emphasis resides in the experience rather than the work product.

Summer interns of my era spent twelve weeks at it, but today's students are often ushered in and out of offices by the month, like patients in the waiting room of an efficient dentist. No matter. The point of the experience in part is to be able to say "I was there," an objective not dissimilar to the Hill tradition of raising and lowering American flags every few seconds so that they can be distributed to constitutent groups with the legitimate claim that they have flown over the U.S. Capitol. Students come, as the internship supposes, to gain insight into the legislative process and, even within such a short time, do indeed make a bowing acquaintance with much of the jargon and ritual of Congress. But the keen competition for positions suggests other purposes as well. The opportunity to gild one's resume does not escape the calculation of students anticipating application to graduate schools; a summer sojourn in government is regarded in yuppie quarters as the hallmark of an educated gentleman. Others see an internship as the equivalent of free admission, and a ticketbook of rides, to a political Disneyland. But in the end the effect is anything but frivolous: Most students feel they have touched the political process, leaving Washington acutely more aware of their own democratic system and, I think, renewed in their sense of civic responsibility.

Danielson enjoyed the usual congressional experience; compared with his life as a state legislator, he must have felt he had reached the big time. His higher office was, for one thing, larger. Instead of two secretaries and an administrative aide, he now had a battery of staff assistants, including those who, for example, possessed specialized legislative expertise or dealt exclusively in press relations. He may not actually have represented so many more constituents than before (nearly half a million in both cases), but he did so with heightened influence and recognition. He had greater resources at his disposal, contended with larger and more newsworthy topics, was addressed by a more illustrious title, and received a bigger salary. Flying back across the continent frequently, while physically tiring, gave him a jet-set élan. All of this went beyond mere social status; as someone dedicated to public service, Danielson was excited by the opportunity to deal in broader national policy, an attitude that infected even the lowliest summer intern. The state and local issues I had encountered the previous summer receded quickly from focus and began to seem less important.

My Sacramento experience did qualify me for slightly more substantive duties in Washington. One of my first assignments was to tally a survey of constituents, whose opinion on issues congressmen regularly solicit. Typically households are queried by means of mass-mailed newsletters and simply asked to mark their answers and send them back. In part, of course, this provides guidance on voting, and the results may be treated very seriously. But other motives lurk. Voters tend to be flattered by the idea that someone cares to know their opinion, and they credit their representative with fidelity to his electorate. ("I want to know what *you* think," the congressman will write, "so I may serve you more effectively.") And unscientific polling techniques permit questions to be tailored that elicit desired replies and can be used to justify controversial votes. (Of course only a small percentage of recipients respond, and those who do so may be motivated precisely because they hold opinions that depart from the norm.) At first I assumed that our tabulation required the utmost accuracy and was daunted to see a growing mountain of returns. "There's a lot of work here," I said with a sigh. One of the congressman's aides graciously reassured me. "Don't worry," he said, "you can count every tenth one. Just so the numbers look realistic."

The episode taught me a first lesson about Congress. Much of its work is geared to public relations and in particular to the imperatives of perpetually impending reelection contests. There is nothing intrinsically wrong with such an orientation of course; Congress is *supposed* to be responsive to voters. Devotion to constituents is one thing, however; creating illusions is another. Yet Congress is quite capable of engaging in make-believe. The *Congressional Record*, a daily "transcript" of floor proceedings, sometimes bears little resemblance to what is actually uttered in live debate given the latitude members enjoy to "revise and extend" their remarks. Congressmen employ computerized typewriters and "autopens" (machines that carefully replicate their ink signatures) in an effort to convey the impression that their letters are personal. Members praise each other as "honorable" and "distinguished" when, like Shakespeare's Marc Antony, they mean precisely the opposite.

These values were made clear to me when I had my official picture taken one day with Congressman Danielson, an essential souvenir of any summer experience. I followed him through the mazelike corridors of the behemoth Rayburn House Office Building to a small room tucked away in a corner of the basement. There our picture was snapped in what might as well have been a Hollywood sound stage: a set consisting of an impressive mahogany desk, formal bookcases, and, instead of a window, a blown-up photograph of the Capitol dome and western facade, set off by elegant drapes to convince the casual observer that it was the real thing. Few in Congress had offices looking out on such spectacular views, so for promotional purposes there was no choice but to create the setting artificially.

It was hard to reconcile these superficial preoccupations and occasional deceptions with the underlying integrity of congressmen and the nobility of their activities. The representatives I observed that summer seemed, for the most part, deeply interested in issues and determined to pursue their respective views of the public interest. Indeed it was a particularly inspiring time to see Congress in action as it tangled increasingly with President Nixon's overreaching assertions of executive power. Why, then, the crass electioneering? Partly because it was an embedded tradition of the institution, lending it the weight of social acceptability. Partly, perhaps, because it seemed to involve only "white lies." Why shouldn't constituents get official-looking replies if they had taken the trouble to write? Why shouldn't statements be published on behalf of their good causes even if congressmen didn't have the time to deliver them personally? What was wrong with calling an enemy "honorable" if it helped preserve a tone of civility? Admittedly these purposes coincided with congressional self-interest. But that may have produced the most compelling justification, as crystallized by the politician who once explained, "We have to save our seats before we can save the world."

Danielson was a bright and energetic congressman, liberal but pragmatic, who applied his organizational skills as effectively within the institution as he did in his home district. Always he walked at a fast pace, as though urgently expected elsewhere, and spoke only in short, crisp declarative sentences, as if anything else wasted his time. Eventually he was rewarded by his peers with a position as a senior Democratic whip, responsible for counting noses and shepherding troops, but years later gladly exchanged this hard-earned status for an appointment as a California appellate judge. Burnout is a phenomenon that affects congressmen at least as much as anyone else and even the most dedicated among them recognize the antidote.

Of course neither a congressman nor his senior staff can spend much time with their student help, and the impressions one takes back from a summer experience come, in large part, from imbibing atmosphere. To an intern Washington is above all a place of political glamour. Famous figures pass constantly in the halls; the hearings that one observes are reported in headlines the next morning; and, as functional as they are fashionable to someone always on the prowl for his next meal, any of a dozen elaborately catered congressional buffets are available each evening for the enterprising intern to infiltrate and forage.

Part of the program is formal. A bipartisan internship committee, for example, provides opportunities for students to see newsmakers in the flesh. Almost every week I joined my fellow interns in filling Coolidge Auditorium of the Library of Congress to hear addresses from such notables of the time as Barry Goldwater, Edmund Muskie, and Charles Percy. (Student to Muskie: "What do you say to the charge by critics that you're too wishy-washy to be president?" Muskie: "I am not wishy-washy! At least I don't think I am.") Interns from the same college sometimes arrange smaller seminars. On one occasion I joined a dozen classmates crowding around the desk of California senator John Tunney to discuss environmental issues, an event that was livelier than expected because his late arrival (by nearly two hours) turned some in our group momentarily hostile. Another time we sat around a table for an hour hearing about House procedure from a Michigan congressman named Gerald Ford. The turnout was smaller owing to the obscurity of the speaker and the nature of the topic, but Ford seemed pleasant enough and his evocative use of football analogies sustained our interest.

In addition interns are known for scouting the congressional calendar in the *Washington Post* every morning to find interesting committee hearings to visit. One day I attended foreign-policy testimony given by Dean Acheson, the former secretary of state. Unrelated to his remarks, I recalled his recent and controversial public reminiscence that President Kennedy had presided over the Cuban missile crisis in the manner of a high school student; in response Senator Edward Kennedy's office had released a letter written by Acheson shortly after the crisis in which he had lavishly praised the president's abilities. During a break in the session I approached him and asked how he reconciled the statements. "Young man," he said, his arms akimbo in his classic pose as he peered at me superciliously, "haven't you ever been to a party where you told the hostess what a wonderful time you had and then, outside, you told your wife what a crashing bore it all was?" At eighteen I neither had a wife nor had I ever been to such a party. (Nor, at the time, did I appreciate the real significance of his comment: that even a man of such stature and forcefulness as Acheson had inhibitions about providing direct advice to a president.) But my spine tingled with the sensation of high Washington chatter; it was clearly not a conversation I could have had in Los Angeles.

Other news events of that summer had special significance to me because of my presence in Washington. The imposition of wage and price controls meant much more having seen Treasury Secretary John Connally testify on the subject before populist Congressman Wright Patman's banking committee. Questions about freedom of the press involved in the "Pentagon Papers" case were rendered less academic when I attended the historic announcement of a decision at the Supreme Court. And when my draft number was drawn in the annual lottery, the process seemed less impersonal for the fact that Curtis Tarr, the commandant of the Selective Service System who was in a position to influence my fate, had recently passed me in the hall.

When opportunities to experience the Washington political scene did not present themselves, I did my best to create them. One morning I learned that President Nixon would be visiting the Capitol later in the day to assist in unveiling the portraits of former Appropriations Committee chairmen under whom he had served many years before as a congressman. He wasn't my favorite politician, but he *was* the president. For a couple of hours another intern and I raced among strategic Hill offices, armed with letters from Danielson and motivated by an insatiable desire to attend the event. Evidently security measures were not so tight then as now, for at the appointed time we found ourselves part of a small, private gathering in Statuary Hall seated behind Defense Secretary Melvin Laird and Speaker of the House John McCormack. (The moment was also remarkable because it was the first time I realized that renowned public figures could be afflicted by ordinary dandruff.) Nixon entered, smiling grandly at his adulatory reception, and for the next thirty minutes stood behind a solitary mi-

crophone like a variety show emcee, delivering extemporaneous rec-
ollections of his years in Congress. Even so, my principal memory of
the event is of the repeatedly whispered exclamation during Nixon's
remarks by a senior Republican congressman seated nearby: "Isn't he
great? No notes!"

I might have considered this the high point of my summer's sightseeing had it not been for another event concerning the presidential
entourage. One day I paid my first visit to the Old Executive Office
Building, an imposing granite edifice adjoining the White House that
quartered the president's staff. Lee Huebner, an acquaintance who had
once served as my summer debate coach, was now prestigiously installed there as a speechwriter. An excursion through these important
executive halls would have been interesting enough, but my visit took
a more dramatic turn as I left the building. Thirty feet ahead I saw
Henry Kissinger and a small group of associates walking briskly away.
The national security adviser had become recognizable to the general
public only recently on the revelation of his clandestine mission to
China. "Dr. Kissinger, Dr. Kissinger," I shouted, running to catch up
and hoping only to say hello and take the measure of this mythic
Washingtonian. I came within two feet of him, my arm outstretched
to shake his hand, and suddenly the men I had taken to be his aides
pulled me violently aside. This was my first encounter with the U.S.
Secret Service, and indeed my most eventful to date. Wholesomeness
must have been written all over my face, for no one asked to see
identification before Kissinger apologized. I congratulated him on the
opening to China, marveled to myself at his unexpected accent, and
reconsidered the juvenile thought of requesting an autograph. Instead,
I walked away contented that the mere telling of the story would epit-
omize the thrill of a first summer on the Potomac.

5

SCHOOLING FOR POLITICS

In the early 1970s, the tranquillity of Stanford University intermittently exploded in student reaction to the Vietnam War. One event after another in Southeast Asia inspired teach-ins, mass marches, and arrests symbolic of the anguish and turbulence of the era. Despite the current events that swirled around me as an undergraduate there, and my own rising feelings against the war, I rarely joined a demonstration. The irony of my summer experiences in government was that, although heightening my interest in politics, they divorced me from the political expression of my own generation, which was predominantly that of antiestablishment protest. The radical assault on existing institutions vilified the government as a defender of the status quo, hostile to the revolution in social values announced by student groups, and incapable of fundamental reform. Indeed the great debate among students was whether useful changes in policy could be made by working "within the system" or whether it was necessary to hurl bombs from the outside.

Yet I had been there, met the individuals who gave the system its actual personality, and felt little such antagonism. True, I did my best to elect antiwar candidates: In 1972 I cheered on our Stanford-area congressman, Republican Pete McCloskey, in his unsuccessful New Hampshire primary challenge to President Nixon; and in the general election I canvassed Palo Alto voters on behalf of Democratic candidate George McGovern. But on the whole I was convinced that, whatever their views, politicians were conscientious citizens who wanted to do the right thing. The problem was not with our democratic arrangements but with the sentiment being expressed by the electorate. The trick was to convince people to vote in new representatives and policies. I felt frustrated, but hardly defeated, when we failed to do so.

My one combat role at Stanford was, fittingly, as a part-time reporter for KZSU, the campus radio station, covering an appearance by President Nixon in nearby San Jose. I stationed myself in the thick of an unruly student crowd outside the building where he spoke, and as his motorcade tried to make its way through the tossed eggs and chanted obscenities, my eyes were stung by a mist of Mace sprayed in my general direction by protective local police. The event, though small, confirmed my predilection toward reforming the world from the comfort of a government office building rather than from the barricades of revolution.

But what exactly would I do toward that end after graduation? It was not necessary to contend with the draft because President Nixon had by now abolished it; the action was enough to make me see new virtue in his administration, since my lottery number had come up a vulnerable "33." (This disclosure is required by the post-Quayle mores of Washington, where what one did during the war has again become a suitable topic of inquiry.) Everyone else, it seemed, was going to law school. Protests had died down, students were starting to think more realistically about their futures, and becoming a lawyer was widely commended as a means of "preserving options." But I was impatient to re-create the enjoyment of my summer experiences in Sacramento and Washington. So in the fall of 1973, thinking it the perfect training ground, I entered the graduate program at Princeton University's Woodrow Wilson School of Public and International Affairs. Here I discovered my first real emotion about national issues, a paradoxical development considering the clinical nature of the curriculum. Classes emphasized the technocratic and theoretical; current events were regarded (perhaps correctly) as being too obvious to warrant teaching.

I recognized my frustration most acutely following the first year. At the beginning of the summer, I traveled with a friend through Italy and Greece. Sated with ruins and museums, we paused in a café and sipped strong coffee, listening to the sounds of animated discussion at the tables around us; we imagined it was political. My friend turned to me and asked about the present-day governments in these countries. Who were their leaders? What were their parties? What issues concerned them? She was a medical student and made no pretense of knowing. I, on the other hand, was a graduate student in international relations. I could have described models of nation-state behavior or drawn curves to depict the principles of exchange-rate stabilization. But current international politics? I knew nothing.

This gap in knowledge caused me to look beyond school for satisfaction, and when I returned in the fall, I found it in so mundane a place as the daily newspaper. I became fanatical in my reading, determined to remedy my ignorance. Events all around me now stimulated my interest. One evening at a party I sat on a waterbed with several others, including Imee Marcos, then a Princeton undergraduate and daughter of the Philippine president. Friends warned me that aggressive bodyguards were stationed nearby and that I should speak to her only circumspectly. From this I deduced that her father's government was probably one of those despotic regimes that I vaguely knew to exist. My scholarly sobriety was so extreme that, rather than calling her the next day for a date, I settled for going to the library and searching for information on the Philippines.

And a funny thing happened: The more I read about current events, there or elsewhere, the more I cared about them. In time I became quite opinionated in my views; I started pasting clippings on my dormitory walls about such odd subjects as the Islamic insurrection in the Philippine islands of Sulu and Mindanao, and, worse, bending the ears of my friends at dinner about them. I began attending extracurricular seminars with visiting public officials more often than I attended classes. When former Israeli prime minister Golda Meir came through, I studied her recent statements, questioned her perhaps too directly, and wondered that no one else seemed as concerned. With classmates I would absent myself frequently to take the train to New York and experience "real-life" sights and sounds. Briefly I even arranged a one-day-a-week internship with *Time* magazine in the city, until school authorities decided I was going too far in my efforts to avoid prescribed classes. The most fun I had was when a friend and I presented ourselves at the CBS studio on West Fifty-seventh Street, somehow talking our way into standing a couple of yards from Walter Cronkite as he delivered the evening news. Evidently this was my personal mecca, a center of those current events to which I was now devoted with almost religious fervor. Observers on the set were subsequently banned, I learned, after someone who gained such admission "streaked," in the fashion of the day, across the screen on live TV. The thought, I hasten to say, never crossed my mind.

And yet no longer did I care to be only a witness to events. Now I wanted actually to do things, to take stands. Campus concern about Vietnam had subsided, but I yearned to involve myself in "issues." I remember particularly being inspired by the example of Henry Kissinger. Opposed though I was to many of his positions, daily stories of his foreign-policy exploits made me covet a life of action. My budding interest in public affairs, and an impatience to participate, made me think about returning to Washington. For a moment Watergate gave me pause; American politics had been tainted by scandal. One of the CREEP conspirators, Jeb Stuart Magruder, had made the sorrowful observation that the nation's capital was no longer a fit place for idealistic young people to pursue their dreams. To many it had become instead a den of political cynicism where ambitious high-level operatives had, in the famous Watergate expression, lost their moral compass.

For some reason I found Watergate a more sustaining drama than Vietnam; perhaps it was merely that I was older. The summer before I enrolled at Princeton, I had returned to Washington to take a job at NASA. Avidly I stole away from mornings of work to attend John Dean's testimony before the Ervin Committee, rushing back to inform my co-workers of the latest disclosures of White House duplicity. (I understood what people meant when they said Watergate was bringing the government to a halt. It was not simply that a preoccupied administration was unable to make decisions on other matters. It was also that we bureaucrats spent much of the day at our desks reading electric stories of these events in extra-large editions of the newspaper.) At school in the fall I joined my friends every night after dinner in front of the TV set in the basement of the graduate commons; with great glee we hooted any mention of the president. When July 1974 arrived finding the Nixon administration on the verge of collapse, I was in Berlin, Germany, for a school-sponsored summer stint at the U.S. Mission there, the official American outpost in that divided city. The Armed Forces Network broadcast the president's resignation speech live around the world, and in the early-morning darkness I made my way to the home of the chief of the political section to see it. As he had long promised in anticipation of such an event, this senior career official of the State Department wasted no time uncorking a fine bottle of champagne to celebrate.

But now President Ford was beginning to restore civil relations in Washington, and there was a chance that Congress would launch an exciting new era of reform. My generation complained forcefully about politicians; weren't we obliged to try to do better? Oddly one last hesitation intervened: Many students at the Wilson School considered employment in the political arena somewhat lowbrow. First of all, such positions were not to be found through the school's formal recruiting process, which was the natural focus of one's job search; you would have to roll up your sleeves and go find them yourself. Opportunities for advancement were limited in the long run unless you actually ran for office. The pay was modest compared with other options. And there was something about the nature of the work that lacked executive character—you would always be working for someone else. Among my fifty classmates, just four became congressional staffers, and only I would go to work in the office of an individual member.

My susceptibility to political pursuits became clear one evening as the first snow fell toward the close of the year. Former Georgia governor Jimmy Carter was scheduled to speak on campus in his seemingly quixotic quest for the presidency, and I eagerly vacated my study carrel to attend. Arriving at the Whig-Clio Building, I found him addressing an informal group of thirty or so Princeton students, those hard-core political types who had an interest in a presidential campaign two years before the election or who hailed from Georgia and recognized the speaker's name.

I was greatly impressed by Carter's remarks. He spoke in a technical vein about the need to improve the delivery of health care services to the rural poor and then touchingly described the Peace Corps work his mother had performed recently in India. But he reserved his most eloquent statement for a finale. Nixon had resigned only months before, and memories of Watergate remained a preoccupation of public debate. Carter stressed his roots far from Washington and then concluded in a soft-spoken voice and with a touch of drama that, as president, he would never lie, evade, or in any way shade the truth. Of course in later years this pledge became legendary, and many wondered how strictly he intended it to be enforced. But hearing it spoken for the first time, I was moved by its solemn simplicity.

The speech was well received, and a group of enthusiastic students gathered around Carter at the front of the room. For my part I gave instant thought to something I had been mulling in previous weeks: taking leave from school to work on a presidential campaign. I cleared my throat and approached Carter; I was ready to volunteer. I searched my mind for a conversation opener that might impress him with my politics and dispose him toward my offer of services. In his speech Carter had disparaged Henry Kissinger's approach to foreign policy as overly pragmatic. This attitude reflected my own, that at times U.S. interests would be served more by an expression of moral values than of *realpolitik*. So I squeezed by New Jersey governor Brendan Byrne, Carter's escort for the evening, and began by expressing my admiration to Carter for his sentiments and also for his willingness to criticize Kissinger, who at the time enjoyed demigod status.

"No," Carter interrupted, "I'm not criticizing Dr. Kissinger. I think he's a very fine public servant." He smiled and declined to elaborate further; I had the impression he thought I was a campus reporter. But it was impossible to square this statement with what I had just heard in his speech. At that point other students approached, and Carter turned to greet them. I simply nodded and backed away. His answer, seemingly the sort of obfuscation he had just sworn to avoid, abruptly drained me of motivation to pursue my campaign interest further.

Yet my desire to return to the political world intensified in inverse proportion to my declining enthusiasm for combing the stacks of a library. So, at the beginning of 1975, thinking I would take only temporary leave from school and return to complete my program in a year or two, I ventured back to Capitol Hill.

6

JOB HUNTING

Congress is full of political jobs, more so than one might expect. Roughly 12,000 staffers work directly for the 100 senators and 435 representatives, and another 3,500 work for their 53 committees and 247 subcommittees. (Many thousands more perform in administrative roles that keep Congress running, or in several auxiliary research institutions that observer Milton Gwirtzman has labeled "staff of the staff.") Each congressman can hire up to 22 assistants (some of whom work in the district), and senators, depending on the population of their states, can have upward of 60 or 70. Committees employ anywhere from 25 to 250 staff members, and subcommittees often half a dozen. Six imposing granite and marble office buildings—Russell, Dirksen, and Hart on the Senate side of the main Capitol Building; and Longworth, Cannon, and Rayburn on the House side—are not enough to contain them, and they spill into several annexes, prompting regular calls for even more expansive facilities. At one time an official study proposed evicting the justices of the nearby Supreme Court.

Amid these riches, it is surprisingly difficult to find a job. The problem? Congress's approach to the hiring of its political staff remains almost entirely ad hoc. There is no personnel agency or master bulletin board to facilitate the process of matching openings and applicants, or even an information window at which a newcomer can ask how to proceed. Occasionally an individual job may be advertised (as, for example, in the bulletin of the House Democratic Study Group), but even then it tends to be done anonymously, as if the matter were of a delicacy reserved for the personal columns of a local newspaper. ("Young member from northeast state with special interest in labor issues seeks energetic assistant with knowledge of computers, and willing to travel to district. Submit resume and writing sample. Listing no. 32.")

Such mysteries awaited when the train from Princeton Junction deposited me at Union Station for my first exploratory foray to the Capitol nearby. For lack of better ideas I headed to the office of Alan Cranston, a senator from my home state of California. My status as a constituent conferred an immediate benefit: The office allowed me to park my baggage in an anteroom on the occasion of my visits. This may also have been the receptionist's way of compensating for the fact that it could do nothing else; Cranston's professional staff was known for its infrequent turnover. At the office of the other California senator, John Tunney, I badgered a secretary with enough questions that she finally summoned a more experienced aide, Martin Franks, to placate me. Franks was someone I would run into again as he himself negotiated the corridors of power and advanced to other Washington jobs over the years, but for now he imparted his wisdom quickly. He told me I was doing exactly as I should: walking door-to-door asking aides like himself whether they knew of any openings. (He did not.) I was left with the impression that if I felt like a Fuller Brush man, I would know I was doing it right. Repeatedly I heard advice to this effect in my early rounds, and always the reassurance that such efforts would eventually pay off.

I did not have endless patience to pursue this tack. If necessary, I was prepared to make several short trips to prospect for jobs. But I was relying on the indulgence of an old Stanford friend to put me up at night, and I suspected that his new wife was thrilled neither with my residence on the couch in their small Dupont Circle apartment nor with plaintive daily tales of my futile efforts. I found it hard to believe that the prescribed methods of job hunting could be the only way to proceed and for a time harbored conspiratorial views that those who had already attained Hill positions were willfully withholding trade secrets from potential competitors.

The realities come as a rude awakening to someone who arrives directly from school, as I did, and is familiar only with the systematic admissions process employed by universities. Indeed many students, long after graduation, never know anything else. My friends who went on to law school immediately from college, for example, followed a well-paved route. Recruiting officers arrived on campus, conducted interviews, flew candidates out to the main office for a fresh round of inquiries, and—*voilà!*—these friends found themselves comfortably situated in a firm where, with some luck, they might remain the rest of their lives.

With a touch of envy for those who can accomplish their career goals so smoothly, job hunters on the Hill find at least philosophic consolation: the thought that the exercise is in fact a necessary proving ground for subsequent employment. Those who steer themselves successfully through the process can consider that they have exhibited the sort of initiative, persistence, and resourcefulness that are the required skills of political work. One finds much the same rationalization in another context, where it is contended that only those candidates who emerge from the crucible of a national campaign possess the true strength to be president. The accuracy of this characterization is beside the point: it serves admirably as a sustaining motivation throughout the process.

The unstructured nature of hiring confers at least one potential advantage on job seekers: There are virtually no rules, and therefore no necessary obstacles, that govern selection. Such conventional employment data as grade-point average, test scores, and record of extracurricular activities won't matter; indeed it is probably rare that an applicant's claims in these areas are even verified. What tends to be important is relevant job experience and the more subjective personal attributes that come across in interviews: political views, communications skills, levels of energy and enthusiasm. There are no stacks of forms to fill out and, once hired, no further bureaucratic delays; you can, if convenient, start the next day. In these respects the arrangements are entirely unlike the regimented civil service procedures and progression of executive branch agencies, giving them special appeal to young people who aspire to climb quickly through the ranks.

At the same time the system has a clear logic from the employer's point of view. Congressmen are sent to Washington to act not as bureaucrats but as political animals. They come with a personal agenda and a broad mandate from the citizens they represent; and their needs change frequently. They may switch committee assignments and suddenly require new legislative specializations on their staffs. A senator may decide he needs a speechwriter instead of an economist or that he ought to replace an administrative assistant whose forte is state politics with one who knows about office management. Thus there is an inclination to accord legislators the widest latitude in assembling staff. Of course they can go too far. Some years back, a staffer successfully sued powerful Congressman Otto Passman for denying her promotion because she was a woman; Congress had exempted itself from equal-opportunity laws. The case reached the Supreme Court, which ruled for the aide and held that there are constraints even upon congressional employment practices.

Many aides advised me to blanket the Hill with resumes and not to be discriminating about jobs or employers, at least at the beginning. Indeed I was made to feel derelict by some job seekers, who claimed that they had not only dropped a resume at *every* office in Congress but had done so more than once. Others urged me to stand near the subway in the basement of the Capitol and press resumes into the hands of passing congressmen. But I had noticed that there was already an elderly man—pleasant enough but generally taken to be deranged—who stationed himself there handing out his own photocopied pleadings *du jour*, and I was somewhat doubtful about my ability to carry this off in a way that would not invite comparisons.

Meanwhile stories were legion about Ph.D.'s who served as receptionists while they continued hunting for jobs of choice—or others who were happy to sit in front offices answering phones, in the hope that their prominent location, like that of Schwab's Drugstore in Hollywood, would cause them to be discovered. As the days went by, I was tempted to degrade my standards. One morning in the basement of the Russell Building I found a small but official Senate personnel office and wondered, as I was filling out biographical forms, why I had not been directed here before. As I exited, the clerk called out, "You forgot to take your typing test." I had stumbled into a clearinghouse for secretaries. But in my anxiety to find something—and since typing was in fact a strong suit—I decided it was worth the try. I scored well but, alas, even my clerical services went untapped.

Walking the halls was not without its dividends. Each congressman had a suite of rooms identified by a boldfaced sign on the front door, and scratching the offices from my various lists was a useful lesson in congressional names and places. It was easy to pick up the gossip that becomes a staple of staff conversation: this member was considering a run for the Senate, that one had a bad temper, another wanted to change committee assignments. Some blessed offices were known as oases for the weary job hunter: Those of Florida senators dispensed complimentary citrus juices; those of Atlanta-area congressmen could be coaxed to produce free bottles of Coca-Cola. I also met many pleasant receptionists (most were not Ph.D.'s, after all, although bright young women for whom Capitol Hill is known), yet I quickly perceived that it was their sworn duty to resist job seekers. Indeed they were so accustomed to the sight of well-groomed young people nervously entering an office that they could instantly anticipate our purpose. In the middle of roundabout questions, and invariably within earshot of other visitors, they would blurt out, "You're looking for a job, right?" As the job seeker would nod sheepishly, the waiting room would echo with the steely refrain: "Just leave a resume."

More than once when I had heard reliably that a senator was looking for a new aide, the receptionist would deny it. It is a remarkable fact that interest in Hill jobs is so great, and the persistence of job hunters sometimes so unpleasant, that offices would rather keep openings secret, seeking candidates privately, than to publicize them at the risk of an overwhelming and indiscriminate response. Indeed the typical approach is for a congressman or top aide to make a few phone calls to colleagues asking for recommendations—and often only as a secondary option to reach for a stack of unsolicited resumes. Moreover resumes have a short shelf life on Capitol Hill; it seems to be assumed that those still in the market, or truly determined, will regularly check back. For all of these discouraging facts, there are not many other ways for a first-timer to break in. Continually I was told that being in the right place at the right time was the key to success and that it was therefore essential to keep in circulation and avoid giving up prematurely.

It was a frustrating business, but as a memento of my labors, stacks of acknowledgments would be waiting for me each day in the mail, written on impressive congressional letterhead and signed in ever so friendly a fashion, it seemed, by the member of Congress whose *aides* I could never even get to see. It was, of course, an easy matter for the receptionist, after waving good-bye, to scribble "job" on top of a resume and drop it in the out-box, indicating to letter writers that it should be awarded a particular form reply. After a recognizable, if imperfect, rendering of my name, and an opening line thanking me for my "recent inquiry," the letter might read something like this: "Although your qualifications are most impressive, I am afraid, after careful review, that we have not been able to identify an opening at this time that is suited to your valuable skills and abilities. Please rest assured that you will remain under consideration should our needs change in the future. In the meantime I am confident that with your excellent background, you will find a rewarding position." And if the words were not soothing enough—on close examination they seemed somewhat ambiguous—for good measure I might be placed on the congressman's mailing list for the next several years, although this was less likely as a deliberate consolation prize than because my name was added to the wrong pile.

In my epic efforts to get past the receptionist, eventually I researched the name of the AA (the administrative assistant, or the one who usually does the hiring) and asked for him (rarely *her*) directly. But this was, I soon learned, a common trick, and, especially in the larger Senate offices, they were rarely "available." In fact their air of mystery assumed such proportions that when I met some of them years later— charming, down-to-earth people, such as Roy Greenaway with Senator Cranston and Joe DiGenova with Senator Charles Mathias—it was difficult to believe they actually existed and were not mere Wizard of Oz creations.

Still, beating the system remained the constant challenge. One day I thought I had devised a scheme to crack, of all offices, the seemingly impregnable fortress of Senator Edward Kennedy. In prowling the halls I had learned that the senator's chief political adviser, Paul Kirk, was located not in Kennedy's office, which would have seemed the obvious place, but in that of the Judiciary Subcommittee on Refugees, which the senator chaired. It was not unusual, I learned, for senior legislators to tuck their personnel into any convenient cubbyhole that could provide a salary. I was only too pleased to suspend moral judgment on this practice when I realized that it could give me a new strategy to elude the front lines. I walked into the modest subcommittee office and found Kirk sitting unguarded at his desk in the middle of the room. Although years later he would become chairman of the Democratic National Committee, he was at this time only another congressional aide unsheltered by a protective cordon of assistants. He could not avoid seeing me, and once we conversed a few minutes, his perfected sense of courtesy in turn gave him no choice but to provide an introduction to the senator's foreign-policy adviser, Bob Hunter. The referral appeared to confer new clout, for Hunter subsequently sat down with me at length to hear my notions of foreign policy and, professing to find them informed, announced that he would recommend my hiring to the senator.

Looking back, I realize that he was talking about only a very junior slot, but at the time I fancied much greater things. Every day I imagined that Senator Kennedy was actively considering my candidacy, perhaps personally reading the school assignments I had submitted as writing samples. Periodically I would check back by entering his legislative office directly from the quiet hall of the Russell Building, opening a tall and unmarked mahogany door to reveal a beehive of exciting staff activity within. Each time, Hunter would beckon me over while he finished a phone conversation, then introduce me to his colleagues with a graciousness that convinced me I would soon be joining them. In fact I never did get a definite answer, and eventually I recognized that Hunter's refined diplomatic skills could be applied not only in the foreign-policy area but also in dealing with job seekers. Having invested so much time only to raise my own false expectations, I reluctantly came to appreciate the usefulness of cold-hearted receptionists.

7

GETTING A FOOT
IN THE DOOR

Fortunately I had been pursuing a parallel track in the office of Senator Hubert Humphrey. His foreign-policy assistant, Dan Spiegel, showed a surprising receptivity when I arrived without notice in the waiting room and sent in a note inquiring of his need for assistance. Initially I took this to signify a possible interest on the part of the senator, but in time I realized that Dan was simply thinking of his own, narrower office needs, which I had arrived just in time to fill.

Although still in his twenties, Dan carried the air of a much decorated Hill veteran. He had worked for Humphrey a couple of years (and before that, Senator Cranston) but, like many Hill staffers, had become restless in subordinate status and was already actively plotting his own advancement. Recently he had begun a four-year night program to earn a Georgetown University law degree and was therefore falling behind in his daytime office routine. A junior aide—making me an assistant to an assistant—would do the trick.

The only problem was that Dan couldn't pay me; the office budget was already fully subscribed. But one of the refrains of job advice I had heard most frequently as I roamed the halls was about the usefulness of "getting a foot in the door." Here was an opportunity to serve in the exciting environment of a powerful senator, learn about the institution at the side of knowledgeable staffers, and earn the cachet of having worked for Hubert Humphrey, which could be the ticket to my next job. Indeed that was to be part of the arrangement: Dan understood that I would, in the course of working for him several months, use my free moments to locate more suitable permanent employment. To some it may be hard to believe that I agreed even temporarily to work without pay, but this was at a stage of my life when I was convinced that money was an utterly trivial consideration in comparison with fulfilling work. Dan did nothing to disabuse me of the philosophy.

Fortunately I was able to afford the luxury. The Wilson School's remarkable endowment had provided me free education and even a small stipend; I had actually managed to *save* money and now had only modest expenses. Looking for housing, I had met a college student from Milledgeville, Georgia, Roy Lane, who was spending the semester working for Senator Sam Nunn from his home state. We agreed to split the rent on a one-room efficiency apartment two blocks northeast of the Senate office buildings. We also split cooking responsibilities, which worked to my advantage; I tended mainly to produce variations on spaghetti, but Roy, whose family operated a small southern diner, was a skilled short-order chef whose menus featured crisp french fries and authentic barbecue. Our apartment was in a mixed-use building, and we shared the end of the corridor with the office of Members of Congress for Peace Through Law, a penurious liberal lobby which lent us a key so that visiting college friends would have couches available for slumber. Not only was this a thoughtful gesture, but it made our habitat all the more exciting: We seemed to live and breathe Washington politics. And we did it all very cheaply.

It was about a month after I had started exploring for Hill jobs that I reported for work at Senator Humphrey's office on the second floor of the Russell Senate Office Building. Already Dan was relishing my first assignment. From under his desk he pulled out a large cardboard box stuffed with hundreds of letters to the senator that, over the past many months, had been referred to Dan but that were as yet unread and unanswered. Humphrey, of course, received large stacks of mail each day, much of which was channeled to full-time letter writers, who relied on preapproved replies. But the mail room singled out occasional letters as deserving of special attention: those that came from

VIPs (big donors, friends of the senator, public figures, etc.) and those that raised issues for which there were not already automated responses. These letters required individualized replies, which fell to the senator's top aides to compose; the senator himself had no time for such drudgery. But now that Dan had his law school obligations, he, too, wished to be spared. So correspondence from British prime minister Harold Wilson, strategic-arms negotiator Gerard Smith, and a notable amount from then Trilateral Commission director Zbigniew Brzezinski sat languishing until my arrival.

To my enduring benefit I quickly picked up the art of congressional letter writing. There seemed to be three essential attributes of the model reply. First, it should exhibit a personal touch—perhaps an opening salutation adapted to the recipient or an overall colloquial tone—that would leave the reader with the impression that the letter had been dictated by the senator himself. Second, it should be restricted to descriptive or vaguely analytical discussion of an issue, thereby preventing the inconvenient documentation of a position on an issue that could later get the politician into trouble. And finally it should be extremely brief, permitting the letter writer to move on expeditiously to other correspondence. Dan was generally sparing of compliments, but his relief at having the cardboard box progressively drained of its contents was palpable.

Meanwhile I would increasingly envy Dan's own less sedentary regimen. He would arrive at work every morning promptly at 8:30 carrying a stack of morning papers procured from Ann's Newsstand, a venerable little shanty situated across from the Senate office buildings through which all news junkies of the era passed at least once a day; it was subsequently razed to make way for a congressional parking lot. Then he would race through the headlines, starting in at 9:00 A.M. on the real business of the day, conducted at a frenetic pace until he had to leave for classes at 5:00 P.M., pulling out of the parking lot—it seemed appropriate even in a time prior to the discovery of yuppies—in a bright yellow Porsche. Except for the much abbreviated evening hours (self-respecting Hill aides often worked until seven or eight o'clock), Dan was the epitome of a bright young staffer, dashing through the corridors alongside the senator, darting in and out of meetings, returning to the large stack of urgent telephone messages. Regularly he would receive a buzz instead of a ring on his phone, and all nearby would grow quiet. "The senator," he would explain to no one in particular as he hung up and in the same motion headed for the door.

It startled me at first to see the power he wielded. With vast liberty he would invoke the senator's authority in coordinating strategies with other Hill offices, requesting answers on important policy matters from the State Department, and responding to press inquiries. Of course he was expected to act exactly as he did, anticipating Humphrey's inclinations and enlarging the sphere of Humphrey's influence by acting as an extension of the senator himself. That was the tacit bargain that gave Hill staff the thrill of power: They would promote their boss's interests, in return for which they would be given the license to pursue them in his name. Even Senator Humphrey, possessed of unsurpassed energy, acted under the mortal limitations of time. One day I delivered to Dan a newspaper article that the senator had clipped for him to see, annotated by a note scribbled in the margin. It was a *New York Times* editorial column concerning the lessons of Vietnam, and Humphrey had written, "Dan—let's start a file on 'lessons' and begin sorting out the issues." Although Hubert Humphrey had been centrally involved for an entire decade in a national debate on the war, even he had not had the time to organize all his thoughts and found it convenient now to delegate part of the task to an aide.

My contact with Humphrey was quite limited, even within the confines of our small Senate suite. The legislative office was several doors down from his personal office, and in the months I worked there, I never saw him enter a part of the suite other than his own; if aides didn't cross his path elsewhere, they saw him only when summoned. This seemed odd, since Humphrey was legendary for his gregariousness, and I had no doubt that had he been convalescing in a hospital, he would have bounded on an hourly basis into every adjoining ward to make new friends. But in time I realized that politicians, like anyone, can have very different public and private personas. I did not formally meet Humphrey until a week after I began work, when everyone gathered snugly around his desk one morning for a staff meeting, the younger among us sitting on the floor. He was far more businesslike than I would have imagined; the man who was known for "politics of joy" matter-of-factly discussed the details of his weekly schedule. Suddenly I could picture him as an actual president and not just a rhetorician: although he clearly depended on his staff—one agenda item was an impending trip abroad, the itinerary of which he appeared only now to be learning—he demonstrated an effortless sense of command.

This demeanor became apparent on a daily basis. It happened that the main FTS (Federal Telephone System) phone line in the office—usable after five o'clock for free long-distance telephone calls—was installed in the short interior hallway between his private office and the desks of his administrative aides. As the most junior legislative staffer, I was assigned to make occasional constituent phone calls (and allowed the fringe benefit of interspersing quick personal ones as well) while the senator and others would skirt around me exchanging papers, pungent political conversation, and bemused looks in my direction. I spoke in a whisper, careful not to disturb the impressive discipline of the inner sanctum. Senator Humphrey may have been beyond the responsibility of staff when he was outside the walls of his office and exposed voluntarily to the electoral hordes, but when he set foot inside, it was expected that they would aggressively defend his solitude. His administrative assistant and principal secretaries had served him for many years, and their hushed tones suggested that they took their duties seriously. If I wanted to talk politics, I was likelier to seek out Betty South, the warm and competent press secretary, who maintained a more relaxed environment in an alcove behind the reception room.

The legislative office, where I usually resided, was presided over by Al Saunders, the chief legislative assistant and a man appreciably older than his subordinates. He did not perform typical legislative functions but instead sat stoically at a corner desk all day long meticulously reviewing every document sent out of the office in Humphrey's name. His presence there was a soothing reassurance that at least it would not be the *staff* that got the senator into trouble. Another aide performed in the area of agricultural policy much as Dan did in that of foreign policy, and although this held special interest for Humphrey, it held none for me and therefore I had little specific notion of what the aide did during the day, even though it was happening only five feet away. Several secretaries and junior assistants filled out our one room, and occasionally a visitor, even a prominent one like actor Lorne Greene, Humphrey's friend, would find it necessary to perch on the corner of a desk if extra chairs were unavailable. Altogether it made for an unceasing clatter of voices, phones, and typewriters from early morning until late at night. If the atmosphere suggested the chaotic environment of a metropolitan newsroom, it was not untypical of legislative activity in any congressional office.

Although Humphrey had served four years as vice president of the United States, and, in 1968, run in his own right for president, he exhibited a remarkable humility in returning to Congress as the junior senator from Minnesota. From what I saw, he expected no special treatment, but it was inevitable that he would be regarded as an elder statesman; a new Foreign Assistance Subcommittee was established for him to chair, for example, because it was thought only right that he should have his own forum in the foreign-policy area. At the time I worked for him, the U.S.-backed governments of South Vietnam and Cambodia were on the verge of collapse, and he was an influential opponent of President Ford's requests for further aid. As such, he did not come across to me as the gabby, out-of-date pol whom we students had raucously derided three years before during his 1972 California primary battle with George McGovern. He seemed, instead, pragmatic and effective. I began to wonder whether campaigns highlighted the real skills useful in holding office.

The office was excited to see Humphrey's name alive again in early rumors of possible presidential contenders for 1976. No one at the time could foresee Jimmy Carter's successes in the Democratic primaries, nor the cancer that would take Humphrey's life the following year. He was the Big Man on Capitol Hill, someone who had served on the national stage during most of the postwar era, and yet these were days when other giants also stalked the Senate. The southern senators were particularly memorable; they looked like they had just walked off the set of *Advise and Consent*: James Eastland, James Allen, Herman Talmadge, John Sparkman, John Stennis, Harry Byrd—if they didn't actually wear white linen suits in the summer, it would have been easy to imagine it. There was the coterie of nationally renowned liberals, who in those days held much sway: George McGovern, Ted Kennedy, Birch Bayh, Frank Church; they were the political heart-throbs of college students. Older-guard figures, such as Mike Mansfield, Stuart Symington, Abe Ribicoff, and Scoop Jackson, were more distant objects of respect; they seemed a link with the liberal past. Newer arrivals, such as Gary Hart and Dick Clark, were activists who moved quickly into the limelight. (Staff had a special affinity for them: Hart was a former McGovern aide, and Clark had been administrative assistant to Senator John Culver, who in turn had been a legislative assistant to Senator Kennedy.) There were the traditional Republicans—Hugh Scott, Robert Griffin, Robert Taft, Barry Goldwater—and the beginnings of a "new right" in freshmen such as Paul Laxalt and James Buckley. And there were the liberal Republicans, such as Jacob Javits, Clifford Case, Edward Brooke, and Mark Hatfield, who often tried to set a high tone of bipartisanship in their dealings. I was not at a level to have interaction with these great figures except in the hallways and observing from the galleries, but even such glimpses made for an acute sense of living history.

The thought that Capitol life was something akin to a movie set had a literal quality to it when I passed the Library of Congress one holiday morning. Backed up to its entrance were several large trucks—the paraphernalia of a Hollywood studio there to shoot scenes for the film production of *All the President's Men*. Off to a side I saw John Brademas, a much-respected congressman from Indiana (and a future president of New York University), apparently as dazzled as I was by the preparations of the sound and lighting crews. He wondered aloud whether there would be any parts for extras, and we agreed to pool our efforts to find out. I spotted Jack Valenti, head of the Motion Picture Association, who was happy to oblige Brademas and let me ride his coattails. For the next two hours we sat through several takes of a scene in which we pretended to be reading books (instructed to turn the pages every ten seconds for effect) in the Library's large main reading room. A few yards away the lead actors (Dustin Hoffman and Robert Redford) themselves pretended to do research. The end of the scene, in which we would appear, was captured by a camera slowly zooming up by pulley to the top of the grand rotunda, thus providing a panoramic view of all of us below. When the movie finally opened, I excitedly awaited our debut, but that part of the sequence, it turned out, lasted about three seconds and made us out to be blurred and totally unrecognizable specks. Was this, I feared, a parable for Washington "extras" in general?

In the midst of such diversions, my letter writing went on, sometimes interrupted by the welcome respite of a staff meeting or a summons to accompany the senator to a speech so that I might tape-record his remarks. On one special occasion I was relieved of the noise and tedium by an assignment to baby-sit Humphrey's five-year-old grandson, Benji, and for much of the afternoon chased rubber balls and other flying objects down the corridors of our building. The omnipresent policemen, usually alert to deviant behavior, must have had a sixth sense about my mission, for it was never questioned.

A more rewarding project occurred one day when Dan, running late, asked me to prepare remarks for the senator to use in connection with a floor debate on foreign-aid legislation, one of Humphrey's areas of personal expertise but not, at the time, one of mine. I did only the casual research that a couple of hours allowed, wrote out the first few arguments that came to mind, then walked apprehensively to the Senate gallery to see what use Humphrey would make of my poor handiwork. I sat stunned as I heard him read faithfully from my text. It had simply never occurred to me that a debate in the Senate of the United States could proceed from such rudimentary efforts and that the principals upon whom such efforts would reflect, such as Humphrey, would not impose more exacting standards. Neither had I appreciated until then that a senator could so adeptly borrow from a staffer's work, making it seem—as Humphrey did through his extemporaneous mannerisms and tone of voice—entirely his own.

But notwithstanding my momentary success at writing speeches, Dan needed me more for writing letters. I imagined that at some point I would be rewarded for my diligence, perhaps by advancement to a weightier policy task, but all I got was more letters. There was no reason for anyone to think of me differently; I was performing well in my limited role, and the senator already employed more than enough chiefs. My interest remained in foreign policy, and the only relevant position to which I could be promoted was Dan's. But he seemed a fixture in the office, and the last person to be considered as a successor would have been a twenty-two-year-old neophyte.

My true status hit home one evening at the annual congressional Democratic dinner, a gala affair held for thousands in the ballroom of the Washington Hilton. Tickets were purchased by corporate sponsors who wished to hobnob with the politicians, but leftover seats were offered as a favor to congressional offices. For others on Humphrey's staff the novelty of attending such functions had worn off; it was just one more tedious professional obligation. For lack of takers I received the one available ticket, which was thrilling for me because it would be a night of politics and glitter. I took my place in the ballroom, greeting the richly dressed corporate titans and spouses arrayed at my table and smugly imagining myself to be more senior that I was. Suddenly I saw Humphrey, in his usual fashion, bound into the hall and begin heading in my general direction. I straightened up, preparing myself for the impressive comment I was sure he'd bestow on me in front of the others, something like, "Do you all know Mark, one of my valued advisers?" I knew he was adept at such public flattery. He did indeed come by, and I held my breath. "Hey," he said, pointing at me and turning to everyone else, "you've got the freebie at your table."

I laughed, but it was time to move on.

PART II

THE HOUSE

Even junior members were now seen and heard. Representative Don Bonker (D-Washington), right, meets Egyptian President Anwar Sadat under the paternal gaze of Speaker Tip O'Neill.   U.S. HOUSE OF REPRESENTATIVES

8

JOB HOPPING

As planned, I used spare moments to canvass perhaps seventy-five other offices. A committee position seemed out of the question. One Senate Foreign Relations Committee staffer, Dick Moose, tried gently to explain that nothing but an occasional research slot would be available to someone barely out of school. He pointed out that my principal job experience to date was dealing with constituents, an exercise from which committee staff, exalted in the congressional scheme of things, were often mercifully exempt. As for personal staffs, other aides I knew—Dick McCall with Senator Gale McGee of Wyoming, for example, and Sally Shelton with Senator Lloyd Bentsen of Texas— informed me that although the Hill was known for conferring unusual responsibility on young people, the Senate was not generally the side for beginners. Once, when Brian Atwood of Senator Thomas Eagleton's staff ushered me into another room for a confidential chat, I was all but certain that I had at last found an office with jobs to offer, but evidently he wanted only to protect my privacy while conveying similar discouragement. Still, I was impressed that these staffers showed me such courtesy—perhaps they did so having once been in my position themselves—and I would remember their example in the count-less times job hunters one day visited me.

There were brief moments of hope. David McKillop, a retired For-eign Service Officer advising Senator Claiborne Pell, defied conven-tion and urged me as his own replacement. The senator, a member of the Foreign Relations Committee and a onetime FSO himself, brushed the suggestion aside and settled eventually on another ex-FSO. Mc-Killop's charitable act restored my battered self-confidence, but it caused me to worry that Pell might think less of my benefactor for his ingen-uous judgment. Meanwhile Senator Richard Schweiker's office, which needed no foreign-policy assistant, countered with the suggestion that I become an "idea man" on the staff. The notion intrigued me—I did not know what it meant, but it seemed invested with great intellectual prestige—yet after extended discussions the staff finally announced that the senator had changed his mind. Whether about me or about the need for having ideas was not made clear.

I had been spoiled by my Senate experience—although the branches may be coequal in the aggregate, individual senators seemed far more influential than individual congressmen—and it was with some reluc-tance that I finally went looking in the House. I photocopied the rel-evant pages of the *Congressional Directory* and started walking systematically into the offices of all the members of the International Relations Committee, which remained the area where I hoped to spe-cialize. I soon learned that senior members rely on full committee or subcommittee staffers earmarked for their use—many of whom rise through the ranks of their personal offices after years of service and most of whom have substantial specialized experience. Junior mem-bers, on the other hand, do dedicate staffers in their personal offices to cover their committee assignments, but no one on the "IR" com-mittee seemed about to make a change.

So I cast my net more broadly and made inquiries at other offices I happened to pass in the halls during my rounds. Ironically it was from these that I received several positive reactions, although none from anyone who wanted a foreign-policy assistant. One day, for example, following preliminary screening by his staff, I was summoned for an interview with Republican Jim Broyhill of North Carolina. He was pleasant and soft-spoken and made me an offer of employment, but at the end of our conversation I politely declined, explaining that the positions he described were probably too conservative for me to serve him conscientiously. With minimum preparation, I might have checked his voting record before imposing on his time. At least I was contrite about the experience, for when similar circumstances arose and Democrat Bill Hughes of New Jersey wondered if I were interested in doing his work for the Judiciary Committee on which he served, I did not allow the process to advance as far before I informed an aide that the subject matter did not interest me.

Finally I heard from the office of Congressman Mark Hannaford of Long Beach, California, which I had applied to only out of nostalgic affinity for my home state. His AA told me I was in luck: Someone was expected to leave, giving the office the opportunity to create a new and senior position. The catch was that it wouldn't happen until the fall. This was an advantage, however, for I had been offered the chance to work at the United Nations for the summer (my addiction to interesting internship experiences had not abated) and the promise of a well-paid job awaiting my return would give me comfort as I incurred the extravagant expenses of living several months in New York City.

What the AA did not explain was that he was the one departing and under clouded, if not bizarre, circumstances. Apparently he behaved quite eccentrically, among other things stuffing batches of constituent letters into the drawers of his desk and locking them away from others' access. His motives were unclear but, as I had come to learn, letters are the bane of a congressional staffer's existence, and while the AA's actions were extreme and inexcusable, anyone who has worked on the Hill will faintly understand the psychopathy that might have brought someone to this point. It was an awkward situation all around, for the AA had been hired as a favor to his father, a prominent supporter in the district, and, handled indelicately, his removal threatened political ramifications. More experienced congressmen knew better than to mix personal and professional relationships.

All of this might have raised questions about the AA's authority to supervise further office activities, but Hannaford was just as glad to have someone else, even a defrocked assistant, working on personnel matters. Congressmen are no better as managers than a cross-section of the public might be, and possibly they are worse: Had they been primarily interested in such things, they might have gone into (or stayed in) private business. Once the AA agreed to leave, Hannaford was not of a mind to disrupt the planned, if gradual, transition. Thus the AA continued to function as always and, with regard to my own situation, simply announced that he wished to hire me, only subsequently bringing me in to see the congressman for final approval.

The AA had not been the first of the office's hiring miscues, and

Hannaford found himself besieged by unaccustomed administrative burdens, which he probably assumed his staff would deflect rather than cause. His senior legislative assistant had a useful expertise in banking—one of the congressman's committee assignments—but lacked a dynamism he desired. Another assistant, an ex-campaign aide, was energetic but single-mindedly devoted to politics; he worked mainly on plotting the congressman's reelection, still a year and a half away. No doubt this would be essential in time, but it did not address the office's more immediate legislative needs.

Although Hannaford was anxious to fill the vacuum, his adverse experiences made him queasy about gambling on other staffers, like myself, of limited Hill experience. This was a rare instance, however, in which my academic *vitae* gave me a veneer of respectability, important to Hannaford as a one-time college teacher. Stanford was a school one of his children had attended and made me seem a little more familiar. He invited me to join his staff as a general legislative assistant, potentially responsible for any subject area in the congressional domain. At first I was concerned that this would sacrifice my narrower foreign-policy interests, but Hannaford argued that specialization was premature at so early a stage of my career; he hedged the point by hastening to say that he hoped to take a special interest in the field. This was helpful persuasion, but two other, more practical, considerations clinched the deal: The position would be committed to me here and now, obviating any further unpleasantness of job hunting; and it would be compensated at the rate of $21,000 a year, a mind-numbing figure at the time for a House staffer of my utter inexperience and undistinguished salary history. Itching to be able to take off for a summer in New York, I accepted on the spot.

When I returned to Washington in September, the congressman welcomed me warmly but in the next breath, and with the look of someone who had been rehearsing this moment for some time, said he had reconsidered the salary and that he could only justify paying me $19,000. He said his constituents would have difficulty understanding how someone my age could make so much on a government payroll; he felt it safe to contradict the AA—who had set the terms— now that he was gone. I made no objection to the news. To my mind the sums were equally stratospheric.

Hannaford had crested into office on the anti-Watergate tide the previous fall, one of numerous Democrats who had prevailed in traditionally Republican districts; his predecessor had retired after holding the seat twenty-two years. At age fifty Hannaford had run for election from his roost as mayor of Lakewood, California, a middle-class bedroom community near Los Angeles, although he served simultaneously as an associate professor of government at a local state college. He was an astute and congenial man, but central casting would not have picked him to play a political candidate. He was short and pudgy— it renewed his confidence, he said, that the Speaker of the House at the time, Carl Albert, was of similar physique—and, despite his intellectual temperament, gave the impression of being almost as wide-eyed at the Washington experience as his newest aide. Cautious by nature, his hesitations in political matters were accentuated by the knowledge that he came from a marginal district where one wrong vote might defeat him in the next election. His good humor and relaxed manner helped him keep his bearings: he and his vivacious wife entertained office staff in their Crystal City apartment, and on visits back home they often took a detour to a newly purchased vacation home in Baja California. Perhaps because he knew his elevation to power might be distinctly temporary, he wisely determined to enjoy it. (He was, unfortunately, defeated four years later.)

The work I did in the office was indeed general in nature. Although nearly nine months into his term, Hannaford had not yet hired a full complement of staff, let alone refined our assignments. In a typical week I might write a speech for him to deliver on the House floor urging an audit of the Federal Reserve System; give advice on bills to establish quarterly adjustments in support prices for milk, and to make revisions in the national scheme of pesticide regulation; and draft a story for the newsletter to inform constituents of Hannaford's role in promoting research on alternative energy sources. Such duties, of course, were interrupted by incessant calls from lobbyists and other offices urging a position on this bill or that, visits to committee sessions, which I covered in Hannaford's absence, and lively political conversation with my office mates—until by the end of each evening my wastebasket would be filled with crumpled phone messages, torn-up first drafts of statements, cardboard cartons I had used to ferry sandwiches and milk shakes from the basement carryout, and Styrofoam cups oozing out the dregs of stale coffee. My work days often lasted twelve hours, but they went fast; it was all great fun.

The office of a junior House member was the perfect place to learn the congressional process. Originally I had conceived of my Humphrey stint as an apprenticeship that would teach me survival skills for work in the legislative branch. What better model to observe than one of the institution's most veteran legislators? But Humphrey's office was ill suited as a training ground precisely because Humphrey was so experienced: Often he conducted legislative activities out of his hat, keeping his staff at a surprising distance. In contrast my new boss was still learning—and his staff would learn with him. Almost every issue and every procedure was new to us. Hannaford sought continual advice and required constant support, and although we may have been even more newly minted than he was, he made us feel invaluable. Moreover my assignments were far broader than I would have found in a bigger and more compartmentalized Senate office. Although coming to the House side had seemed a step down, now I realized that it was actually a more exciting and logical place for a young aide to start.

Unfortunately Hannaford had little enduring interest in foreign affairs and certainly no influence. When Secretary of State Kissinger initialed the Sinai disengagement pact during this period, congressmen rushed to the floor to voice ringing endorsements. Hannaford asked me to prepare remarks, and while I generally offered praise, I also attempted to raise concerns about possible dangers. He said he agreed with the points but was not prepared to express them: it would appear out-of-step with his colleagues. This incident provided my first glimpse of congressional groupthink. It was not that Hannaford had any constituency in his district that would have been offended, nor even any newspapers or colleagues who likely would have noticed. His reluctance at bottom reflected a forgivable human tendency: Following the crowd, in Congress as elsewhere, takes the least effort. U.S. policy in the Mideast was not high on the list of his legislative priorities, and he would have felt the need to invest precious time learning about it in detail to feel comfortable departing from conventional wisdom; there was little incentive to get involved.

Only days later he asked me to substitute for him at a breakfast meeting on foreign policy. Excited by the discussion, I participated intensely, apparently attracting the attention of a congressman in attendance, who asked afterward whether I had an interest in joining his staff. Unlike Hannaford, this congressman—Don Bonker of Olympia, Washington—served on the House International Relations Committee and was therefore engaged daily in my favorite area. He, too, had assumed office in January, but had delayed hiring a legislative assistant in order to assess the needs of his office. Toward the end of the year he decided to find someone who would specialize in foreign affairs, reflecting his major committee assignment and anticipated allocation of time.

I couldn't believe my bad timing. All my efforts to find a foreign-policy position had been thwarted—until now, when I was no longer looking and had settled for something different. Taking the offer was out of the question; I had been with Hannaford only two months. The frustration was excruciating, and I smiled weakly in telling the story to friends. Much to my surprise, they scoffed at my inhibitions and uniformly advised me to ignore the customary sensibilities of the outside world about switching jobs. "That's the way the Hill works," they said, referring to the transient environment of congressional offices.

As I was to learn quickly, it is commonplace for aides to transfer among offices as though they are merely different departments of the same company, which to some extent they are. Movement within individual offices is often limited, and an alternative avenue of advancement is through other offices; staff of the various congressmen and committees work side by side, and available jobs become highly conspicuous. In other lines of work lengthy tenure is considered a virtue; on the Hill someone who has remained at the same job for too long may be looked upon as perhaps lacking appropriate drive and ambition. Many staffers are young and highly mobile. Far from being hesitant about making job changes, many seem engaged in a perpetual search for new and superior positions. And Hill employers themselves set the tone: House members eagerly run for the Senate, and senators for president. Almost nothing seems sacred when it comes to professional ambition.

Still, I rebelled at such wisdom and began thinking differently only when I described the events to Hannaford. He shook his head. "You don't owe me loyalty," he said. "None of us is here long enough to worry about that." Perhaps the ex-professor was accustomed to lenient college policies allowing semester credits to be added and dropped; he insisted that I be faithful only to my own interests. "If your driving ambition is really foreign policy, you can't let a chance like this slip by." At the same time he offered an inducement to remain. After a short additional training period, he said, he would make me his AA. It was an undeserved opportunity, one usually reserved for much more experienced aides and available to me only due to Hannaford's generous nature and the extreme vicissitudes of his office.

For several days I wrestled with strongly ambivalent feelings. Finally I called Bonker, half-hoping he had found someone else. His offer still stood, so I told him that I had decided to accept. I was beginning to yearn for recognition as a specialist—and for the opportunity, in the area I most cared about, to influence legislation. Being an AA, I knew, might have more status; but at this particular juncture foreign affairs offered more professional fulfillment. Hannaford congratulated me and even insisted on holding a going-away party in the office; he could see I needed confirmation in my decision. We stayed friends for the remainder of his congressional years, and of course his office hardly noticed my absence. The enduring impact of the events was on my own frame of mind. Having changed jobs to such positive effect, I would be less hesitant in the future as new opportunities arose. I began to think of the Hill as a series of rewarding experiences, not a career path; I convinced myself that a certain restlessness was a sign of intellectual vitality. I had heard about the mobility of young congressional staffers, found the mystique appealing, and felt proud now to have become, so effortlessly, a part of the culture.

9

THE PECKING ORDER:
LIFE WITH A FRESHMAN

So I went to work, in late 1975, for Congressman Don Bonker from Washington State. Don's name had a ring to it that, in addition to providing rich material for plays on words, seemed to sum up his obscurity as a freshman member of Congress. He was, in fact, an able representative and a very decent human being, but that had little bearing on his influence within an institution where rank often depends on either seniority or renown. And since the clout of aides rests vitally on that of their employers, the fact that few had heard of my boss was a matter of consequence to me as well. The ambitious freshman agenda would challenge us to find ways for him to transcend his anonymity.

Don represented healthy new blood for the institution. He was the prototype of a junior legislator, starting with the fact that he insisted on being called by his first name. Indeed his earnestness and lack of pretension almost made him seem a part of my own generation. Just shy of forty, he was hardly the youngest member of his class; others, like Tom Downey of New York, were as young as twenty-five, the Constitutional minimum. But he had a youthful mop of hair in the manner of John Kennedy, complemented further by a wife who had the stylish look, and even the silken sotto voce manner, of a Jackie Kennedy. And he typified the "Watergate babies" of Congress—like Hannaford, those new members elected in the wake of Nixon's resignation—in much more than the matter of age. He was a moderately liberal Democrat, one determined to reverse many of the policies of the Nixon era. In addition he had a reformist attitude about the political process itself, as did many of the seventy-five new House Democrats, that went beyond mere party position. A well-educated group, they were inclined to challenge received wisdom and eager not only to install new ideologies but to repair the workings of the government institutions that had produced the old ones. They seemed to share a feeling, perhaps bred in the college rebellions of the 1960s or in the presidential campaigns of Eugene McCarthy and George McGovern, that they heralded a different sort of politics, a collective breath of fresh air that would blow away the antiquated customs of a stodgy Washington establishment. Here I was no bystander; like most aides my age, I found this viewpoint refreshing and did what I could to abet their activism.

This temperament coincided well with the times, for there was much to question: the seniority system in Congress, government secrecy, the arrogance of a powerful executive branch. Congress did not seem an egalitarian institution but the preserve of superannuated southern committee chairmen and other passive figures who deferred too readily to the wily maneuvering at the other end of Pennsylvania Avenue. The Gulf of Tonkin Resolution, ratifying American involvement in Vietnam, remained fresh in younger minds, as did Nixon's pattern of budget impoundment and assertions of executive privilege. The Church committee, as I arrived, was beginning to unearth evidence of CIA assassination plots and other foreign-policy scheming about which most of Congress had been kept deliberately in the dark. Whenever the freshmen gathered to discuss their purposes, there was a distinct new attitude in the air: "Never again."

Yet as much as they seemed to resist old-fashioned, smoke-filled-room "politics," ironically they introduced a kind of their own. True they were serious-minded, cause-oriented, and less prone to compromise. But in time they brought forth impressive new political techniques. If they didn't possess institutional power, they would learn to issue press releases and address television cameras; if they came from marginal districts, they would apply their high-tech sophistication to computerized letter writing and direct-mail fundraising; if their numbers were still small, they would begin to enlist sympathetic national constituencies in their battles. Eventually this sort of permanent campaigning proved so effective that it often produced a politician's ultimate trophy of success: perpetual incumbency. By the late 1980s—these practices having been widely imitated—almost no sitting congressman would lose a bid for reelection.

Like many of the other new arrivals, Don was impatient to exercise power and had staged precocious bids for office. He served first as a county auditor in Washington State, building a popular reputation on his support for voter registration by postcard, then boosted his name identification by running a respectable, if unsuccessful, campaign for secretary of state. On the fortuitous retirement of a veteran congresswoman, Julia Butler Hansen, he was ready to switch gears and run for Congress. He won a tough contest and came to Washington, D.C., where he had served ten years before as an aide to Senator Maureen Neuberger of Oregon. Although now a bona fide representative himself, he would often hark back to that period as his glory days (I could begin to identify), and he seemed proud of his return as though he had personally fulfilled the promise of Lafayette.

He should have been proud. Although staffers rub shoulders enough with congressmen sometimes to imagine themselves as peers, they are not. And while an occasional aide does run for Congress, and others daydream about doing so, the vast majority are quite content with their derivative power. Aides frequently tell themselves that they can exercise much the same influence as elected officials without having to accept the practical disadvantages: commuting long distances, trimming positions as required by constituencies, shaking hands at fundraising affairs late into the night when one would rather be asleep. Yet the real separation between aides and bosses runs deeper: One has public recognition, political support, and financial backing—and the other doesn't. Most staffers have settled in Washington and maintain little connection with potential constituencies. When Senator Warren Magnuson's AA, Norm Dicks, was elected to the House, observers were not entirely facetious in saying he had taken a demotion. But elective office carries a prestige and an independence that are hard to quantify and act as powerful attractions; it is the concrete difficulties of getting elected that give one pause. Once, when I heard that Senator Sam Nunn of Georgia had started out as a House committee aide, I began to imagine the possible leaps one could make from such a station—until I learned that the committee chairman who had hired him, the well-known Carl Vinson, was his great-uncle. I realized then that his staffer's background may not have been Nunn's only leg up.

The area Don represented was largely rural—vast forested areas, such as the Olympic Peninsula—and hardly seemed a natural constituency for a Democrat whose positions resembled those of an urban liberal. But it was in part a blue-collar area of loggers and lumber mills— small towns with names like Longview and Centralia—susceptible to populist Democratic politics. (One of Don's winning issues in the 1974 campaign, for example, had been his opposition to unbridled log exports, which were depriving constituents of processing orders for the raw product.) In addition, like any congressional district, it valued representatives, no matter their politics, who brought home the federal bacon. Congresswoman Hansen ensured her place in Congress when she became head of an Appropriations subcommittee on interior affairs, a position of tangible relevance to the region. So, too, did Don eventually establish a secure seat as he learned the electoral value of "constituent service," a term euphemistically describing the government favors—such as intercession with Washington agencies to obtain Social Security benefits—that a congressman seeks to bestow on voters back home.

Such work is often considered one of the more beneficial things congressmen do, but the motivation goes beyond mere charity; personal touches typically matter to voters as much as larger issues of ideology, voting record, or even public reputation. As a result, constituents occupy almost deified status in the eyes of Hill offices, a flotilla of paid aides poised to handle their problems. Too bad for a challenger who can do nothing more than walk the district at his own expense. It is also possible to wonder about the *net* benefit of constituent service. An office's intervention with an agency on behalf of one citizen may simply bump to the back of the line another who has not been clever enough to enlist such help. And the aid that constituents request is not always so innocent. A recent example has been that of the Keating Five, senators accused in 1990 of seeking to thwart a financial regulatory investigation; they defended their efforts as service they would render any constituent. But that their activities did in fact go well beyond the norm was obvious not only from the large campaign contributions involved and the attenuated claim of constituent status (four states for one man), but by the highly unusual fact that it was the senators themselves, not their staffers, who made direct contact with midlevel agency personnel. Don, for his part, stuck to much smaller, perfectly legal, but equally effective measures.

This was not a skill he learned from me, because from the beginning I pushed him in the direction of national issues, an emphasis that appealed to my own values but that was, if anything, a source of resentment on the part of his constituents. I had not yet come to appreciate the truth (at least for Capitol Hill) of Speaker Tip O'Neill's aphorism that "all politics is local," and its special significance for freshmen whose status at home is still fragile. But Don had departed the path himself, having been assigned on arrival to the International Relations Committee. This was justified to him—as in turn we would justify it to constituents—on the grounds that the Pacific Northwest lacked representation on the panel, but in fact the appointment reflected a freshman's lack of clout to win a better committee assignment. (Each House member served on one principal committee designated by party caucus.)

Foreign affairs may be the privileged domain of presidential candidates, eager to demonstrate a worldly expertise, or of frustrated secretaries of state, determined to travel the world and pronounce on profound issues of war and peace, but to ordinary members of Congress it is sometimes a minefield best avoided. Those congressmen who serve must regularly defend themselves from charges by opponents that they care more about the peoples of far-off continents than about citizens at home. Some are even defeated on this account: William Fulbright, Frank Church, and Charles Percy, each in his time an illustrious chairman of the Senate Foreign Relations Committee, were successively turned out of office at least in part because of such grumbling. We heard some of this, too, as Don, partly under my influence, became involved through his committee assignment in topics of such peripheral relevance to the Third Congressional District of Washington State as Africa and human rights. I was oblivious of his local imperatives, but fortunately he was not. Prodded by his politically attuned AA, Dave Yaden, Don recognized that if he could do nothing about his committee assignment, at least he could capitalize on his subcommittee assignments. Several years later he joined the International Trade Subcommittee, and through persistent effort not only turned it into an important congressional voice on the subject but also an effective vehicle to advance his district's local interests.

Another drawback of Don's original committee assignment was that it offered little potential for attracting campaign contributions. Such a consideration, however crass, can never be far from the minds of congressmen, who continually must be devising ways of raising the tidy sums of money required for their next election campaign. In the mid-1970s, House members could expect to spend in the range of $50,000 to wage a creditable effort; by the late 1980s, bitter contests in expensive media markets ran in excess of $1 million. An additional consideration for congressmen elected before 1980 (when the rules were changed) was that unused campaign funds could be converted, incredibly, to a congressman's personal use upon retirement.

Whatever the motivation, amassing large war chests has become a congressional preoccupation. Members of the Finance and Appropriations committees, for example—those that exercise influence over taxes and spending—are typically well favored by interest groups eager to curry their favor. Political-action committees in particular, the source now of many large contributions, are especially disposed toward those who control the pursestrings of government; these congressmen are the ones whose actions impinge most immediately on their interests. "PAC" money is no idle matter; by 1988 nearly $100 million of it was being awarded to congressional candidates, and for a majority of House members elected that year it provided at least half of their campaign funds. A congressman's most vocal constituencies—auto workers who want import tariffs, elderly citizens worried about Medicare benefits, corporate managers concerned about depreciation schedules—also recognize helpful committee membership. As a result there are few more direct means for a congressman to promote his own reelection than to offer himself as a source of influence to groups that can provide him money, foot soldiers, credibility, and votes.

Thus the problem of the House International Relations Committee. Practical-minded congressmen cringe at the thought of the fund-raising difficulties it presents. Foreign governments are prohibited from contributing to congressional campaign coffers, and domestic foreign-policy lobbies, with rare exception, are not known for rich endowments. Emblematic of the realities, the committee's roster as published in the *Congressional Directory* during Don's first term contained three long dashes at the bottom of the Democratic list, an embarrassing indication of vacancies. (This also had political significance. Since the Democrats had a substantial majority in the full House chamber, they were entitled to a similar apportionment of committee seats. Not filling them hampered their ability to control the results of committee voting.)

Congressmen who take membership on a foreign-affairs panel often rationalize it as an educational or philanthropic mission. Don was somewhat different; although it may not have been his first choice, he was heartfelt in his interest. In part this resulted from the strong religious convictions that he brought to his work. A born-again Christian, he sought divine inspiration for his decisions, actively associating with other evangelicals in the Congress. They seemed to be divided into two schools: those who, it was said, wrapped the Bible in the flag, invoking severe moral standards to justify conservative positions; and those, like Don, who wrapped the flag in the Bible, their tenets counseling tolerance and compassion. As a result Don's religious outlook reinforced his instinctive liberal opinions, and his appointment to the House International Relations Committee, in particular, provided a perch from which he could articulate his concerns about the moral aspects of foreign policy.

In addition, although he lacked an obvious expertise in the subject, Don was able to claim a demonstrated interest, citing the fact that he had taken courses in international relations as a college student in Oregon many years before. He was the first to admit, however, that he had not intended to make this field of study a professional pursuit. Indeed Don had decided to hire a foreign-affairs specialist partly to perform (and so he would introduce me) as his personal tutor. His diligence was impressive, but if he found me suitable, it had less to do with my limited knowledge than with what he would glamorously describe as my "Princeton credentials." Don must have been trying to flatter me, because the reaction of his constituents was quite the opposite. One of the newspapers there, the *Daily Olympian* of Olympia, Washington—disparaged by some for its one-note conservatism as the "Daily Zero"—was moved to editorialize that Congressman Bonker had lost touch with his constituency. Its prime evidence of this fact was that for foreign-policy advice he had chosen to rely not on a homegrown product of his district but on an "ex-Ivy League graduate student," as if the term summed up the most unwholesome of possible influences.

Don was deliberate in his method and determined to learn. One evening early on he invited me to his home to review background materials for an upcoming committee hearing. His ever-gracious wife, seeking to minimize diversions during valued study time, phoned out quietly for pizza. Don had been assigned to the subcommittee on Africa and needed to acquaint himself with the issues in its jurisdiction. Eventually he was to become one of the most knowledgeable congressional spokesmen on the subject, but for the moment his background was scant. "Let's get a map," he would say, searching for various countries. He was eager to learn his facts, even down to the pronunciation of names. When we came to Zaire's president Sese Seko Mobutu, he found it a tongue-twister, and we practiced it many times. It was a tribute to his application that he never hesitated to ask elementary questions, and it was fortunate for me that he did: I was only a step ahead.

Of course Don had other responsibilities and could sandwich in such homework only occasionally. For long periods he would turn his attention away from issues of foreign policy and address himself to matters more pertinent to his constituency, such as the need to dredge a deeper local port. (Luckily for Don, he had one other committee assignment—Merchant Marine and Fisheries—which, while not as important as International Relations in the congressional scheme, was of greater significance to his coastal district.) I would be left to cover hearings on my own, gamely explaining Don's absence to other aides, who in turn would tell similar stories of why their bosses weren't there either.

Even when Don attended, his participation was quiet and restrained; I despaired at the slow rate at which it appeared we would transform American foreign policy. But Mike van Deusen, a long-time aide to Congressman Lee Hamilton of Indiana, offered me encouragement one day when he commented that Don reminded him of his own boss in his early days. He said that Hamilton—at this point one of the most respected members of the committee—had acquired expertise and self-confidence only gradually but had been well served by working at a methodical pace: he had gained respect precisely because he avoided the occasional showboating antics of other members. Mike predicted that the fact that Don husbanded his energies and maintained a generally low profile would cause his colleagues to pay more attention on those selected occasions when he did express his views, and I think time proved him right.

Committee meetings were frequent, but the attendance of members often sparse, a phenomenon that revealed much about the workings of Congress. Committees (and subcommittees) are the workhorses of the institution, expected to produce, scrutinize, and expedite legislation. Sometimes they convene for investigative hearings—the questioning of administration witnesses and outside critics about events and policies— and at other times for "markup," when their purpose is actually to draft and approve laws. Many hearings of the International Relations Committee had a perfunctory quality, such as when it was merely discharging its jurisdictional obligation to review foreign-aid authori-

THE PECKING ORDER: LIFE WITH A FRESHMAN / 81

zations. Others addressed individual members' pet topics—whither Armenian refugees?—intended to please constituencies or gain local TV coverage although they held little general interest. Under the best of circumstances, Kafkaesque congressional logistics created hurdles to attendance: committee and floor activities often occurred simultaneously, and all of this during coveted office time when congressmen had appointments to keep with staff and visitors. But at times hearings concerned colorful front-page news topics or featured witnesses important enough to fill a room with network television cameras; the testimony of a cabinet secretary was treated as a celebrity appearance. On such an occasion the expectation of extensive news coverage nearly assured that a full complement of members would attend—and that an entire morning would be consumed in a competition among them to denounce or defend administration policy in a way best calculated to win sound bites on the evening news. The purpose of a hearing was often less to learn new information than to press preconceived points, less educational than accusatory. Motivations varied, of course. Some congressmen sought personal publicity; others felt deeply about the issues and knew that this represented their chance to bring a point of view to public attention.

In the event of an important committee meeting I would typically proceed with Don from our personal office suite down assorted elevators and escalators into the adjoining Rayburn House Office Building and then through long halls to the main committee room. Our respective roles would be obvious to the trained eye of passersby: Don strode purposefully, saluting or remarking to other congressmen we passed along the way, and I would follow a half step behind, trying precariously to balance the overflowing folders and notebooks of background material that I brought to hearings for possible consultation. (Most of it would prove unnecessary.) Faced with only a few available minutes to impart all the information I had spent the previous afternoon gathering, I would hastily summarize expected points of testimony and provide intelligence on the intentions of Don's colleagues.

Reaching the large oak doors of Room 2172, I would proceed to a place in the audience while Don joined other committee members at the dais; a clerk would immediately set a nameplate in front of him, fill his water glass, and direct his attention to the set of prepared remarks that a witness at that moment would be paraphrasing. (Except for chairmen, who are needed to call the meeting to order, congressmen almost invariably arrive late, knowing that they will be missing only the ceremonial formalities.) Meanwhile committee staff would be taking their places behind members, frequently to be called on for whispered assistance. Old hands such as Marion Czarnecki, Jack Brady, Bob Boyer, and George Berdes—knowledgeable committee aides who coordinated closely with administration officials—might have prepared recommendations so that action could be taken swiftly on motion of the chairman. And personal staff sat indistinguishably among the public, making the always-present distinction between themselves and committee staff even more visible than usual.

From where I watched, facing the committee, the setting seemed at times excessively august. Rich wood paneling and bas-relief designs covered thirty-foot-high walls, mammoth navy blue draperies framed towering windows, and the raised platform on which committee members sat made them seem to peer down at witnesses from Mount Olympus. About thirty-five congressmen comprised the full committee, physically arrayed in two curved and elevated tiers in a cavernous modern hearing room, obviously built prior to concerns about energy efficiency. There was a nice symmetry to the arrangements. Democrats were assigned to the left, Republicans to the right; senior members above, junior members below. They were a hodgepodge of backgrounds and styles, but a sociological typology might have identified three broad categories among the Democratic majority, the shifting weight of which tended to decide committee action: old guard, great compromisers, and young Turks.

The "old guard" consisted of veteran members, who had arrived at least fifteen years earlier and come up through the ranks during a very traditional era when Congress was highly deferential in its dealings with the executive branch on foreign policy. They seemed alternatively startled and bemused at the increasingly assertive character of their younger colleagues. The chairman of the committee, Thomas P. "Doc" Morgan, a Pennsylvania Democrat, epitomized them. He was large and jolly and presided quietly and inoffensively; it was a tribute to his personal popularity and longevity of service, distinctly more than his contribution to foreign affairs, that explained the committee's action on his retirement to name their hearing room in his honor. If Doc Morgan rarely stated a personal conviction, other long-reigning congressmen who sat alongside him rarely said anything at all, tending to vote as a bloc behind the chairman. One exception was Clem Zablocki, a Wisconsin maverick given to expressing candid opinions and frustration with other members, although the fact that his visage and facial expressions faintly resembled those of Popeye tended to soften the occasionally harsh edge of his words. He would become chairman in the succeeding Congress, although not without resistance from several members whom his manner had annoyed.

The "great compromisers" occupied the pivotal ground in the committee, showing sympathy with the concerns of their younger colleagues yet maintaining more than a sentimental attachment to the traditions of the institution. Their backgrounds were a reflection of the mosaiclike diversity of the Congress. Jonathan Bingham was white-haired, thin, and craggy, at once as patrician and progressive as his one-time service to New York governor Averell Harriman might have suggested. Dante Fascell of Florida was his perfect opposite. Short and squat, he wore colorful polyester; where Bingham was reserved and precise, Fascell was effusive and colloquial. Ben Rosenthal was a feisty New Yorker, as wise in the ways of Congress as of the streets of Queens, which he represented. Lee Hamilton was the incarnation of his own sober Hoosier constituency: quiet but solid. All of these men possessed an extraordinary ability to get to the point of issues and to articulate practical solutions. They indulged the iconoclastic opinions of the younger members, simultaneously seeking their acceptance of a more incremental pace of reform. It was not their intention to introduce wholesale changes into American foreign policy but to preserve the consensus that they felt to be its essential backbone. Yet more than the old guard, they knew the issues, cared about them, and had the intellectual agility to identify a middle ground. Any committee action that departed from the norm was usually the result of the persuasion that could be exercised upon this group by the next one.

And the "young Turks" (the group to which Don belonged) were determined to do so. They were not strident or unpleasant, but there was no mistaking the seriousness of their views. Michael Harrington of Massachusetts was a sort of prep-school revolutionary; his muted voice and elegant words veiled deep skepticism about American foreign policy. Helen Meyner, the cheerful wife of a former governor of New Jersey, gave the appearance at times of an innocent housewife who had wandered onto the stage not entirely on her own. But looks were deceiving; she had strong liberal opinions and supplied important votes. And Leo Ryan's adventurous turns of mind were evident not only in the provocative comments he made at hearings, but ultimately in a trip to South America, where he was shot dead following his visit to Jonestown, Guyana, an action that apparently helped to trigger the mass suicide there.

But perhaps the prime example of the species was freshman Stephen

Solarz of Brooklyn. It was clear that he considered himself from the beginning to be a foreign-policy specialist as much as a congressman, discoursing in long and detailed passages about highly technical issues, and showing no special deference to his congressional elders. About him it might have been said that he had never met a piece of legislation he did not want to amend. He was indeed sophisticated and articulate, but for the tastes of some seemed too much like the classroom prodigy who raises his hand furiously for recognition during every discussion. His dedication to the subject became evident in his record-setting number of trips abroad (in one year forty-five countries in nine separate tours); but his travels were also known for their serious purposes and heavy workload. Over the years Solarz's manner softened somewhat, and he developed an impressive ability to bridge factions, contributing effectively to the committee's work. But by that point, of course, he had transcended the "young Turk" stage and had come more nearly to resemble the great compromisers.

As for the Republicans, several were individually quite eloquent, but they were scattered over the ideological spectrum and therefore not notably influential as a group. I particularly enjoyed two members from Illinois, Ed Derwinski and Paul Findley. Everything about Derwinski was hearty: his build, his manner, his humor. He stated his views in an earthy way, often with sarcasm, but his keen intelligence and wit made him popular even with adversaries. Findley was more academic—actually, he was an ex-journalist—and always seemed, if not politic, ever so *rational*. Charles Whalen of Ohio was a similar voice of moderation; indeed their larynxes literally seemed to be set to the same pitch, a modulating, comforting, radio announcer's tone that exuded credibility. Millicent Fenwick, the famous pipe-smoking congresswoman, and John Buchanan, a onetime southern preacher, were as liberal on many issues as any Democrat. Bill Broomfield, the soft-spoken ranking minority member, was more traditionally conservative, but not prone to battling uphill. Committee membership is, to a large degree, self-selected, and it may be that congressmen who accept a foreign-policy assignment tend toward a more worldly—and less jingoistic—perspective than others. There were in fact a number of issues on which Democrats and Republicans worked closely together.

Meanwhile Don's junior status was placed in bold relief by the fact that he sat at the very end of the rostrum; Solarz and Meyner, his fellow freshmen, had won their committee assignment only moments sooner, but that was enough to put them a notch ahead. The positions had a potential significance: Were they all still around by the time subcommittee or even full committee chairmanships came vacant, the others would have prior claim. The only tangible impact for the time being was something far more mundane: questioning of witnesses proceeded by seniority, and when all members attended an important hearing, it could be hours before Don had his chance. By that time the audience had lost interest, and the television cameramen, who had shot more than enough footage for the evening newscasts, would be noisily disassembling their equipment.

In such circumstances I would look on anxiously from the audience, wondering what would be left for Don to say. It was not that I hoped he would do anything dramatic—junior members (and their staffs) often feel relieved to have the controversial points raised by others better able to tangle with expert witnesses—but it seemed to me that his allotted five minutes presented a rare opportunity for him to shine before his peers. The simple act of making a thoughtful, cogent statement could go a long way toward establishing his reputation. Perhaps other members would gain new respect for his abilities, administration officials come to see him as more influential, and the press flash his name across their wires. Of course this was more the stuff of daydreams than reality, for there was only so much that could be addressed in five minutes, and if it had any significance, it would probably have been said already.

Moreover, congressmen did not always do what their staffs hoped. It was a common reaction among aides to sigh that their bosses had not asked the questions nor made the statements that they had prepared for them so carefully. Often the materials would be rephrased beyond recognition or simply discarded in favor of spontaneous inspiration (which, of course, could be incisive and dramatic, or not so at all). At the other extreme, some congressmen were known for sticking all too faithfully to their scripts—complete with blank stare and a mouthful of mispronunciations. The best use of staff, it seemed to me, was to provide succinct summaries of background material that congressmen would not have had the time to research and study themselves and to suggest significant lines of inquiry they might otherwise neglect. Congressmen are keen judges of general public concerns, but they are usually not specialists who keep up, as staffers do, with day-to-day developments on given issues. In addition they vary in their abilities to absorb information and their aggressiveness in using it.

If congressmen failed to read their staff memos (or, for that matter, the morning paper), they could come to committee hearings surprisingly unprepared. One day this fact gave us an opening. Secretary of State Cyrus Vance was to testify, and I had prepared questions for Don to ask about covert U.S. aid to Zaire, a matter of great controversy that newspapers had revealed during the preceding several days in repeated stories. We believed fervently that such aid was misdirected (Zaire's government was corrupt and unreliable), and, in any event, that it should be extended only on congressional authorization, which had not yet been given. Don wanted to raise these points publicly with administration officials, but we commiserated before the hearing that more senior members would surely exhaust the topic before he had his turn. Yet to our surprise, once Vance finished his testimony and questions began, one congressman after another omitted to ask about it. Suddenly we realized that, dead last though he was, Don might be the one to do so. As his turn drew near and I sensed that the press had all but given up hope that someone would broach the issue they so obviously wanted to cover, I raced over to alert them to Don's intent and suggest that they stay. The scenario materialized perfectly: Don asked about Zaire, Secretary Vance gave hesitant responses, Don pressed further, and reporters scribbled furiously.

The next day front-page articles citing administration comment on the issue invariably noted that it had come in response to questions posed by Representative Don Bonker at a congressional hearing. Even more dramatically, the *Washington Post* editorialized against aid and congratulated Don in print for having been the only one to challenge the administration on the issue. We were not under an illusion that this would decide many votes back in the district, but it did serve momentarily to advance Don's standing among his colleagues and to earn me my own enhanced prestige in the eyes of my boss. Most of all we had helped place an important issue under the public spotlight, a motivation that had brought both of us, on our different paths, to the Hill.

But such episodes were rare, and usually Don remained obscure. In melancholy moments as I waited interminably for his turn to come, I would gaze across the tiers of congressmen in the committee room and find it almost impossible to imagine that he would ever progress to the top rung—or that his staff could ever attain concomitant seniority. Yet turnover on committees is more frequent than one may suppose, and within a few years Don had climbed quite a lot, although I was no longer with him. Among the Democrats, there were retirements (Morgan, Bingham, Harrington, L. H. Fountain, Lester Wolff), committee switches (Cardiss Collins), campaigns for other office (Don Fraser), indictments (Charles Diggs), electoral defeats (Meyner, Robert Nix), sex scandal resignations (Wayne Hays), natural deaths (Zablocki, Rosenthal), and bizarre murders (Ryan). The evolving committee membership was an interesting commentary on the fate of congressmen. More to the point, it allowed Don, by 1988, to advance nearly to the top of the roster. But that year, his sights having risen even faster, he ran for the Senate—unsuccessfully—and in the process gave up his own safe seat as a congressman. He never did make it all the way.

10

"LA"

For weeks I had studied the intricacies of Pentagon arms transfers to foreign nations: the various grant and commercial sales schemes that had made America munitions merchant to the world. My concern mounted as I learned that each year we shipped over $10 billion worth of lethal military equipment to countless authoritarian and unstable regimes, a radical expansion from only $1 billion six years before. The United States, as a result, was exporting more weapons than all other nations of the world combined; we had become, for example, a major supplier of both sides in the arms race between Iran and Arab states on the other side of the Persian Gulf. Here, I thought confidently, was an issue tailor-made for reformers. No doubt Don would want me to start girding him for battle.

Armed with a large sheaf of briefing papers, I entered his office and joined him at a couch and coffee table. I had told him we needed a few minutes to discuss an issue, something we did often, but had not warned him that this time it might be in the nature of a scholarly seminar. I was proud of the detail I had so recently absorbed and was anxious to share it.

"Now, let's begin with the FMS credit sales," I said, employing my new jargon and beginning to sketch diagrams and numbers. Don, who probably expected that I would simply ask his opinion about cosponsoring a bill, drew back. "Mark," he said, "is any *action* required on this?" I looked up. "Well, no," I admitted, "not at this time." Don shrugged. "Don't misunderstand," he said. "I want you to pursue the issue. It's important, and I want to be involved. Just wait until you have something for me to sign off on before you tell me more."

From that moment I began to recognize the vastly different perspectives of congressmen and aides—and the wisdom of Don's judgment. A congressman's time is severely constrained: committee meetings, floor votes, constituent visits, speaking engagements, fund-raising obligations, social rounds, and paperwork pull him constantly in a hundred directions. Leisurely reflection is an expendable luxury. Many aides, on the other hand, are compartmentalized in much narrower areas and live and breathe the same subject all day long. They come to have strong attachments to their field, and at times seem to exist for those moments when they can engage the attention of their bosses; this represents their most obvious opportunity to translate personal musings into public action. As a result staffers can be somewhat trigger-happy, tending to see given issues as considerably more important than do their employers.

In fact an effective aide shows restraint, screening matters closely and advancing them only sparingly to his boss's agenda as decisions are required, preferably with recommendations attached for specific courses of action. Congress may be called a deliberative body, but it makes its influence felt less in classic floor debate than in the committee hearings and reports, press releases and phone calls, and bills and amendments that a controversy produces. Whatever it may have been in the past, Congress today is an action-oriented institution. Members concerned about an issue want to know what they can *do* about it. And on matters where their interest is more passive, they have the time to apply themselves only where an issue is forced, as when they must finally vote on it. Staffers, for their part, often have an ambivalence about their boss's involvement. When Don turned his focus to local politics and away from foreign policy, I could feel neglected; on the other hand that is when I was often given my greatest latitude and authority, since he was depending on me even more at those times to represent him.

The weapons-sales issue was characteristic of my work as a legislative assistant. Don simply did not have a sufficient number of available hours to invest in academic study of the subject and therefore expected me to delve into it for him. I should have realized that he would want to be spared the details: My role was to help shoulder work, not add to it. Having been encouraged to proceed, I participated over time in the staff-level drafting of proposed legislative restrictions. Later, at the appropriate stage, Don requested a briefing and recommendation, signed on, and helped engineer the support of many of his colleagues. The arms-sales ceiling that came out of the process marked an extraordinary congressional departure from the deference traditionally shown the executive branch in these matters—so much so that President Ford vetoed the eventual bill. By the time I worked on my next issue, human rights, I had refined my technique. Congressman Don Fraser of Minnesota was pioneering work in this area, and it seemed another obvious cause for an idealistic freshman. Knowing Don's general support for "morality in foreign policy," I did not hesitate to attend extensive strategy sessions with others before I bothered him with the details of our proposed initiatives. Typically aides would coordinate with subcommittee staffer John Salzberg, or meet with Fraser himself, who might bring along a leading dissident such as former Chilean foreign minister Orlando Letelier, later to be assassinated in Washington by agents of his government for exactly such agitation. Preliminary work accomplished, Don would tend to approve my recommendations and commend me on my initiative.

Legislative assistants—"LAs" as they are universally known in Washington—are quintessential staffers of Capitol Hill, intellectual go-getters at the heart of the legislative process, expected to flag opportunities, reason out sophisticated positions, and help maneuver to victory. They prompt their bosses with lines of argument for committee debate and ghostwrite their statements for the floor, summarize issues and recommend votes, monitor and challenge activities of the executive branch, negotiate with colleagues, and, always high on the list, devise bills and amendments, other good deeds, or at least persuasive explanations to impress important constituencies. In a sense they are the connecting link between congressional politics and substance. Much of a legislator's office, after all, is not geared to legislation: Like a small business, congressmen employ administrative assistants, office managers, mail clerks, personal aides, publicists, customer-relations specialists ("caseworkers," in Hill lingo), secretaries, and receptionists. More than these others, it is the LAs who plunge into actual committee and floor activity and who tune in to the details of national policy. They work in the front lines of legislative battle, and perhaps it is for this reason that, able to indulge their Walter Mitty fantasies considerably more than ordinary people, they often seem to enjoy their jobs so much.

A typical congressman may have two to four LAs, a senator sometimes twice as many. The numbers have leaped over the years along with that of congressional staff generally; throughout much of the 1950s, Senator John Kennedy represented the state of Massachusetts with a single LA. Portfolios are often divided along the lines of committee jurisdictions or generic policy topics—one LA may cover banking, housing, and energy, for example, while another looks after armed services, agriculture, and taxes—with the result that individual responsibilities can be of a rather motley character. In other cases an LA may focus more narrowly on an area of special interest; a congressman who aims to make a name for himself on the Commerce Committee may want an assistant who can devote nearly full time to telecommunications policy.

House LAs tend to be young, commonly in their twenties; theirs can be an entry-level professional position requiring no previous Hill experience. (Committee staffers, in contrast, tend to be more specialized, and therefore older and of greater experience.) Their workaday world is informal and often frenetic: It helps not to be encumbered by family nor spoiled by the habit of regular working hours or a predictable daily existence. Although during recesses the Congress is a land of relative slumber—abbreviated hours are the fashion among those unfortunate enough not to be on government-financed travel—in high season it is literally a place of flashing lights (the omnipresent TV cameras) and clanging bells (a cryptic aural code that announces impending votes and other parliamentary maneuvers). Fifty-to-sixty-hour work weeks are not unusual. Under constant time pressure and a multitude of urgent assignments, LAs typically switch among projects and topics by the half hour; they learn to write quickly, think politically, and argue combatively. In crowded offices, their desks nudged up against each other in ways that would affront a fire marshal, they do their own typing, photocopying, and phone-calling. They then suspend any calm reflections until things settle down again at six or seven or eight o'clock at night, and they think of walking up Pennsylvania Avenue with friends to unwind at a local watering hole, such as upscale Jenkin's Hill or the earthier Tune Inn.

My quarters typified the environment of a House LA. I was tucked away in Room 1514A of the Longworth House Office Building, an address that, to arbiters of social status, signified the lowly position of freshmen who drew last in the biennial housing lottery. The first 1 in the room number indicated that, of the three House buildings, we were in Longworth, the oldest and least commodious; the 5 meant we were on the fifth floor, in a building known for its exasperatingly slow-moving elevators; and the A expressed the fact that some of us who worked for Don resided in an annex of the main office, which is to say an outpost separated by another congressman's entire suite in between. The halls of Longworth were shadowy and uninviting, the views out our window were of another office building, and the decor within could be described most generously as utilitarian. It was a sufficiently out-of-the-way place that Elizabeth Ray, the voluptuous secretary hired by Representative Wayne Hays for purposes other than typing, maintained her desk and theoretical duties in a room around the corner.

The annex was a space measuring about fifteen by twenty-five feet and housing, besides me, another LA, a part-time staff assistant, a secretary, various storage supplies, and one or two pieces of noisy, if fancy, automated typing equipment. At one end was a door to the public corridor, which we tried to keep open to reduce our sense of claustrophobic isolation; at the other end a window with heavy blinds, through which we would regularly peek when we heard sirens blaring and wanted to see which illustrious person's motorcade was arriving at the entrance below. In between were floor-to-ceiling walnut shelves and cabinets, which overflowed with aging *Congressional Records* and other dust-collecting items that had been evicted from our front office.

At the desk adjoining my own was a likable young high school teacher from the district, Ron Lundberg, who thought a stint in Washington might provide him a constructive civics lesson. He was quiet and philosophical, resistant to the quick pace of congressional life, and all in all too much a passing observer to qualify as a typical LA. In his corner he often pushed back from his typewriter, musing aloud to the rest of us upon the foibles of Congress and how he would try to describe them to his impressionable students without diminishing the luster of the democratic process. In one sense he communed admirably with his new environment: After a couple of years on the job Ron returned home with one of the office secretaries as a wife, a heartwarming interoffice romance that, although I worked in the same few square feet with both parties, had characteristically eluded my notice until the day they announced their impending wedding.

Rounding out the legislative office was our part-timer, Phyllis Rov-
ine, a mother who had raised small children and was returning to the
work force. Her excitement about issues no doubt had to do in part
with her own sensation of professional renewal, but it was infectious
and lent our little annex the occasional intellectual aura of a Left Bank
Parisian café. In time we had one other confrere, who joined us from
across the ocean for a few months, his purpose to study the American
political system. This was Nicholas Soames, a grandson of Winston
Churchill, whose acquaintance Don had made through a religious fellowship. Nicholas, rotund and imposing in the manner of his fore-
bears, was fabulously funny and perceptive—and startled by the activism
of younger members, on which he offered us running commentary.
Motivated by his new perspectives, he went back and energetically gained
election as a member of Parliament, a more spirited backbencher for
his exposure to junior members of the U.S. Congress.

Our main office was most nearly the nerve center of the operation.
Dave Yaden, the AA, sat immediately beyond the desks of two receptionists and not far from an all-important interior corridor leading to
the photocopy machine and coffee maker. A further clue to his importance was the fact that his desk was hidden from view by two jerry-
built six-foot-high partitions, from behind which he could address the
discreet personnel and political matters in which AAs tend to specialize. A friend of the congressman's who had assisted during the campaign, Dave was imported from Oregon for the job. He was both
intellectual and streetwise, and although he hailed from across the
river and not the district itself, he knew its geography and, far more
importantly, its political landscape. He was the perfect AA, responsible
and mature, measured in his utterances, and, in his mid-thirties, sufficiently older than the rest of the staff to command our natural respect, yet close enough to Don in age to be considered a peer and
relied on for frank advice. Jim Van Nostrand, our fireball of a press
secretary, looked every inch the part: hair unruly, shirt untucked,
mumbling under his breath constantly about assignments and deadlines; the office would have seemed empty without him. Other aides
came and went. Donna Inserra, a dynamic young lawyer who had
served briefly on the staff but earned immortality by affectionately
nicknaming our boss "the Bonk," checked back frequently from her
new position as a CBS News assistant and pronounced our environment to be tame in comparison.

Several aides served locally in the district, although I had little contact with them except as questions arose that required my consultation.

They would then call and hesitatingly inquire, "Well, I don't really follow these things, but was there a foreign-aid bill passed recently?" The situation bred some social tension: LAs in Washington take pride in their "big picture" mentality and sometimes dismiss local concerns as "parochial." Aides in the district, for their part, seem to alternate between feelings of inferiority about their imperfect knowledge of national politics and resentment that young people in Washington without roots or real interest in the district have the ear and the time of the congressmen. Of course local aides perform an essential job in minding the home front, and Washington staffers who recognize their own interests are in fact most grateful.

Perks were a symbolic matter. Congressional aides are deprived of some that might be bestowed, for example, on young lawyers: private offices, personal secretaries, generous expense accounts. But those they do receive give them a sense of power. Soon after arriving in Don's office I was supplied with business cards made to look impressively official by the presence in the upper left-hand corner of an embossed gold eagle symbolizing the authority of the Congress. In the House barbershop I could sit alongside congressmen and feel all the more a political insider (as well as receive a subsidized haircut and shoeshine). When I tired of the warehouselike Longworth or Rayburn cafeterias, I could take lunch in the more exclusive Members' Dining Room of the Capitol, and although unaccompanied aides were admitted to only one of its two sections, congressmen would spill over into it, creating the impression of a political Polo Lounge, which never failed to excite out-of-town guests. If I wanted to attend President Carter's inaugural or State of the Union address, or a joint session of Congress to hear King Juan Carlos of Spain or French president Valery Giscard d'Estaing, tickets flowed freely.

My real power, of course, came from my derivative position. Although I may have been only one of the many aides within both my office and the Congress, to the outside world I represented an elected official, and the line could easily blur. When I called the State Department, I could cloak my own inquiries as those of "the congressman"—I was, after all, working on his behalf—and in this way command large amounts of time and attention from the executive branch. Officials at the other end, whatever their suspicions, had no way of knowing the congressman's real involvement, nor did they care to take chances. Lobbyists would treat me as though I were a direct line to my boss, even though my purpose was often to spare him from having to deal with, or even know about, their interests. (The arrangement suited them as well: they could claim to have talked with congressmen even though by this they really meant their aides.) And when I had occasion to phone constituents, the shivers I sent down their spines to announce I was calling from Washington were nearly audible.

Office life had its decidedly perfunctory aspects as well, perhaps best epitomized in the omnipresent task of answering constituent mail, something I naively imagined to have left behind with my lower-caste position in Senator Humphrey's office. Although legend has it that there are still congressmen who eagerly read and answer their mail personally—those, such as William Natcher of Kentucky, who have served many years and whose habits may be a relic from another age—more commonly it is handled in routinized fashion by staff or machine, although at least the AA will usually approve drafts of form letters or of important individual ones. Congressmen know that correspondence is a valuable source of information about voter sentiment and recognize that they may be judged on election day according to their responses. The problem is the sheer volume, often hundreds of letters and postcards a day addressed even to the office of a junior member. Much of it is generated en masse by organized interest groups, sometimes from outside the district, and may deserve its impersonal treatment. Properly handled, however, it can present a public-relations opportunity. An unpopular position can be explained in a more compelling way; a congressman's prompt response or gracious language can impress constituents with his diligence and thoughtfulness.

Happily for Don, our AA was quantitative in bent and dedicated to introducing us to the era of computerized mail. Eventually he had us filling out continual forms for our letters, so that information could be entered into a data bank and constituents identified by legislative interests for targeted follow-up. Coded entries made for easy retrieval of original correspondence, and "ticklers" reminded us that responses were due. Computer-generated mail permitted the composition of modular letters from a wide selection of stock paragraphs. In turn this allowed for the tailoring of replies in terms of both issues and points of view: a constituent might receive a different form letter depending on whether the comments made were classified as "pro" or "con." ("I share your feelings about this vital issue and appreciate your support . . ." or, "This was a difficult decision, but I ultimately decided to oppose the bill, for the following reasons. . . .")

My impression is that these ploys persuade most constituents that their letters are personally read and absorbed by the officials they address. To this day some of the most educated and sophisticated people I know inform me, without a trace of irony, that Congressman Smith knows about something or other because they have written him about it. Congressmen, of course, encourage the fiction. In theory, they could send back *mimeographed* replies stating, "I hope you can understand that the number of letters I receive prevents an individual reply. But for your information, enclosed is a statement of my position on the issue that you raised." Instead offices employ high-speed "robotype" machines to produce individually typed letters, and autopens to affix the member's authentic-looking signature, and congressmen become adept at pretending to remember constituents and their letters when they return home. (One golden oldie congressmen tell on themselves is about their colleague who asks the constituent how his mother is doing. "She's passed away," comes the reply. "And did you get my flowers?" asks the congressman, not missing a beat.)

Our AA did his best to inculcate the new computer culture into us, but for some it didn't take. I myself preferred simply taking a sheet of congressional letterhead, sticking it in the typewriter, and drafting a short and immediate response without having to fill out accompanying invoices. Jim, the press secretary, kept a sign on his desk: "See it once, handle it once." This was meant to remind him of the efficiency of dealing quickly with incoming assignments, but the admonition, while aspired to, ultimately went unheeded, a fact reflected in the perpetual chaos that consumed his desk. My own work area was only slightly more virtuous, but I took the aphorism far more seriously when it came to my letters. They were something I didn't care to linger over.

A not insignificant portion was referred to as "flake mail," letters from those inspired to write because they had learned of a sinister worldwide conspiracy and wished to warn officials in the most alarming tones about it, or who wholly misunderstood an issue or misconstrued a representative's position and wanted to take exception with all the bigotry and irrationality at their command. Regularly we were apprised that Nelson Rockefeller was preparing to overthrow the government, or that the government was in fact already in the hands of a nefarious cabal such as the Council on Foreign Relations. (When I later became a member of this organization, I was most disappointed to learn that it had no such power, although one group of critics continued to list all the members' names in one of its mailings and label us "the world's unelected leaders" to my great delight.) Many of those who wrote were well-known repeaters who were never satisfied with our answers. They earned unenviable reputations within the office and even the honor of having their latest missive taped up on a desk divider for public display.

Such skeptical treatment of constituent mail may be surprising considering the hallowed place it holds in democratic myth: "Write your congressman" is the timeless injunction offered citizens seeking to express a grievance; in the climax of the movie classic Mr. Smith Goes to Washington, boxes of constituent letters are hauled onto the Senate floor to make a point. Sometimes letter-writing campaigns are effective, particularly on an issue where a representative may not otherwise hold a strong opinion. (If they don't actually read the letters, congressmen are certainly interested to know the "pro" and "con" tallies.) At other times letters won't change a thing. Perhaps the baldest example is the regular maneuvering over a congressional pay raise. Polls invariably show vast public disapproval of such action, and letters pour in accordingly, but for some congressmen the question this begs is not whether they are in tune with constituents but how to disguise or defend predetermined positions. It is common to hear the private explanation "If only people back home realized how much it costs to live in Washington, and maintain another residence in the district, etc., they'd agree." And, of course these congressmen may be right. It should be remembered that even Jimmy Stewart, portraying the noblest of representatives in the Mr. Smith movie, stubbornly ignored all those constituent letters—because they opposed him—but in the end was vindicated for his independence. Yet in 1989 a public uproar helped to defeat a proposed 50 percent pay raise, although many congressmen still thought they could have won it if only Speaker Jim Wright had more artfully avoided a direct vote.

LAs probably take more interest than other aides in "issues," yet there sometimes seems to be a tug-of-war going on in their minds over whether they are generalists or specialists. On the one hand they consider themselves quick studies who, as lawyers might describe members of their own profession, are trained to take on almost any subject, gather relevant information, and discern key points. When they need detail, resources are available in abundance. From Don's office, for example, I could order an individual analysis or stock "issue brief" from the Congressional Research Service on almost any topic. (The CRS, a part of the Library of Congress, is dedicated to such inquiries; 850-employees strong, it receives nearly 300,000 requests a year for information from Hill offices.) The Democratic Study Group and House Republican Conference, among other in-house research organs, also produced cogent and readily available policy analysis. Alternatively I could pick up the phone and call a subcommittee specialist or perhaps a desk officer at the State Department. For outside viewpoints I might query a scholar at the Brookings Institution, a university, or one of the nearby public-interest lobbies, such as the Council for a Livable World or the Coalition for a New Foreign Policy. Even when it came to writing actual legislation, all I needed to do was take Don's inspirations, or my own, to the office of legislative counsel, where a battery of lawyers would craft them with jargony legislative language into the fine points of law. At times I was left to feel like a contestant on an old television game show where the object was, using a telephone and available directories, to find the answer to a question before the buzzer sounded. Time constraints made "quick and dirty" efforts a necessity. In effect I was a middleman between the politicians and the experts— parties that, in a more leisurely world, might have talked directly.

Indeed LAs are valued as much for this knowledge of process as for their familiarity with particular issues. They know procedures and customs, and many have established elaborate networks among their peers and honed interpersonal skills as much as congressmen themselves. (Some overdo it and are sneered at by others as "Senator" Such-and-such, so aggressively do they perform their roles.) Accordingly newly elected members of Congress often confer coveted staff positions not on loyal campaign aides but on "permanent" Washingtonians who already possess institutional experience. I was an example. My entire knowledge of Don's district consisted of having traveled through it during a twenty-four-hour period on a family vacation nearly a decade before. But even my limited Humphrey and Hannaford experiences gave me the aura of a wily native guide who could compensate by navigating unfamiliar Washington terrain.

At the same time LAs almost inevitably come to identify with specialized areas. Some do so in part for professional purposes, seeing in their work a chance to cultivate expertise that will help advance them to other positions on or off the Hill. For example, one friend, Bonnie Caldwell, a talented aide for many years to Congressman Henry Gonzalez of the House Banking Committee, wisely gained a reputation in housing finance; eventually she was lured off the Hill to become a vice president of the Public Securities Association. Quite apart from any commercial motive, LAs typically experience deepening genuine interest in their assigned areas and enjoy the specialization. Again my case was typical. As an LA for foreign affairs, I began to define myself rather narrowly. My day, after all, revolved around specific matters in my field: a subcommittee hearing on establishing a naval presence in the Indian Ocean; communications from the State Department on the Moroccan invasion of the Spanish Sahara; "Dear Colleague" letters from fellow congressmen taking sides in the dispute over Cyprus; public debates over whether to withdraw troops from Korea.

Far from being so dull as a recitation of these topics may suggest, the actual nature of my activities made it a lively, hands-on experience—one that stimulated interest in the same way that otherwise soporific museums entice children by letting them push buttons and turn dials. Hearings, constant phone calls, memos and letters, huddles with other aides and our bosses: Minute-by-minute there were urgent things to be done. In the hall I might trade ideas with counterparts in other freshmen offices—Tim Lovain with Congresswoman Meyner, and John Isaacs with Congressman Solarz—who always seemed brimming with creative new angles on issues of the day. Sometimes I would find fellow aides in the carryouts or cafeterias and, as we waited in long lines for notoriously mediocre food, engage in great debate about pending bills. On other days there was no time for lunch. But if I were lucky the events on my schedule would themselves replenish me: strategy sessions over breakfast, luncheons with lobbyists, afternoon teas with visiting dignitaries, multiple evening cocktail receptions, and more rarefied but equally culinary seminars over dinner.

The daily papers became a basic resource, suggesting legislative initiatives or, a more common fallback, statements in Don's name for the *Congressional Record*, which would, in the frequent interludes between actual legislative activity, signal the world that Don remained vigilant. The newspapers also reminded me that Congress's ordinary concerns were matters of worldly importance; seeing my daily assignments in the neon lights of the *Washington Post* revived any flagging interest. Indeed the underlying significance of the work was its own motivation. Here, still in my early twenties, was a chance to deal in momentous public topics, ones I had come to care about so much myself, and to do so in the wings of a great national stage and in the company of idealistic young congressmen and fellow staffers who felt we really could change the world.

Thus I became a foreign-affairs junkie, irretrievably absorbed in the minutest issues and thrilled at the unaccustomed sensation that I was beginning to possess a specialized knowledge. I began racing with myself to develop expertise. Sometimes I felt transported back to a graduate-school study carrel as I tried to pore through the voluminous literature that interested groups sent to our office. With even more eccentric discipline I required of myself that I read every foreign-affairs-related article that appeared each day in either the *Post* or *The New York Times* (which together nearly define the universe of recognized knowledge in Washington) and that I read them down to the last word, making a point, in sophomoric but useful fashion, to memorize facts. (Admittedly I might supplement these sources with an occasional scholarly article from *Foreign Affairs* magazine.) I even picked up the habit of reading while walking so that I could begin this laborious exercise on my morning strolls to work—although I was also encouraged in my idiosyncrasy during the period when I lived in "redeveloped" southwest Washington and had little else to look at during my passage along stretches of highly unscenic concrete. Unfortunately my return in the evening tended to occur in the darkness, and I was left to tote home crumpled batches of unfinished newspaper, which I would then continue reading, in the obsessive manner of those who devour the sports page, until I fell fast asleep and the cycle began again the next morning with freshly delivered papers.

The technique was straightforward, and it repeatedly surprised me how effective it could be. I had assumed, as many do, that foreign-affairs expertise is the product of long-accumulated professional experience, or unique assets such as extensive travel or access to classified information. But it turns out that vast amounts of detail are available for unimpeded daily perusal in the pages of the major newspapers. Of course it is not natural to read on and on, day after day, about the inner struggles in the governments of Sri Lanka or Botswana. Yet for the effort I would frequently find myself better informed on particular issues than State Department officials, who regularly rotated through new areas, and light-years more knowledgeable than many members of the House International Relations Committee, let alone others in the Congress, who had so much else to occupy their time.

One moral I drew from this was that the constant congressional demand for information is somewhat misdirected. The working assumption of the institution seems to be that the way to learn about a subject is to summon experts or high officials before committees, arrange briefings, take fact-finding trips, or hire more staff specialists. These, of course, can be helpful. But it always seemed to me that if a congressman merely read the relevant sections of *Time* magazine once a week—examining the daily newspapers would be pure extra credit—he would profoundly deepen his knowledge of current events. A congressman's demanding schedule, however, does not always leave the opportunity for that; moreover, some believe that "details" are for staff. At the same time, Congress recognizes that the public expects to see it gathering information. So hearings are scheduled, whether they are attended or not; travel is arranged, whether it is essential or not; and bevies of highly qualified specialists are employed, whether they are used or not. If anything, congressmen sometimes have *too much* information. The aides who provide it are therefore destined to spin their wheels; there will never be enough time to process even a fraction of their work.

There were other constraints on my role as an adviser. Unlike Senate counterparts, personal staff in the House are not generally allowed on the chamber floor, or to sit behind their bosses in committee; probably the rules have something to do with their greater numbers and often younger age. The House gymnasium is even more exclusive, so much a sanctum, it is told, that a special House rule had to be adopted during the period when House Speaker Carl Albert stood next in the line of presidential succession, so that his newly acquired Secret Service escorts might accompany him inside. This meant that Don could conduct many of his most pertinent conversations beyond my access: He was such a basketball fanatic that when his secretary told me he was "on the floor," she lightheartedly meant that he was playing a pickup game in the gym.

For all this, staff often imagine themselves to be more important than they are. One day I was invited to a roundtable luncheon on foreign policy. I was proud of the work I had done on the arms-sales issue and, in making comments, casually spoke of myself as having "written" legislation on the subject as I had heard other aides say among themselves in private conversation. I noticed that Henry Waxman of California, a congressman who attended the session, seemed to wince at my remark. I assumed he was simply impressed that a staffer of such youth had played so important a role. Years later, after my attitudes about staff had been leavened somewhat, it dawned on me that his perspective may have been quite different. By the time legislation winds its way through the process, many have exaggerated ideas about their contribution. Moreover "writing" laws is in theory a function reserved for elected officials, and there is something unseemly about staffers, even if they have played a part, advertising that fact. So I now realize that Congressman Waxman was probably sitting there thinking not "What a cool guy," but "What a jerk!"

I should have appreciated staff's real place sooner. Sometime before, I had read a piece in the *Times* one morning on arms sales; it was written by Cyrus Vance, then a Wall Street lawyer but known to be a likely candidate for secretary of state in a future Democratic administration. Here, I thought, was a chance to express myself to someone who might one day be in a position to take action. I wrote a statement for Don applauding the column, and he submitted the two items together for the *Record*. The next day, after they were printed, I sent a copy to Vance and enclosed a note making my own further comments on the subject.

A few days later I happened to arrive at work early and began to sift through the large stack of morning mail waiting at the doorstep of the main office. A letter with Vance's name and return address caught my eye. My heartbeat quickened; I assumed it would be for me. In fact it was addressed to Don and marked "Personal." Disappointed, I waited in the expectation that he would share it, certain that it would at least offer a reaction to my ideas. Time passed, but Don said nothing. Finally the letter arrived in my box without comment; Don had routinely routed it to me for reply. It began, "Dear Congressman," and contained both thanks and another point or two on arms sales. But it made not the slightest mention of me, my ideas, or my note.

Later, as a more experienced LA, I would realize that it was not important what *I* thought. My views assumed significance only as they were taken to be those of the elected official for whom I worked. "My boss believes . . ." is often simply the preface for a clever LA's own views. Clearly if I needed more direct personal recognition, I was in the wrong business.

11

WAR BETWEEN THE BRANCHES

From my modest redoubt in the Bonker annex, I had looked forward to staging occasional forays into hostile territory (usually considered to be status quo foreign policies of the Republican White House). But I had not imagined that I would actually help Congress mount an assault against the executive branch so furious that it blocked a major foreign-policy initiative. This was the episode of congressional opposition to U.S. intervention in Angola, a flurry of events between 1975 and 1976 that briefly vaulted Don to national recognition and gave me, his lowly aide, a heady sense of influence over national affairs. More importantly, it was the sort of event that gave junior members encouragement that Congress remained a vibrant institution that could, at their prodding, take up good causes and make a difference. It was also an example of new interbranch tensions bred by legislative activists through the expanding use of staff.

The congressional setting in which these events took place was ripe for revolt. Institutional reforms to restore legislative power reached a peak in 1975, when Don's freshman class helped to topple entrenched chairmen Wright Patman of the Banking Committee, W. R. Poage of Agriculture, and F. Edward Hebert of Armed Services—members who had come to Congress in 1929, 1937, and 1941, respectively. The new members held frequent meetings and on some issues threatened to vote as a bloc; the very fact of their election signaled that reform was a potent issue capable of deposing incumbents. Norm Mineta of California, a young Asian-American elected as their leader, was not a firebrand but someone more effective: a soft-spoken and responsible negotiator who commanded wide respect.

The proliferation of subcommittees helped to decentralize power into the hands of younger members. Eventually some proponents of this development would come to rue its unintended consequences: rising jurisdictional conflicts and daily demands on members' time. But in the early 1970s the House Democratic Caucus proudly propounded a "bill of rights" allowing committee members to establish subcommittee membership and competence; previously these matters had been within the nearly sovereign domain of the chairman. Later it required that all committees of more than fifteen members maintain at least four subcommittees. By 1976, as a result, many congressmen were to have six or seven subcommittee assignments; on the Senate side, the average was a stupefying fourteen. A reflection of the change was that there were now more *subcommittee* staffers than there had been full committee staffers ten years earlier. With a total of 268 subcommittees at the high point (the number was not much different as of 1990), many relatively junior members were given a chance to chair panels and originate important work; and even the freshmen in these smaller ponds began feeling like bigger fish.

There were limits. On the House International Relations Committee five subcommittees existed when Don arrived, but a consensus developed to add more. Majority leader Tip O'Neill lobbied for nine, enough to allow fellow Massachusetts congressman Michael Harrington, a second-termer, to take a chairmanship; appointments tended to be made by seniority. Committee elders were willing to acquiesce in some change, but Harrington was too distrusted a maverick; moreover this would have left Steve Solarz, the first-ranking of the committee's freshmen, just one position shy of having his own subcommittee, another threatening prospect. A compromise set the number at eight—still, from the reformers' point of view, an impressive benchmark of progress.

The subcommittees were given staff and performed as miniature committees, flagging issues, summoning witnesses, and writing reports. Some became quite active and on certain issues seized the spotlight from the committee itself. (Much depended on the chairmen; in the case of the Inter-American Affairs Subcommittee, the incumbency of Gus Yatron, a former ice-cream manufacturer from York, Pennsylvania, did little to stimulate creative staff activity. Several years later, however, an energetic successor, Michael Barnes of Maryland, made the panel a national focal point for debate of U.S. policy in Central America.) By now there was no space in the committee's Rayburn suite for the subcommittee apparatus, and it had spilled into converted rooms of the old Congressional Hotel, renamed House Annex No. 1, catty-corner from Longworth. My visits there made me feel like an inspector of tenements. The presence of a uniformed police officer at a desk in the lobby signaled that one had entered a government building, but I always walked by with the sense that a shooting the night before had occasioned the security. The elevators to the fifth- and sixth-floor subcommittee quarters were slower even than the legendary conveyances in Longworth but, once aboard, the ride was far more dramatic. In a claustrophobic cell passengers bumped along, halting abruptly at every floor, eventually reaching their destination by stepping out carefully into a hall that was often six inches above or below the elevator floor. Beyond the worn carpet and the musty smell were many neatly arrayed offices, although one had to peek into cubbyholes and behind boxes to find the staffers.

"Europe and the Mideast," one of Don's two subcommittees, had typical arrangements. Mike van Deusen served as the knowledgeable staff director on whom subcommittee chairman Lee Hamilton leaned heavily; except for Mike's habit of sporting flowery ties against conservative suits, he was as self-effacing as he was efficient. Allison Brenner was the minority counsel, another congenial staffer whose purpose was to assure Republicans that their point of view would not go unheard. Her boss, however, was Pete DuPont, the moderate ranking Republican—this was long before his more conservative incarnation in the 1988 presidential primaries—and in practice she and Mike worked quite harmoniously. But if one side won personnel, the other reacted, and an escalating staff race ensued. Democrats accepted the justification for Republican subcommittee aides but argued in turn that their own two-to-one majority entitled them to greater resources as well. And so a new position—"staff associate"—was created to provide research help for the majority. In the case of our subcommittee the slot was filled by Ron Soriano, a recent graduate of the Johns Hopkins School of Advanced International Studies, something of a local feeder to Hill foreign-policy jobs. He provided much intellectual grist, which his superiors leavened with political perspective.

Thus the halls vibrated with feverish legislative activity, reflecting the evolution of the Congress from a small and cooperative branch of government to a growing and emboldened one. Staff seemed to serve as both cause and effect. Obviously they were put there, and unleashed, because the Congress had decided to assume a more determined posture. But once installed, they performed diligently and presented the Congress with many of its opportunities. What was happening in the subcommittee structure was echoed in freshmen congressional offices, perhaps more so because aides there were younger and had less sense of institutional responsibility. As an LA I continually sought outlets for my own opinions and legislative ideas. Inevitably this meant challenging the administration, since it tended to set the foreign-policy agenda. Staff activity, which to the White House seemed nettlesome, to the Congress seemed noble: We were monitoring an executive branch known in the immediate past for its excesses and mischief.

The freshmen argued for "new directions" in foreign policy; their specific positions were not always more precise. What they did make clear was a strong aversion to the pragmatism practiced under the regimes of Nixon, Ford, and Kissinger. Their goal, paradoxically like that of right-wing critics, was the introduction of a more palpable moral tone in U.S. policy. So much emphasis had been placed on superpower relations, they argued, that events elsewhere in the world were seen unduly through an East-West prism. Vietnam had produced an ennui about fighting battles over communism; and détente with the Soviet Union and rapprochement with China had raised questions about the black-and-white character of supposed U.S. interests. At the same time the ethical transgressions of Watergate made many nostalgic for bedrock values. The sixties counterculture had given young people a new affinity for the downtrodden and oppressed—and this would now be broadened to include peoples of the Third World.

Don's committee reflected the times, having voted, in a fit of avant-garde sensibility, to replace the "foreign affairs" in its name with "international relations," a semantic transformation intended to imply a consciousness of the interdependence of nations and the multidisciplinary nature of issues. After all, crises now crossed international boundaries, and one nation's problems—energy shortages, refugees, inflation—impinged potentially on everyone else. All this was true, but there was something in the attitude that reminds one, looking back, of the era's other charming excesses, such as the renaming of factory supervisors as "forepersons." Within a couple of years the committee mellowed and changed its name back again, notwithstanding the recurring cost of replacing its vast stockpiles of stationery.

Roused in part by its younger members, Congress was in a mood to rebel, resentful that it had lost its status as a coequal branch of government, and determined not to be misled and outmaneuvered again. In its assertive frame of mind it championed the idea of "consultation," an appealing but ambiguous principle intended to suggest that the president should take the Congress into his confidence in deciding even the most sensitive of policies. Passage of the War Powers Act in 1973, requiring such consultation prior to the introduction of American forces into hostile action, symbolized this determination. The same sentiment drove Congress the following year to establish a whole new budget process, an area of domestic policy considered a similarly presidential domain, and stimulated anew the practice of enacting "legislative veto" provisions, giving Congress the authority to overturn administrative regulations. President Ford objected to almost all such restraints on his power (the legislative veto was, in fact, later ruled unconstitutional) but, prodded by Secretary Kissinger, seemed especially exercised by congressional efforts to restrict his freedom of action in foreign affairs. Here he was persuaded that the effectiveness of policy depended on secrecy and executive mobility. Unfortunately the more he urged his thesis upon the Congress, the more suspicious it became of his designs.

Consultation was ineffective to forestall this conflict because the very term took on widely different and inconsistent meanings. Congress thought its advice would be sought in the *formulation* of policy; the administration felt it complied if it merely informed Congress prior to the execution. Even this communication typically was confined to a very few senior—and, not coincidentally, conservative—members. Don, for his part, would generally learn of administration initiatives through newspaper accounts; and when he expressed an interest, he was often treated curtly. If, for example, we wrote the secretary of state to question a policy, invariably we would receive a superficial reply signed by the assistant secretary for legislative affairs. Although the stationery was impressively embossed, we knew from our familiarity with bureaucratic routine that it had been drafted by a junior desk officer. In one typical instance we sought background information on a dramatic sevenfold increase in military assistance to a particular country. The explanation, no more than two paragraphs, was notable only for its circularity: The request was being made, we were informed, because it was deemed to be in the U.S. interest. This was hardly the basis for an informed decision, yet Don, as a member of the committee that had oversight of U.S. foreign policy, was expected to make one.

To some extent the attitude of the administration was understandable. Congress flooded it with inquiries and requests, and the State Department would have been left with little time for diplomacy had it dedicated its resources to thorough responses. Moreover it knew that congressional interest was often expressed as a courtesy to groups or constituents and that members might be as pleased to receive an acknowledgment that their opinions were valued as to effectuate actual changes in policy. The administration also resisted collaborative policy making because of fear that Congress, lacking sophistication in foreign-policy issues, would clumsily interpose itself. But it was equally predictable that Congress would take offense at being left out. Congressmen had been elected to express their opinions; they could not be told lightly that these didn't matter. At times it seemed that Congress faced a dilemma in exercising its responsibilities: Either it left the administration alone, in which case it risked being criticized for dereliction, or it took matters into its own hands, in which case it could be charged with interference.

Was there not a middle ground? Vice President Rockefeller argued that Congress had a right to review foreign policy but not to conduct it. Of course at one level this was indisputable. Congress simply didn't possess the resources, the detailed knowledge, or the enduring interest to participate in day-to-day foreign-policy decisions. Nor did its 535 members have anything resembling unified opinions. The historic responsibility of the president in the foreign-policy area had an obvious logic. Yet it was hard to see at times what constructive contribution Congress would be allowed to make by a president at odds with its positions. The record was littered with "sense of the Congress" resolutions that, given their nature as mere advisory opinions, had been all but ignored. The executive branch tended to take advantage of loose constructions, not necessarily because presidents were mischievous but because it was in the nature of leadership to press to the limits of their authority. How, then, was Congress to establish even broad outlines of policy? Apparently on a selective basis: The role of Congress would be to exercise a veto power on those occasions when an administration wandered beyond the bounds of strong public sentiment. Thus it was the feeling of the younger and more activist members that when the Congress stood up to the president, this was not a gratuitous meddling but its only choice in conveying general guidance. Like the Supreme Court, it reserved to itself the right to choose an occasional symbolic occasion on which to establish a broad and important precedent.

It was against this background that the explosive issue of Angola came to the fore at the end of 1975. Reports surfaced of secret U.S. aid to "pro-Western" guerrilla factions battling for control in this former Portuguese colony in Africa. In Congress there was little immediate reaction; news accounts did not yet warrant banner headlines and were of too arcane a nature to stir public emotions. I became familiar with the issue early but inadvertently. In reading documents that the administration presented for its annual foreign-aid request, I was startled to realize how generously we aided various of the world's most corrupt and unpopular governments. My young blood simmered: This was just the sort of policy that the new congressional generation questioned. What could be done about it? I asked more experienced committee staffers, and their answer was simple: If a member didn't like an item in the administration's program, he could propose to delete or modify it during committee markup. If his motion failed to carry, he could try again by way of amendment when the reported bill came to the House floor. It seemed too easy; we could reverse the whole foreign-aid program in an instant.

For several evenings one week I went to the Library of Congress nearby, determined to document the excesses of the regimes we supported. The Congressional Reading Room was an inviting, yet largely undiscovered place. It had high decorative ceilings, lavish marble adornments, cozy leather armchairs, several attendants, and almost no other guests. The public was barred by a forbidding signpost in the corridor outside: CONGRESSIONAL VISITORS ONLY BEYOND THIS POINT. But even those authorized guests were conspicuously absent. Most were too busy to use the facility; fortunately they had others who could do research for them. Congressmen, after all, had staff—and staff had the CRS, the CBO (or Congressional Budget Office, a similar but more numbers-oriented support agency), and others: armies of impressive professional specialists who could synthesize, summarize, and otherwise answer almost any question.

Not having learned these tricks yet—and my intellectual ambition, imported from graduate school, still intact—I buried myself personally in reference materials. The best source turned out to be recent newspaper stories that had been neatly clipped, date-stamped, and filed away in countless folders designated by country, year, and subtopic. A note to the clerk, "Bolivia—1972–75, Economic and Political," was enough to summon bulging folders from an inner office, discreetly laid in front of me for use in the crepuscular lamplight of my reading table. In time I pulled together data on Brazil's military rule, Kenya's censorship of the press, Philippine martial law, repression in Indonesia, official graft in the Dominican Republic, and intolerance of political dissent in Korea.

But in a category by itself, it seemed to me, was the nation of Zaire in southwestern Africa. President Mobutu behaved tyrannically, hanging cabinet ministers, jailing political opponents, and living in regal splendor even as his managerial fiats roiled Zaire's economy and produced one of the world's lowest per capita incomes for his citizens. Moreover his government did not seem particularly stable, reliable, or sympathetic to American interests (he had recently ousted the U.S. ambassador on a tenuous pretext and even hampered the rescue of kidnapped American students). Despite all of this the administration proposed a greatly expanded aid program. The mystery of our interest in Zaire unraveled somewhat when newspaper speculation raised the possibility that the aid would be funneled elsewhere: to underwrite reported U.S. involvement in the battle for succession in neighboring Angola. President Mobutu was said to harbor designs on oil-rich Cabinda Province there; his brother-in-law, Holden Roberto, headed one of the major guerrilla factions staging raids on Angola from sanctuaries in Zaire, and some of Zaire's own military equipment, in part American-supplied, had been spotted in use across the border. As a result U.S. aid to Zaire raised not only the issue of U.S. support for an undeserving despot but the even more alarming possibility of indirect U.S. intervention in an African civil war.

Nothing created as much concern among younger members of Congress as the thought of "another Vietnam," a specter espied now in foreign-policy decisions much as a previous generation had everywhere seen the ghost of Munich. Was it necessary once again to choose sides in a complex tribal conflict on the other side of the world? Administration officials testified that the United States had no inherent strategic interest there, but only a concern about balancing Soviet support of another faction and ancillary consequences such as diminished influence over neighboring sea lanes. Could it be that this was happening so soon after Congress had at last written an end to American involvement in Southeast Asia? And was it possible that the administration had secretly promised assistance without consulting Congress?

I of course was scandalized. But then I was all of twenty-three years old and possessed of a *Weltanschauung* that had been formed only in the previous three years. Editorials commented occasionally on aid to Angola, but in Congress no one seemed to have noticed until one day John Franzen, a young aide to Congressman Harrington, approached me with the idea of having our bosses cosponsor a committee effort to stop it. I had been planning to propose a number of amendments to Don, but had begun to realize the impracticality of too aggressive a battle plan. Arguments needed to be prepared and rehearsed; colleagues would have to be corralled and persuaded. There was only so much time to do it, and other members had only so much patience to listen. Congressmen who tried too hard became tiresome and ineffective; we needed to be selective.

Here, however, was an amendment focused on what seemed to me the most questionable of the administration's requests and, alluringly, one already drafted and ready to go. It was in fact just a few sentences, but contained legalistic expressions ("notwithstanding any other provisions of law") and obscure statutory references ("under Section 532 of the Foreign Assistance Act of 1961 as amended") that, in view of my inexperience, convinced me it would be helpful to work with someone of more evident legislative skill. We could, moreover, share the work of preparing briefing materials and phoning other staffers—and our bosses could share any potential controversy. Don agreed almost immediately to sign on, and although I was gratified by his somewhat uncharacteristic willingness to embrace a new cause so quickly, (he tended to weigh pros and cons more painstakingly than I did), neither of us considered it in the tones of high drama that it assumed weeks later. Harrington, whom Spiro Agnew might have called a "radic-lib," was more impulsive about such things, and Don's sensible concern was whether his association might prejudice our chances with moderate committee members. In fact Harrington had recognized that possibility himself and, I was told, sought Don's help deliberately to strengthen the amendment's credibility with that group.

Within a fortnight the Angola controversy leaped to the lead column in the newspapers; American involvement was read to be the first test of U.S. international intentions in the post-Vietnam era. Moreover in the aftermath of Watergate the press seemed to feel a heightened obligation to challenge presidential claims and to report the views of officials who dissented. In turn, escalating press attention assured a deepening congressional interest. It was not that congressmen were mere publicity hounds (although no normal human adult can be indifferent to having his name, his picture, and his words broadcast to the world). But something about national media interest acted as a seal of approval upon an issue, vouchsafing to members uneasy about their own judgment in the area that it did indeed justify their time and involvement. This phenomenon went a long way toward explaining why an issue dormant one day could incite such attention the next and why congressmen only faintly familiar with an issue could suddenly become so outspoken. They had not actually become overnight experts, but they had absorbed the general terms of the debate and, in combination with reassurances and prodding from better versed colleagues, were willing to lend their names. The fact that editorials and columns began pouring out in support of the congressional rebellion did nothing to prompt their reconsideration.

As public debate proceeded, Don needed to offer a more formal explanation of his position for the benefit of colleagues and constituents, and that is where staff come in. As is typical in such cases, I was given carte blanche to draft a statement, which would take the form of a speech supposedly delivered on the floor of the House of Representatives. In fact nothing was ever uttered. Don simply reviewed the text quickly, changed two or three words, signed his name at the top, and handed it in to a parliamentary clerk, who saw that it was reprinted the next day in the *Congressional Record*. He could have written his own statement, of course, which might well have been better. But as frequently as public officials are expected to pronounce their positions, they are left with little time to do so personally. The result is the ritualistic, if minor, fraud perpetrated in the *Record* nearly every day by nearly every office, no less remarkable for the fact that it is commonplace. Thus was it sobering to see how congressional debate on Angola could be so artificially manufactured. Obviously I knew Don's general disposition on the issue, but for the detail I took liberties. I argued, for example, that Soviet efforts to grab power were self-defeating, since African nationalist movements (so I had been assured by our public-interest lobbyists) historically asserted their independence. They might seek temporary assistance from one of the superpowers, but it was an illusion to think that the relationship would be more than a tenuous marriage of convenience. (Here I was on more confident ground, having read so much to this effect about Zaire.) U.S. intervention in such a situation promised only to prolong a brutal conflict and in the end deliver an uncertain result: Either the side we backed would lose, earning us the enmity of those who prevailed; or our side would win, and we would be expected to sustain a questionable regime indefinitely in power.

Armed with copies of Don's speech, I buttonholed fellow staffers, drafted notes for my boss to send other House members, and notified sympathetic reporters. Enlisting media support, colleagues frequently advised me, was an integral part of modern-day political battle. Don's name soon appeared in laudatory newspaper columns which, in a satisfying if circular way, lent his further statements on the subject somewhat more weight. But other politicians now joined in, and while we were pleased by the rising interest, it meant that those of greater status would rob us of our leadership role. In the Senate, John Tunney of California, facing reelection the coming year, proposed an amendment to a pending Department of Defense conference report so as to strike funds that could be reprogrammed for Angola. It was not the sole action required, but the defense bill was the most readily available vehicle, and the Tunney amendment fit the need for a symbolic first gesture that would focus attention on Senate sentiment. With one California senator involved, the other, Alan Cranston, was not to be left out. Foreign-policy aides in both offices besieged us with phone calls for information, but only curtly informed us of their own plans. They were high-powered assistants to well-known senators and no doubt considered themselves of a station superior to Congressman Bonker, let alone myself. Their voices dripped with disdain, as if to say, "Stand back, this is a job for the Senate."

Even within the International Relations Committee, Don became overshadowed on his own amendment. On administration request the top-ranking members hastily rescheduled the planned markup session to accommodate a closed-door briefing by Undersecretary of State Joseph Sisco, who urged Congress to act with restraint. Ultimately the committee watered down the Harrington-Bonker amendment considerably, notwithstanding growing public expressions of concern about a new foreign entanglement. Instead of forbidding aid to Angola (either directly or through Zaire) as our amendment directed, it allowed such aid so long as the president certified it to be in the national interest and Congress did not disapprove by concurrent resolution. This language was something of a legislative charade: Such presidential action would be as exceedingly likely as the prescribed congressional action would be unlikely. It was a typical loophole written into foreign-policy legislation. Congress could claim to be administering serious restrictions without in fact compromising essential presidential authority. But it did have an important implication from our point of view: It placed the committee on record—and by a very substantial majority—as voicing misgivings about current policy.

Although the Congress at this point appeared to have acted, we had one further moment in the sun. Neither the committee proposal nor the Tunney amendment was expected to reach the House floor prior to Christmas recess, and Don felt that Congress should state its opinion more fully before leaving: Developments in Angola were breaking fast. So together with other freshmen Democrats—George Miller and Norm Mineta of California, Toby Moffett of Connecticut, Tom Harkin of Iowa—he circulated a resolution on the floor urging that foreign powers stay out of Angola and that the president refrain from providing aid until it had been specifically approved by the Congress. Several hours' effort was enough to gather an impressive 140 signatures. It is true that the "Bonker resolution," even if passed, would not have been binding; and more conservative House leaders were not enthusiastic about bringing it to an actual vote. But it served well as a gauge of House sentiment, and we did not delay in trumpeting the accomplishment as evidence of strong congressional opposition to continued administration policy.

It was spine-tingling to witness the sudden ascension of the freshmen class. It had staged a grass-roots action in an institution known for its hierarchy, much as its members had learned to conduct insurgent political campaigns in running for office. I remember Congressman Miller—a bright and warm-blooded bear of a man who, with his shaggy hair, looked something like my idea of an aging U.C. Berkeley teaching assistant—coming into our office late in the evening, his sleeves rolled up from hard labor as a signature solicitor. All of us pulled chairs up to a vacant desk near the front door to compare petitions. Straining to decipher the penmanship, he and Don would exclaim to each other as they recognized improbable names: "You got him? That's amazing!" They leaned back and congratulated themselves. It was only the end of their first year—and already they were leaving a mark.

In time the Tunney amendment passed both chambers, and Don's resolution became superfluous. The administration was forced to end its program of covert aid—or so it claimed. Just as a later generation would learn that a determined executive could evade seeming prohibitions on funding for the Contras in Nicaragua, so we sensed that congressional directives on Angola might not be entirely heeded. Ford and Kissinger continued to scold Congress for its myopia and interference and pledged, in a common refrain of the time, that the United States would not let its foreign friends down. Reports persisted that the factions they had supported still enjoyed generous assistance and were even being helped to recruit mercenaries to fight in their behalf.

As a result our Angola offensive continued as we demanded facts about administration compliance with stated congressional intentions. We wrote everyone who had a part in carrying out the policy—Defense Secretary Donald Rumsfeld, CIA director George Bush, presidential assistant Max Friedersdorf—but always we received qualified assurances, merely raising our suspicions. For a while I busied myself in the library again, this time studying methods of executive-branch circumvention: use of unobligated previous appropriations, transfers among accounts, possible arrangements with other countries to provide aid that could later be replenished, reselling of food aid, disguised provisions in other bills. Most particularly we remained suspicious that aid to Angola was being laundered through Zaire, a charge the administration repeatedly skirted. We kept up our volleys for the next year, not entirely thwarting the administration but perhaps harassing it enough to make it think twice about carrying out possible deceptions.

Our allies helped stir the pot as well. We relied for much of our information on public-interest groups such as the Washington Office on Africa, a knowledgeable, if provocative, left-of-center lobby whose director, Ted Lockwood, proposed such activities as teach-ins at the Capitol. At the end of the year I returned for the holidays to Los Angeles and was invited to a New Year's party with a group of prominent local liberals, who were thrilled to have in their midst a veteran fresh from the Angola battles of Washington. My table consisted of Hollywood politicos, such as the star of the weekly TV show *Chico and the Man*, and it hummed with promises to "deliver" the California delegation on any necessary vote.

The State Department had its artillery out, too, although it tended to rely on the softer persuasions of officials like Bill Schaufele, assistant secretary for African affairs, whose white hair and careful diplomatic manner belied unyielding aversion to our stance. Once, he invited staffers over to his office for a drink in the evening, a sociability that was probably as clever as it was forced, and I could see him taking my measure as we were introduced, no doubt wondering what crazy world could require someone of his age and background so submissively to be greeting someone of mine. Behind the scenes the brass was steaming. A friend I came to know later, Ken Adelman, had served at the time as a Pentagon official and recoiled to learn that I once worked for Don Bonker. Well-meaning though we meant to be, Ken could only remember the colossal headaches our activities had given him during the Angola affair. He was, of course, right—but the feeling was mutual.

12

HAVE YOU HUGGED YOUR LOBBYIST LATELY?

Growth in subcommittees, staff, and the power of junior members has been followed closely by a proliferation of Washington lobbyists. The number of public-relations consultants, trade-association officials, corporate representatives, lawyers, embassy personnel, and others who try to influence legislation was estimated to be about three thousand in the early 1970s—and ten to twenty thousand in the 1980s. The surge has been no coincidence. As more subcommittees and individual members have become involved in crafting bills and amendments, lobbyists have been faced with greater obligations and opportunities. Moreover larger staffs have given them far more points of contact; lobbyists know the importance of staff recommendations, especially on the smaller and more detailed matters that typically concern special interests but don't engage the attention of congressmen.

Like other aides I had mixed feelings about these agents of influence. On the one hand, their narrow concerns and mercenary motivations tended to be fairly blatant and gave me a sense of unease about letting them use our good offices to advance their objectives. On the other hand, they could be exceptionally well informed and pleasant, represent important constituent interests, and provide useful data and perspectives that spared me burdens of research. To some extent we saw them as the main incarnation of the public in Washington: They argued on behalf of real people and entities that stood to be affected by legislative action. Their presence on Capitol Hill was far more vivid—both in person and in force—than what we saw of constituents, who tended to visit in connection with sightseeing excursions (when the requirement of obtaining gallery passes to see the House chamber conveniently brought them by our office and reminded them of the name of their congressman) and had no such explicit agenda.

Foreign embassies were active in their lobbying efforts on the Hill, and it was hard to blame them: Congress exerted what must have been to them a startling influence in the foreign-policy-making process. Indeed in its negotiations with foreigners, administrations even found it convenient to exaggerate that influence; predicting that "Congress won't buy" an agreement can make an effective bargaining point. Many diplomats came from countries where such decisions were virtually the *diktat* of the executive, and even those accustomed to functioning legislative branches knew little of the openness and dispersion of power that increasingly characterized the U.S. Congress. The most effective among them adapted and tried to present their arguments in terms of benefits to a congressman's constituency (e.g., trade benefits for Mexico would reduce the number of illegal aliens flooding across the border and competing for jobs). Sometimes there was no such argument to be made, and they were forced to speak grandiloquently about the dividends for U.S. security that good relations would bestow.

Another resort, however, was simply to skip the intellectual approach and try to win favor by dint of sociability. Foreign governments are prevented from contributing to political campaigns and therefore must invent other means of getting their message across. As of the mid-1970s a week in the Washington social calendar seemed empty without a glamorous party hosted by Ambassador Ardeshir Zahedi of Iran (who might have imported both Persian caviar and actress Elizabeth Taylor for the occasion), Count Wilhelm Wachmeister of Sweden (whose sprawling party I once attended to see my own screen idol, Liv Ullman, regrettably sidetracked in conversation with the ubiquitous Henry Kissinger), or socialite Tongsun Park of Korea (soon to be put out of business for his excesses). These "A-list" soirees were mainly for congressmen, but there were more than enough other embassy events to compensate, including one country or other's "national day" several times a week. This was literally true: 260 weekdays during the year were barely enough to absorb the 150 countries' dates of independence, revolution, or other epochal events that needed to be celebrated.

Diplomatic parties were a pleasant diversion, even a cultural experience, particularly when they rose above ordinary reception fare and featured exotic native cuisine. The mingling itself was entertaining; foreign-embassy personnel seemed to spend much of their lives attending each others' parties. Bejeweled women in chiffon dresses and men with slicked-back hair and double-breasted suits reappeared regularly at these affairs, confirming the stereotype of a "diplomatic circuit." Uniformed military attachés of all nationalities were also in abundance, weighted down with braided epaulets and decorations, giving me the impression as I weaved around them that they were extras on a Hollywood sound stage. At times an inverse relationship seemed to exist between the importance of a country and the size of its embassy or lavishness of its party: This was logical, since the whole point of embassy social life was to impress those who needed to be impressed.

Making the rounds was great fun, but on the whole I could sympathize with Gerald Ford, whose campaign travels made the different cities he visited such a blur that he was famous for mistaking his location. Just as he might have confused Cincinnati for Columbus, I lived in fear of greeting a host from Romania and asking how things were going in Hungary. Meeting embassy representatives separately was much more satisfying since it allowed for uninterrupted and focused conversation; nor did it require any alimentary deprivation since they did their part to keep the city's finest dining salons thriving. During lunch at La Bagatelle, the Panamanians talked to me of their need to restore sovereignty over the U.S. Canal Zone; at the Montpelier Room the Pakistanis forswore their intention to acquire nuclear weapons; at Jean-Pierre the South Africans explained their plans for dismantling the rules of "petty" apartheid. As a general rule repressive regimes seemed the most hospitable, perhaps because they had a harder job of persuasion—and expense accounts approved by fiat.

Although I came to admire the abilities of many "political counselors" and "second secretaries," I had a hesitation about dealing too extensively with them, perhaps because national interests seemed so tangibly involved, and I worried that even casual relationships could lend themselves to misinterpretation. An experience concerning something so mundane as a Korean wristwatch showed the validity of such apprehension. Even as a junior member of the International Relations Committee, Don became a prime target for the pleadings of interest groups, and our office became fertile ground for foreign emissaries who requested continual appointments to express what they inevitably deemed to be grave and urgent concerns. The entreaties were so numerous that, except perhaps where an ambassador was concerned, visitors generally had to settle for seeing only me. One day officials of the Korean embassy came calling. In the course of our discussion they made repeated requests for appointments with Don, testing my abilities to invent ever-new diplomatic excuses for his chronic unavailability.

The Koreans, it turned out, were equally creative and, in addition, undeterred by etiquette. Several days later, in its impatience, the embassy simply dispatched two officials, Colonel Choi and Mr. Ohm, to seek an unscheduled audience. They presented themselves at the office and interpreted the receptionist literally when she said Don was in a meeting, replying that this was fine because they had time to wait. They then stationed themselves in the front room, through which Don eventually had no choice but to pass. Their determined efforts wore us down. Don reluctantly invited them in, summoned me to assist in reciting pertinent facts about our bilateral relations, and permitted the Koreans to discourse for about twenty minutes on their subject: the need for further military assistance.

In the manner of East Asian visitors, sometimes obsessively courteous, they left behind a small gift-wrapped package. Don opened it and found a digital watch. Such items were still a novelty in those days and widely, if perhaps erroneously, assumed to be of great value. Thinking it an expensive gift, Don returned it. The incident, however, was not forgotten. A couple of months later I attended a dinner party given by a gracious old friend, Norma Gilbert, at her Capitol Hill town house. Someone made a lighthearted comment about how I was being showered with free food and drink, and I responded playfully, "That's nothing, the Koreans give us watches." Norma, it turned out, was a friend of *Washington Post* gossip columnist Maxine Cheshire, and before the evening was out had a phone call from her and innocently reported this latest nugget; she knew Cheshire was investigating foreign influence peddling in Washington. The next morning Cheshire called Bonker. He confirmed the incident and, when pressed repeatedly on the value of the watch despite his disclaimers of expertise, said it looked valuable and guessed that it was worth perhaps $150 or $200. That was enough research for Cheshire, who promptly reported for all Washington to read that Congressman Don Bonker had been the recipient of a $2,000 watch—a premier status symbol, as she put it, favored by Hollywood celebrities. Whether Cheshire's appraisal was a typographical error or a deliberate one, we never learned. The Koreans, of course, later insisted that the watch was worth no more than $30 (slightly below the maximum value of permissible congressional gifts at the time). Also lost in the account was the fact that it had not been kept.

But the embarrassment did not end there. When another reporter called for a follow-up story, I dropped the other bombshell. The Koreans, I allowed, may also have offered women. My justification for this remarkable charge was that sometime after his meeting with Don, Colonel Choi had called me to suggest that, should Don wish, an "attractive" Korean woman could be "made available" to see him about matters of "mutual interest." Admittedly this was not definitive evidence of what I imagined to be a possible meaning of these expressions. But I had taken it seriously enough at the time to report it to a newly constituted committee panel that was investigating alleged excesses in foreign lobbying. Again the Koreans subsequently offered an explanation: The woman was a visiting member of Parliament.

All of this occurred, however, in the immediate aftermath of the Elizabeth Ray scandal, when the press was on the prowl for new stories of congressional misbehavior. Among other things, it was beginning to unearth titillating details of Tongsun Park's opulent parties for congressmen, which appeared to be orchestrated by the Korean government, so the lobbying activities of Korea were coming under particular suspicion. In short order the *Chicago Sun-Times* ran a banner headline across its front page: KOREANS OFFER CONGRESS WATCHES, WOMEN. And then the subhead: "But Freshman Don Bonker Is One Who Says, 'No Thanks.' " Other papers quickly picked up the story. At first the reports made Don seem heroic; he had, after all, rejected the proferred gifts. But then inevitably came the questions: Why hadn't he reported these matters sooner? Why was he dealing with the Koreans in the first place? Had they given him something before? Why did they think they could buy his influence?

The problem with scandal is that, in the vague public memory, everyone involved is potentially tainted. And so it was that long after readers had forgotten the details, many remembered only that Don had something to do with the Korean scandal. (I was reminded of this years later when I had occasion to mention the name Archibald Cox to a young law student. "Do you remember him?" I asked. "Sure," the student replied. "He was involved in Watergate." Pause. "But," he said of the special prosecutor who helped bring the conspirators to justice, "I don't remember which side he was on.") The other problem the story produced for Don was ribbing from his colleagues. No one realized how the press had come into possession of the story and therefore tended to think that he had volunteered it to tout his own virtue. In so doing, some grumbled, he had left the impression that other congressmen—the ones who had not reported contact with Koreans— were less pure.

Thus had my foolish cocktail-party chatter brought this on, although to a degree staffers are caught in the middle. They are supposed to have a passion for anonymity, but the fun they have, and even the objectives of their jobs, can carry them away. It is rare to see congressional aides quoted by name; they know that is bad form. But it is common for them to speak with reporters on an unattributed "background" basis. Sometimes the object is to help "spin" a story in a way favorable to their boss or their cause, or to disclose information that may elicit desired action. Headlines, if positive, are generally among the most coveted of staff attainments. At other times they are tempted to talk for the simple pleasure of disbursing coveted information or seeing their words given the authority of public quotation.

In the case of young Hill aides, as I was, problems with the press are often the result of mere momentary indiscretion: Without experience, it is difficult to imagine the consequences of even a minor slip. The Hill has few rules, and the atmosphere is informal. Staffers have come there for the enjoyment of dealing with opinion makers and discussing politics; it takes unusual self-control to resist point-blank questions from prominent reporters who make you think you are a valued source. It is even more difficult to gag yourself in what you assume to be ordinary social circumstances. A few formative experiences, however, are enough to season one's perspective. I suppose it is superfluous to say that both Don and I would have preferred that the whole Korean watch incident had never happened. Years afterward, when I would come by to visit, invariably he would introduce me to new staff members with his practiced one-liner: "Mark here is the one who got me involved in the Korean watches." At that point, fortunately, we were able to laugh.

Yet contact with lobbyists was an unavoidable aspect of working in Congress; indeed, depending on a group's popularity and political clout, congressmen were only too happy to cultivate close relationships. In the case of domestic lobbies, an obvious motivation was money. There were, of course, the time-honored campaign contributions, which flowed liberally to members who showed sympathetic attitudes. More striking, however, was the trend in "honoraria"—personal payments awarded congressmen for articles, speeches, or mere appearances ($2,000, plus expenses, for attendance at a golf outing in Palm Springs or simply a breakfast meeting in Washington). Although the totals at one point were capped at 33 percent of official salary, congressmen throughout the 1970s and 1980s had available to them ready income supplements, as well as the political benefit derived from giving additional amounts to charity. Objection was made to this system on the grounds that it gave them an incentive to ignore their legislative work in favor of outside activities. The more serious indictment, of course, was that the fees were thinly disguised inducements to take a point of view or allow donors undue access to make their cases. We would hardly allow special-interest groups to reward congressmen directly for their votes with bundles of cash, even if it could be claimed that they would have taken the same position anyway, yet honoraria accomplished the same result. Indeed, executive-branch officials who engaged in identical practices would have gone to jail.

From the point of view of staffers, the concern about contributors tends to be more parochial: Congressmen (or their campaigns) get the money, but their aides do the work—writing the speeches, performing the research, making the arrangements. The work also includes providing various services (not simply positions and votes) often expected in return. One of our benefactors was a warm and amiable Seattle rabbi who, although he and his congregation were from outside our district, naturally assumed that his largesse would open the congressman's doors and phone lines as needed. The rabbi's interest was in the foreign-affairs area, and therefore I was the staffer who handled his visits and calls. On a typical occasion he phoned frantically to inveigh against the administration for allegedly breaking promises to Israel on amounts of foreign aid and to urge that Don resist fiercely. Staff, among its other missions, has a key function to act as a buffer in such circumstances, taking action or forestalling demands as it would expect its boss to instruct. I knew Don would want him treated courteously but not extravagantly. I drew up a memo stating our friend's concerns but recommending that we avoid expressing them officially; I was unconvinced of the usefulness of our intervention. Don agreed, but at least we could say that the matter had received the congressman's personal attention. On another occasion I lent my services to one of the rabbi's colleagues who was visiting Washington and wished to obtain funding for an Israeli school that educated Soviet refugees. To this end I escorted him through half a dozen offices at the State Department and made many more times that number of calls. His was a noble cause, even if it was not obvious what benefit my activities were producing for our immediate constituents. The availability of staff resources spared Don a possibly awkward involvement, and yet knowing that there were aides like me to help may have encouraged the request for assistance in the first place.

Still others who combined personal relationships and secular legislative objectives passed through our office. Don himself belonged to the Fellowship House of Washington, an energetic group of high government officials that sought to encourage international religious brotherhood. It organized prayer breakfasts, hosted out-of-town VIPs, and otherwise expressed its evangelism by bringing together prominent citizens of different lands, even those of other religions. I was involved only inadvertently as participants in its programs visited Don's office. One evening I helped welcome to Washington the secretary-general of the Organization of Petroleum Exporting Countries—OPEC was widely held responsible by Americans for the chaotic energy shortages of the time—but he was a most pliable and interesting companion as we toured the nightspots of Georgetown. A more serious chore was to help devise an expanded U.S. aid program to the Sudan, then sell it to the administration, in part because Sudanese president Nimeiri was another Fellowship participant. His country was poor and pro-Western, and the cause seemed logical enough, but this alone might not have proved sufficient to move the Congress. It was the extracurricular friendships and interests of a particular member that provided the spur to action, which in a busy and preoccupied institution is not only understandable but often quite essential.

PART III

THE SENATE

Senate Budget Committee, 1977. John Heinz listening to chairman Ed Muskie, while I try (unsuccessfully) to think of something helpful to whisper.
U.S. SENATE

13

GOING FOR THE GLAMOUR: THE UPPER BODY

While I became enamored of foreign affairs, Don gradually grew disengaged. Having taken such a high initial profile, his burden now was to show constituents that his concerns went beyond the high-minded distractions of foreign policy. My own job satisfaction required just the reverse: sustaining the big-picture national activities which I had found so exciting. I admired Don very much, and he had become a friend, but working as an aide to a junior House member began to seem routine. Some LAs remain in the same office for years, waiting for their break to come when their bosses are senior enough to win them committee staff positions. Don, I knew, was likely to become a sub-committee chairman two to four years hence, and I would have been the natural candidate to be his staff director. But I had come to the Hill for rewarding experience, not job security, and I desired a more dynamic involvement. What was the route to more responsibility?

The comparative ranking of Hill staffers probably parallels the influence of their bosses. An aide to a senior or well-known House member perforce carries more weight than an aide to one who is junior or obscure. Committee staffers have special influence because they work closely with chairmen and exercise direct control over committee work, where much of Congress's most important activity takes place. (To a lesser extent this would hold true for subcommittee staff as well.) Senate aides typically outclass their House counterparts for the same reason that every representative would prefer to be a senator and never the reverse. But just as an important House chairman might have more influence than a novice senator, so a Senate LA might gladly switch positions with a House staff director. (A senator couldn't switch, because the seniority system would prevent him from becoming a House chairman for many years.) Within an office an AA outranks even a chief LA, if only because he is the chief of staff; but in terms of influence there will be exceptions depending on an aide's personal relationship with the member or his standing among staff colleagues. So, too, a staff director sits at the vertex of a committee hierarchy.

For those of the right party, administration positions are the plums of a Washington existence. Being a Democrat at the time, I might have sought one myself. Jimmy Carter had just taken office, and in fact I had helped Don draft a memorandum on foreign policy to aid in the transition. Yet it never occurred to me that there might be executive-branch jobs plentifully available to aides who worked in the offices of the president's congressional supporters. I assumed that there were mainly the top positions that the public hears of—cabinet secretaries, undersecretaries, ambassadors—and that in any case all slots would go to Carter's certified original supporters. It surprised me to learn that there were over two thousand political appointments to be made and that nearly all that mattered were one's party affiliation and political connections; having volunteered for campaign work was helpful but not essential. After Carter's election many of the same people showed up in office who might have served in a Hubert Humphrey, Morris Udall, or Birch Bayh presidency. Dan Spiegel (Humphrey's aide) reappeared as a special assistant to the secretary of state, Sally Shelton (Bentsen's aide) was nominated as an ambassador, and Dick Moose (of the Senate Foreign Relations Staff) became an assistant secretary of state.

Not surprisingly every administration finds Hill staff a fertile source of appointments; a president can score points with their congressional patrons and, more importantly, place on his team officials skilled at working the legislative branch, an increasingly central aspect of effective executive-branch policy making. The tradition hardly let up with the arrival of George Bush in 1989. In one case a top aide to Dan

Rostenkowski, the liberal Democratic chairman of the House Ways and Means Committee, was selected as the administration's number-two trade negotiator. It was a much-coveted position, but the selection of a political opponent was no fluke. The administration wisely recognized that having a respected Democratic staffer inside its tent during negotiations would help to sell a potentially controversial product outside.

I did make one, almost inadvertent, effort. Shortly after Carter's nomination Congressman Solarz had hosted foreign-policy specialist Zbigniew Brzezinski at a seminar of congressmen and staff, and I was designated with a friend to give Brzezinski a ride to the airport. He made the mistake of asking my opinion about various issues, and I replied with prolix observations from my recent travels. Afterward I wrote him still further thoughts and was impressed when I received prompt personal responses. Following the election, when he was slated to become Carter's National Security Adviser, it occurred to me to write him about a possible White House job. I did so, but heard nothing back. Months later when I was cleaning my desk, I found a yellowed telephone note that was dated about that time and indicated he had called me. But by then it was too late—I was leaving Don and had accepted another Hill position.

That job was back on the Senate side. One day I crossed the Capitol for a meeting and, freshly reminded of my Humphrey days, began to think about returning. It seemed somehow grander, more important. The halls felt wider, the aides appeared older, the legislators themselves were surely better known and (since there were only one hundred of them) more influential. For someone who wanted to influence policy, *this* was the place to be. I dashed off some letters to the new batch of senators who had just been elected and were arriving to take office. Over the years I have found that making cold calls for jobs is a notably ineffective means of getting them, but in those days I didn't have enough contacts at senior levels to rely on an old-boy network. That I heard promptly from a senator's office can be attributed only to the freakishness of his employing a young aide, unconstrained by conventional routine, who thought it would be rational to read his incoming mail.

That aide, Geoff Garin, had been scouting for new LAs to staff the office of John Heinz, a Republican from Pennsylvania, whom the electorate had just promoted from the House to the Senate. Geoff had come with him in the transition, as had several others, but Heinz's new office would be much larger. They had waited to learn their committee assignments and precise needs, but were now anxious to hire. Heinz, scion of the 57-variety pickle and ketchup family, epitomized the mystique of the Senate: He was wealthy (surveys regularly showed that a large proportion of senators were millionaires), had a well-known name, and, given his family's close identification with Pittsburgh, seemed the very incarnation of his state. (Later I was to learn that Philadelphia—"eastern Pennsylvania"—considered itself quite different.) When he stood up on the Senate floor to speak, he would be representing twelve million people; the galleries might even know who he was. No wonder so many representatives sought elevation to the Senate: It *was* the upper body; it was the big time.

But the job Geoff wanted me to fill was in the domestic-affairs area; ironically my search for fulfillment in foreign policy had now led me astray. I hesitated, torn between the greater fascination of a Senate job and the steadier progression in my chosen field that staying with Bonker represented. But Geoff, bright and irreverent, said, "You're too young to be secretary of state. Why not have some fun first?" Immediately I began to rationalize a decision. Perhaps it could be a useful detour, I thought, remembering that the State Department encouraged domestic sabbaticals for its diplomats in order to broaden their perspectives and reacquaint them with American culture. But now I see my choice as a turning point. No longer would I regard foreign policy with such inner compulsion; once I had switched, I could do it again. I would indeed find other areas rewarding, and I would become accustomed to the idea of changing among them as necessary to sustain my interest. The price of this, as a foreign-affairs specialist, Bill Barnds, once observed to me, was a sacrifice of credentials. It would be hard to document my qualifications in the future if I wanted to return to the foreign-policy fold. But, at the time, the excitement of a new challenge outweighed any doubts.

The job was still contingent, of course, on Heinz's approval, but Geoff implied that this was a near certainty. My main concern was to consult Don. I hoped he would give his blessing; although turnover on the Hill is frequent and always half-expected, I did not want to disrupt the smooth functioning of his office. I called him at home that night and told him of my plans. It took him more by surprise than I had anticipated, perhaps because I had tried, probably mistakenly, never to hint at my restlessness; I had wanted to be a good soldier. He was obliging as always, however, recalling idyllically his own stint as a Senate aide, and said he would be tempted to do the same in my place. His more practical concern was finding a replacement. Fortuitously an FSO had recently applied to work for us as a "Congressional Fellow." This was a popular program of the American Political Science Association designed to give executive-branch officials, academics, and journalists a several-month experience in the Congress, and it allowed us to arrange a quick succession. (Moreover at the end of the FSO's tour another able young man, Alan von Egmund, happened along to take the spot on a permanent basis. I was—so I learned with a mixture of relief and consternation—readily replaceable.)

When Don came in the next day, though, he had clearly been thinking further about matters and had one more question, which he asked with a furrowed brow: "But, Mark, why a Republican?" Until then, I had not really thought about it. There were surely many members for whom I would not have worked. A congressman's political philosophy was of critical importance to me, yet it did not seem connected necessarily to party labels, which often provided only broad definition. The GOP had conservatives like Goldwater, but it had progressives, too, like Javits and Mathias. By the same token, George McGovern may have been the Democratic standard bearer one year, and epitomized to many the liberalism for which his party was either vilified or revered. His, however, was hardly the only strain of thought the party encompassed: Scoop Jackson, John Stennis, and even Hubert Humphrey articulated different points of view; in the 1980s there would be liberals like Paul Simon, moderates like Bill Bradley, and conservatives like Sam Nunn. It seems entirely possible to imagine politicians of different parties (say, Democrat Bradley and Republican moderate Mark Hatfield) who are closer philosophically than members of the same party (say, Hatfield and conservative Jesse Helms—or even 1988 running mates Michael Dukakis and Lloyd Bentsen).

The party loyalty of staff also seems a secondary consideration to employers themselves. Only rarely in my own experience did I encounter a congressman who insisted on, or even cared very much about, employing only registered Democrats or Republicans. (A significant exception was after I took a prominent role with independent John Anderson, a situation I discuss later.) It may be they consider their aides already self-screened: If someone wants to work for them, their politics must be compatible. This is, interestingly, a radically more carefree attitude than the White House tends to take; there the personnel office has been known at times for scrutinizing not only demonstrated loyalty to party but even to a particular wing of the party. Perhaps it is simply that legislators exert closer control over their employees and are therefore less fearful of their deviations than are presidents, who must entrust large programs and departments to their appointees. In any case Heinz was known in those days—before the expression became discredited—as a liberal Republican, a concept that helped to blur party distinctions. Geoff, I later learned, was himself a Democrat, as were most of Heinz's other LAs. Indeed Heinz never questioned me directly about my party affiliation, because I did not, in the end, talk to him before starting. I was supposed to, but Geoff called me shortly to say it wouldn't be necessary: They had discussed me, Heinz would trust Geoff's judgment, and I could simply meet him my first day on the job.

I can imagine John Heinz saying this. Probably he had every intention of interviewing his new employee personally but had become preoccupied with more urgent matters. He was quick and dynamic, enjoyed juggling a multitude of simultaneous projects, and delegated well; I found him among the most industrious of senators. He had entered the Senate two months before (in January 1977) along with an impressive group of other new Republican faces: Richard Lugar of Indiana, Jack Danforth of Missouri, John Chafee of Rhode Island. Many remarked on the similarities among the group: relatively moderate and intellectual in disposition, devoted to good government, articulate, and even photogenic. They held the promise, it was said, of reinvigorating the Republican party on a nationwide scale, and while this prediction turned out to be bolder than the reality, over time they made significant marks as legislators.

John's privileged background ironically created a hurdle to his success. Formally he was Henry John Heinz III, although in an effort to cultivate a more egalitarian public image he eventually dropped a name and the numeral and became, even on his formal letterhead, simply Senator John Heinz. Like my previous boss, he also insisted on being called by his first name. But at thirty-nine, and endowed with his family name, wealth, and refined good looks, he inescapably carried the air of a young American aristocrat who, in a spirit of noblesse oblige, had given himself to the public service. He had gained national attention by spending $2.8 million in his Senate campaign, then a national record and much of it contributed personally, causing opponents to charge that he was trying to buy his way into office. The criticism nearly cost him the election, and afterward he seemed determined to prove that no representative of Pennsylvania worked harder nor more single-mindedly for the interests of the state.

In this pursuit he was effective and became immensely popular within his constituency, but as a result he also suffered somewhat in his reputation among Washington opinion makers. Over the years I heard him criticized around town as "too parochial," apparently meaning that he sometimes placed Pennsylvania's interests above broader national interests. Senators, of course, are supposed to represent the voters who elect them, but paradoxically Washington reserves its greatest approbation for those who rise above constituency politics. In the ideal, it seems, senators are expected to ask aides, "What do you think we should do?" on this or that issue, as if the book is entirely thrown open to moral or philosophical disputation on proper public policy. John, it is true, was more likely to ask, "Who have we heard from about that?" But it was hard to fault an elected official for taking pains to measure public opinion. Perhaps he did not do it subtly enough; the trick may be to envelop narrow objectives in loftier public rhetoric than he was willing to use to make his points. Moreover on notable occasions, as I shall describe, he *was* eager to do the right, and not simply the politic, thing.

Another complaint had to do with his personal manner. Among his colleagues John developed a reputation for wanting to speak on too many subjects, amend too many bills, and defer only reluctantly to others in between. In another calling this might have been taken to reflect impressive initiative and energy, but in the clubby United States Senate it was seen as veritably antisocial behavior. Where other junior senators might have spoken with great deliberation on the floor or in committee, only after exhibiting utmost deference to senior members, Heinz sometimes conveyed an air of exasperation. With his own aides he showed an occasional irritability, particularly if the factual information he continually demanded was not at their fingertips. But while his intensity perhaps caused a more-rapid-than-usual staff turnover, I found reason to appreciate it.

Employee satisfactions often rest on much simpler things than political philosophy, and at the same time can transcend matters of personal style. The fact is that John's personality gave staff a vital and gratifying role within his office. He worked us hard collecting information, insisted on expert and detailed advice, and drained us of every possible legislative idea and initiative. Many times a day he would summon us into his office for consultation or simply walk back into the legislative enclave at the end of the office suite and pepper us with questions about this bill or that when the answers could not wait. In all of this we were left with the feeling that our contribution mattered, that our boss relied on our talents and energies and absorbed what we said. If we asserted that a federal program worked a certain way, or how a fellow senator would vote on an amendment, John was apt to say, "Do you know that or are you guessing?" Sometimes his unrelenting interrogation was hard to take, but in a way it was just his way of demanding excellence; in first-year law school classes, I was to learn later, people would gladly pay large tuition bills for such treatment.

Aides were made to feel more important on the Senate side of the Capitol. An LA, for example, could make his way through the gaggle of lobbyists in the Senate reception room, register at a desk, clip a badge to his coat, and walk onto the Senate floor at almost any time. (Staff movement was frozen during votes, when senators poured into the chamber and needed no further help creating noise and commotion.) If I came in Heinz's company to assist him during debate, youthful pages would scurry to bring me a folding chair where I would sit nudged closely against his assigned desk (an antique writing bureau complete with inkwell and historic senatorial lineage). Here I might leaf through file folders looking for useful rebuttal materials, converse with other aides who came quietly to my side to ask Heinz's intentions, pass my boss scribbled ideas for debating points—and perhaps daydream during lesser orations about how, as a senator myself, I would stand up and passionately challenge what had just been said. At times I would be summoned into the cloakroom to help explain a provision of a pending amendment to another senator or to take a call at the bank of telephone booths; or I might walk back simply to relieve the tedium of floor debate, momentarily sitting among senators to catch the news or a baseball game on television and overhearing in the process the latest catty gossip about various Democrats.

At other times I would go to the floor on my own to follow a matter of particular interest, in which case I could take a place on the leather couches at the back of the chamber. (This was in the days before closed-circuit TV allowed aides, and senators, to watch from the relative comfort of their offices.) During exciting moments of debate, space was at a premium, and I would be forced to balance precariously on the edge of a cushion, lest I be asked to leave by attendants, who strictly required that aides be seated during proceedings. Even at duller times decorum was enforced. Once I saw Senator Stennis, a craggy southern senator of ramrod-straight bearing, enter the other side of the chamber, stop abruptly in his tracks, and begin glaring in my direction. I searched around in vain to see what had drawn his attention, but he kept on looking. Suddenly I realized that I was slouching. I picked myself up hurriedly while Stennis lingered in his gaze for another few seconds and finally turned away. The floor had become such an accustomed workplace, I had needed to be reminded: This *was* the United States Senate.

The pace of office activity was fevered. For my own part, I reported to work unfailingly at 7:30 A.M. and left about that time in the evening. Occasionally we would stay much later if the Senate remained in session. I wrote reams of long and complex memos, and the miracle is not that so many were produced, but that a United States senator would read them in full as John did. Today I look back and think that to a degree my effort was excessive: Heinz hardly needed such abundant information to decide positions on the fundamentally political basis that senators often use; and even his frequent requests for more facts could have been satisfied by material that was less voluminous in character. But at age twenty-four I was bound to take my role with an exaggerated seriousness of purpose. A job at that point is often the main source of one's self-esteem, and one possesses such pent-up apprehensions about performing in the workaday world that a Calvinistic instinct to toil is only natural. I wanted to prove myself, and the frenetic quality of life the Heinz office provided suited my masochistic cravings.

In time, however, I had an experience that softened my perspective. One day word spread that Hubert Humphrey, now ailing with inoperable cancer, would be speaking to the Congress—a momentous farewell to his friends and institution. I wanted more than anything to see it, but I was in the middle of writing a memo that I was determined to have on John's desk as soon as possible. I felt that my work needed to take precedence; I could read about the speech in the morning paper. I have thought back on that moment often, yet I have never been able to remember what project I was working on; I am sure that, at best, it had only a small and passing importance, and that only I was aware of my sacrifice in doing it. What I do remember is my empty feeling the next day about missing the speech. I would retain my workaholic habits, but in the future try to leaven them with better judgment concerning the world around me.

Senate offices, even for a freshman, were far larger than those in the House. Staff allotments were based on seniority, committee assignments, and the population of the state represented. Heinz had a staff of about sixty, although a part of it was detailed to branch offices in the major cities of Pennsylvania, there to help constituents understand Medicare formulas or trace lost correspondence with government agencies. The heart of the operation remained palpably in Washington, and a visit to an office in the state, as Washington-based LAs had only rare occasion to make, seemed to be a journey to a remote part of the world. Yet our main office, while preoccupied with the larger picture of national politics and policy, never lost sight of local interests, presumed as they were to be predominant in the thinking of voters. Almost everything we did was weighed in terms of how it would help or hurt areas of the state, how it would "play" among different constituent groups, or what the reaction might be of local organizations or prominent individuals. This was of course one reason why Heinz would be reelected in future years by wide margins.

Our AA, Sam Goldberg, was a witty and urbane former State Department official who, to his credit, seemed somehow too intellectual and traditional to fit into the burgeoning new age of computerized public relations. That was just as well; he was kept busy enough fielding John's ceaseless inquiries and instructions. Eventually Sam left to take a more tranquil and remunerative corporate position in New York. A good deal of focus in the office was on our press shop, presided over by Larry McCarthy, an adept wordsmith and spirited promoter who helped package our unvarnished legislative ideas into more compelling public form. Every Hill office had its press secretary but—not unusual for the Senate—now we had an entire press office, rounded out by a deputy press secretary and one or more press assistants. (In later years, I am told, even an "executive assistant for communications" was added.)

Letter-writing activities were also performed on a grander scale. Instead of relying on LAs to handle routine constituent mail, the office boasted a special corps of "legislative correspondents" dedicated to the full-time churning out of form letters, reviewed by the LAs to whom they reported. As if the grinding nature of this work were not enough to assure their second-class status, the "LCs" were segregated in a room several floors below the main office and filled to capacity with noisy machines that barely permitted even shouted conversation. Visiting them in their quarters brought to mind movies about slaves on galley ships, except that the workers here were effectively chained to automated typewriters instead of oars and were exhorted to perform at battle speed merely by an inner compulsion to win promotion to another job that would remove them from this tedium. Remarkably the work force was supplemented by retirees, who volunteered their services as if this were the highest-minded and most constructive contribution to the electoral process. Meanwhile, all day and night, even unattended by a human supervisor, computers spewed out individually typed letters while other automated contraptions forged signatures a thousand times over, all of this in a calculated effort to convince constituents of our unyielding personal concern for whatever their plight.

Capitol Hill in general was notorious for cramped working space. The problem might have been solved by cutting back on staff, but that was sacrilege to a community that had persuaded itself that ever-larger numbers of staff facilitated the legislative process. Thus the preferred solution was simply to jam in more bodies and, as a matter for the long run, to press for expanded space. At my own desk, if I turned too abruptly in one direction, I faced the elbow of my colleague Connie Maffin, our specialist in federal housing programs. Connie was warm, hardworking, and truly an expert; she dedicated herself to her subject with a zealotry that even Heinz, with his penchant for detail, could not equal. I always learned something talking to her, although I could not, for the life of me, keep the various housing programs straight— and she referred to them, in jargon, continually: "The committee has a great bill on Section 8 moderate rehab, but it totally ignores SROs." Connie's area was of considerable importance to Pennsylvanians, but even so our office could not take full advantage of her relatively narrow expertise. Eventually she decided to chuck Hill life and become a realtor, which was my own good fortune, for within a few months she had sold me a condo in northwest Washington that provided me elegant shelter the next several years and rapidly climbed in value.

Connie's place was taken by Gwen King, an expert not on housing but on human-resource issues, which the office had decided better warranted staff attention. Fortunately Gwen was charming and talented, for her first day on the job she was handed Connie's old folders on housing and told there would be a committee markup on the subject that very week, through which she would need to guide her new boss. (Gwen subsequently went to work for the Pennsylvania state office in Washington and in 1989 was named by President Bush to be Commissioner of Social Security.) If I turned to my other side, usually to pound at the typewriter, I was likely to harass Tim Gillespie, our transportation LA, whose ears were only inches away. Luckily for me, Tim was easygoing, and his habit of keeping several months' accumulation of answered phone messages compressed on a desk spindle tended to be his most visible display of emotion. Such a presence nearby had a calming influence in an often frazzled environment; moreover, having worked for Heinz in the House, Tim was valuable in interpreting our boss's mood and desires. Tim, too, wanted to build on his specialty, and after a while left to become director of congressional relations at Amtrak.

Beating too hasty an exit from my desk to the door nearby was likely to disturb any papers left atop the desk of Bill Reinsch, our LA for trade and energy. Bill and I were hired at roughly the same time for comparable positions, but I always regarded him as someone of far greater maturity and stature. A onetime schoolteacher, he was a little older, but more than that he had an impressive sense of self-discipline and authority; every morning he would unload his briefcase of papers he had read the night before, as though they were corrected school assignments. (Bicycling to work as I often did, a briefcase was out of the question.) Trade was an area of special relevance to Pennsylvania, given the state's steel plants and other import-threatened older industries, and over the years Bill was to learn the issues systematically to the point that he became recognized as one of Congress's reigning professionals in the field. He was also the only one of our original crew who remained more than two years into John's first Senate term—and, at this writing, is still there.

Finally there was Geoff, whom I have already mentioned, slightly more distant from the line of fire. He enjoyed similarly incommodious circumstances, but at least he had the benefit of sitting in a corner. This special position was due to his designation as chief LA, although as a result of his being younger than all the rest of us, he was somewhat self-conscious about his elevated status and frequently declined his prerogatives. I was unusually young for a Senate aide—most, including the others in our office, were in their late twenties or early thirties—but Geoff had even me beat by a few months and moreover he was in a position usually occupied by someone at the farther end of the range. The other LAs were responsible for relatively narrow areas, selected because they represented Heinz's committee assignments or particular interests, but Geoff allocated daily responsibilities to be sure nothing that John needed went uncovered. He had served with Heinz for several years, earned his trust, and more than anyone else on the staff had developed so personal a relationship that he might occasionally see the Heinzes on a social basis.

The rest of us did not generally fraternize with the Heinz family, except for a Christmas or office party, where sociability was, for a few hours, virtually obligatory, or when Heinz's wife, Teresa, a spunky and attractive Portuguese woman often given credit for bringing her husband down to earth, breezed through the office with one or more of their three small boys in tow. (On such occasions she was known to hand out tickets to Mstislav Rostropovich concerts at the Kennedy Center or even to invite us to join her at lunch in the senators' dining room.) Typically it is rare for aides and employers to mingle in the after hours, unless it is in the nature of a drink after work. Late one evening, for example, after three of us had accompanied him to a television news show taping, Heinz offered his aides a ride back into town. He drove us to his own home, and when we alighted from the car in the alley behind the garage, there was never any question that we would simply part ways there to find taxis. (It was not difficult; Heinz lived in the heart of Georgetown.)

Geoff, like Teresa, was a model of spontaneity. He had the disheveled appearance of Woody Allen, and even a comparably offbeat sense of humor, but his most impressive attribute was that he refused to take things too seriously and never hesitated to use his clout with Heinz to intervene on behalf of fellow staff members. By the time I came to know him, he appeared almost to be coasting in his role as Heinz's political aide—although it may have been just the fanatical habit of a New Yorker to begin his day by spreading the sports pages out on his desk. In time he left to commence a new career as a political pollster, where he has since excelled as president of Peter Hart Research. Similarly Larry McCarthy, the press secretary, became a successful media specialist, working successively for the Senate Republican campaign committee (which Heinz, in recognition of his organizational abilities, was tapped to head) and political consultant Roger Ailes (where he produced adroit TV ads, such as the one where a pack of bloodhounds tracks down a senator who, instead of voting, is away in sunny resorts giving speeches). From their vantage point in the U.S. Senate, Geoff and Larry shrewdly sensed that politics, in the modern age, involved much more than legislation.

14

COMMITTEES
AT WORK AND PLAY

Although to most appearances I functioned as a Heinz LA during this period, I was technically an aide of the Senate Budget Committee and listed on its payroll. This anomaly reflected the complexity of employment practices on the Hill, a situation driven by Congress's continuing demand for staff. Junior senators complained in the mid-1970s that they needed more help competing with senior members, who could tap committee resources. So the Senate voted them new funds to hire an additional aide to assist with each of their committee assignments but, to avoid criticism of ballooning personal offices, created the fiction that the new employees belonged to those committees.

For reasons that remain obscure the positions were formally designated to be "task force investigators," although they were more colloquially known as "S. Res. 60s," a reference to the Senate resolution that created them. But few used these terms or appreciated the convoluted arrangements. In deference to the technical points, however, I was required to maintain a desk in a converted former hotel across the street from the Senate, where the Budget Committee, for lack of space elsewhere, had been lodged. Here I shared a room with Charlie

Gentry, my counterpart from Senator Pete Domenici's office. I tended to visit for no more than five or ten minutes each day, the minimum that the committee staff director, John McEvoy, assured me would keep our names out of the *Washington Post*.

Just like the annexes on the House side, this building had seen better days and had been appropriated out of the continuing imperatives of congressional *Lebensraum*. If there was a difference, it was only that the Senate had a more glamorous heritage, and amateur historians could point with pride to the fact that it had been the Carroll Arms—the onetime hostelry—that served as the site of some of Senator Jack Kennedy's allegedly epic extramarital liaisons. Other senators had also been known to go in and out of the Carroll Arms for various reasons, and it was appropriate that McEvoy, a memorable storyteller, should now be presiding from a large suite at its entrance. He was an effective leader of the committee's seventy-member staff, not least because he enlivened many afternoons by regaling audiences with colorful tales of the Senate. He had served as AA to Senator Edmund Muskie of Maine, now the committee chairman, and at the slightest inducement would recount the details of his boss's fabled private outbursts. It did not surprise those who knew John that in 1987 he was publicly quoted as saying that his friend, former senator Gary Hart, would have no trouble in his presidential campaign "as long as he can keep his pants on," a statement credited with hastening Hart's downfall. John had always been as candid as he was witty.

When I arrived on the scene, the Senate Budget Committee was a recent invention reflecting the era's new fiscal concerns. Its purpose was to help rationalize federal spending: setting priorities and matching expenditures to receipts. Until this time national budget policy had been essentially an executive function. The congressional tradition had been to authorize programs almost haphazardly—on the merits or politics of individual cases—rather than by comparing them to other spending possibilities or to the availability of revenue. Only the most casual regard was paid to the total budget-impact and economic-policy implications of all these bits and pieces of spending. An appealing program had the presumption of support: Somehow it would be financed. And it was further assumed that justifications for programs already approved over the years were at this point beyond challenge.

In the 1970s, Congress began to acknowledge that resources were limited and that claims on the national budget were in competition. Thus the Budget and Impoundment Act of 1974 was greeted with great acclaim, as though Congress had finally accepted the self-discipline that critics had said would inherently elude it. The legislation established a Congressional Budget Office to provide analysis independent of the executive branch's often partisan advocacy; a new annual budget cycle requiring Congress throughout the year to set tentative and then binding allocations for each major area of spending; and House and Senate budget committees ("supercommittees" in the eyes of some) to superintend the whole process.

A key objective was to flag long-term issues that could become a wedge for future spending. Senators began to appreciate distinctions between immediate "outlays" and the arguably more important concept of future "budget authority," which could determine the direction and magnitude of overall spending commitments for years to come. Henceforth, the theory went, the Congress would weigh the case for new programs on the basis of the larger "missions" it sought to accomplish. For example, it would decide on a figure for the "050 function," otherwise known as defense, on the basis of answering broad questions about desired military goals: Should the navy emphasize "sea control" or "power projection"? Should the armed forces continue to rely on volunteers? In the natural-resources function, basic questions included whether energy conservation should be encouraged—through government-sponsored programs of research, utility-rate reform, and loan guarantees—and whether development of a strategic petroleum reserve should be accelerated. So, too, were choices posed for commerce and transportation, education and employment, and in other large spheres of governmental activity.

All of this required the assistance of a large committee staff, top-notch specialists who could collect and synthesize data, identify major issues for their bosses' attention, and work with other committees, the CBO, and the administration to coordinate action. Given the political nature of the beast it was designed to tame, the budget process was bound to have its limitations. Indeed the passage of the Gramm-Rudman-Hollings law in the late 1980s, dubbed a meat cleaver even by its supporters, signified the quaintness of Congress's early efforts. In practice half the budget consisted of "entitlements," such as Social Security payments for which recipients automatically qualified by formulas already in the law; an additional fourth of the budget was considered "relatively uncontrollable," meaning that it supported programs previously set in motion that could not now be reversed except by breaching contractual obligations or announced government intentions. Despite these facts Jimmy Carter had been elected on a promise to balance the budget, and Congress was jumping on his bandwagon. What were they to do? The Budget Committee staff calculated the means by which the deficit (then only $63.2 billion) could be wiped away: an increase in taxes of 16 percent or reductions in the nonentitlement area—including many popular defense, energy, environment, education, and jobs programs—of 25 percent.

That these options were not politically feasible suggested the considerable futility of the Budget Committee's task. Its chairman, Senator Muskie, tried his best to rise above crass realities and daily implored his colleagues to impose order on the budgetary sprawl. His speeches, delivered in a throaty baritone, his voice rising and falling with large waves of emotion, were all the more impressive because they had to do with a subject—the numbers of the federal budget—that would not seem to lend itself to such eloquence. The point he made over and over was that because the advocates of every program can make it seem worthy, the objective of the budget process was not to weed out "bad" programs (for there were none) but to perform the much more difficult labor of eliminating "good" ones.

Muskie was by this time one of the most distinguished members of the body—a vice-presidential standard bearer for his party almost ten years before and a presidential candidate more recently—and had been selected for the job because he commanded widespread respect. Even so, there was a feeling that "old Ed" could say these things because he was an elder statesman who probably had only limited electoral plans in his future. (Indeed in 1980 he would retire from the Senate to accept appointment as Carter's lame-duck secretary of state.) Other senators joined him in talking grandiloquently about painful choices but, in the end, always demurred when it came time to vote on cuts in popular programs: medical care for the elderly, educational benefits for the disadvantaged, retirement benefits for the armed forces.

One day, for example, Senator Cranston, the outspoken California liberal, arrived for markup on the defense portion of the budget. As majority whip, he was often preoccupied on the floor and could rarely attend such sessions. Some assumed that his presence meant the committee would be considering a particularly important weapons system that he was determined to oppose. There was such a weapons system on the agenda that day—the B-1 bomber—but Cranston had come to battle *for* it. "He's holding his nose today," said Hal Gross, his usually cheerful aide, himself cringing. It hardly needed to be said which state's factories produced the B-1.

Still other senators came only sporadically, depending on press or constituent interest. Illustrious witnesses such as cabinet secretaries Joe Califano or Harold Brown had drawing power, as did markup sessions which could be used to raise larger or more newsworthy issues. Senator Joseph Biden of Delaware made a dramatic plea one day for federal assistance to states burdened by court-ordered busing. The budget allowance for this item was trivial, and some thought the use of the committee's time inappropriate, but Biden's colleagues were tolerant because they knew that on their own issues they might expect reciprocal treatment. Biden was only in his early thirties, but at times seemed younger; his animated comments could amuse as easily as offend. Once, a committee staffer who had been called to the witness table to answer members' questions got caught up in the Biden-inspired spirit and made a quip himself. "No editorializing by staff," Biden snapped back. (Like others, Biden "grew" in office and, especially after his well-publicized presidential campaign and health catastrophes years later, tempered his manner and gained new respect.)

Several of the committee's senators were notably high-minded and frequently abetted Muskie in his efforts to forge consensus. Henry Bellmon, a once and future Oklahoma governor, served as ranking Republican; he was a quiet and gentle man whose moderate disposition reflected his politics. That he often elected to support the chairman's position was a point of pride, for it was his belief that the committee would exercise its greatest influence if its positions were bipartisan. Lawton Chiles, a Democrat of Florida, and Pete Domenici, a Republican of New Mexico, were similarly helpful. Both were refreshingly down-to-earth: Chiles had gained fame in his first election by walking his state for votes; Domenici would greet committee and other members' staffs by first names and tell us during breaks what he had done with his numerous children over the weekend. These senators seemed honest, solid citizens, not practiced politicians, and it was such a type that responded best to Muskie's appeals.

The heart of the committee's work was marking up concurrent budget resolutions, which fixed spending limits for each broad function as well as an overall total. The committee staff prepared thick black notebooks for senators that, in many cases, only their aides had the time to peruse. Although the materials were voluminous, they were composed with a paint-by-numbers simplicity. Starting with a figure for "current policy"—jargon that denoted existing programs plus an allowance for inflation—they outlined major proposals for new spending in each area. Using these guidelines, committee deliberations sometimes became an amusing spectacle as senators with only partial knowledge of budget details casually proposed numbers with an air of authority. No sum smaller than $100 million occupied the committee's attention, and generally references were denominated in billions. Aging Senator Hayakawa of California, in addition to becoming famous for dozing off at these times (in his defense, the numerical recitations could be tedious), also gained note for the comment that a billion here and a billion there pretty soon added up to real money, thus updating Senator Everett Dirksen's line years before about mere *millions*.

When it came to the education and employment function, to take an example, Senators Muskie and Bellmon, seeking to spur bidding like an auctioneer, might jointly propose figures of "6.6" and "6.7" referring, in the arcana that had become commonplace, to outlays and budget authority—in the billions, of course. (Their staffs might have met for several hours to settle on these numbers, arriving at them by starting with "current policy" and adding one or two new programs that they believed to command broad support.) Senator Cranston could at this point move to raise the figures to "6.9" and "8.2" in order to accommodate an increase in funding for the Head Start program; Senator Chiles might then move to *decrease* the numbers to reflect possible elimination of a program that, in his view, Head Start duplicated; and Senator Hayakawa might suggest slashing funds for the Comprehensive Employment and Training Act. Such proposals, and accompanying votes, would go on and on, and once the committee got rolling, could proceed well into the evening.

Disputes could involve great passions though of only marginal significance. Once I attended a House-Senate negotiation that bogged down on the question of whether the mark for the defense function should be set at $118.5 billion or $118.7 billion; both sides announced as a matter of high principle that they would not budge. "Current policy" in practice assumed an almost inviolate status, and it was considered a triumph if the committees simply held that line; they were not expected actually to roll spending back. Moreover Congress began resorting to budget tricks to show progress: delaying the effective date of outlays so that they would fall outside the fiscal year for purposes of measuring the deficit, changing economic assumptions to produce higher estimates of tax revenue. (Staff had some compunction about supplying these solutions, but that was their duty.) The Budget Act had naïvely supposed that mere legalisms—deadlines, points of order, budget waivers—would suffice to modify age-old congressional behavior. But the sovereignty of other committees and the political imperatives of individual members were more than enough to thwart fundamental change. Even in 1989, after Congress had resorted to the severe discipline of the Gramm-Rudman law, critics would complain that its targets were being met only by sleight-of-hand.

Regularly I worked with committee specialists such as Charlie Flickner, the committee's onetime mailroom employee, now its international-affairs guru, who, in a rapid staccato, would recite data about "paid-in capital" for coming "replenishments" of multilateral development banks; Karen Williams, the general counsel, who could explain the mysterious budget "reconciliation" process, which David Stockman would later exploit to enforce spending limits; and Van Ooms, the economist, who would offer GNP growth forecasts and critique invariably optimistic administration predictions. Sid Brown, director of budget review, was the committee's most indispensable aide. Pencil poised on ear, he was always at the ready to supply or explain any number that appeared in massive budget documents arrayed around him. Other staffers might be given a first opportunity to answer questions, but when all else failed, everyone turned to Sid. Many of his colleagues came and went every two or three years, but he was the institution that kept the committee running smoothly for the decade he would be there.

My closest association was with the small cadre of Republican staffers. Although the Democratic majority staff functioned as a resource for all committee members, the minority felt a need for its own source of advice. Even I was conscripted to cover a function (veterans affairs), my responsibility being to alert our side to issues where we might want to take a different stand from the Democrats. I was miscast here, knowing nothing of the subject, and, for background, needed to consult the majority staffer, which obviously defeated the purpose. Fortunately Becky Beauregard was a lovely woman of great charity who answered my elementary questions and mercifully taught me only what I absolutely needed to know.

Partisanship did not come naturally to the GOP team given Senator Bellmon's moderation and the fact that his top aides, Bob Boyd and Bob Fulton, were similarly civil and broad-minded. Charlie McQuillen, the sharp-witted designee of conservative Senator James McClure of Idaho, was more outspoken; and Bill Stringer, our economist, although quiet and scholarly, espoused supply-side economics long before the fashion swept Washington. Under their collective influence, and the fact that I began focusing more on these issues, I became increasingly conservative in my economics and began to question such things as levels of government spending, tax burdens, and bureaucratic solutions to problems. Although I remained in theory an advocate of congressional bipartisanship, in practice I proved capable of tactical party politics. Fortunately, on the Budget Committee, my two allegiances only occasionally diverged.

Heinz tended toward moderate positions, in part no doubt as an imperative of Pennsylvania politics. Party registration there was overwhelmingly Democratic, and Republicans won only by virtue of their seeking support from beyond the margins of their own party. In recent times they have had considerable statewide success—Hugh Scott, Richard Schweiker, Richard Thornburgh, and Arlen Specter, to name others besides Heinz—but they have tended to find their followings by carving out positions that veer away from national party dogma. Heinz himself, a Harvard MBA and onetime executive of his family's food company, probably had an inborn proclivity toward economic conservatism, but this was complemented by an interest in constituent preferences, not to mention all the classroom instruction he had doubtless received in the techniques of marketing.

Still, Heinz recognized his occasional apostasies and sought opportunities to prove an underlying Republican loyalty. At the beginning of the Carter administration he used his membership on the Governmental Affairs Committee to launch broadside attacks against Bert Lance, Carter's chief budget adviser, whose previous banking activities in Georgia had been much criticized. The Senate Budget Committee also presented targets of opportunity. On taking office, President Carter proposed an economic-stimulus program to counteract high unemployment and idle manufacturing capacity; it included such elements as countercyclical aid to local government public-works projects, and new public-service jobs. He also proposed a onetime tax rebate to encourage consumer and business spending; his advisers argued strongly that the state of the economy required it and leaned on Congress for support. Suddenly Carter reversed himself, admitting the move might be inflationary; the rebate proposal would be dropped.

Senator Muskie was furious about the reversal, having personally campaigned for it on Carter's behalf; he felt, moreover, that an eleventh-hour change injured the integrity of the budget process, which had assumed a major tax reduction in its concurrent resolutions. Eliminating the rebate, he knew, would mean additional revenue in the budget—which in turn would produce new pressures from congressmen to fund their pet projects. Republicans had never defended the rebate, arguing that tax relief should take the form of permanent changes in rates, but even the more gentlemanly among them could not resist an opportunity to twit the administration for its vacillation.

Jacob Javits of New York convened Senate Republicans to devise an attack. He strongly supported a tax cut and urged that committees invite all possible economists to testify on the issue. Whatever their persuasion, he was sure they would be of one mind that economic circumstances had not changed since Carter first made his proposal. The result would be to expose the new administration's inconstancy of purpose; the Republicans were successful in this and in so doing helped to lay the groundwork for a reputation that plagued the president to the end. Senators William Roth and Jack Danforth also advocated broad tax cuts and wanted to charge while momentum was building. The GOP was trying out its new battle cry of economic growth, taking to voters a seemingly esoteric message about the need for capital formation, enhanced productivity, and limitations on government spending as a fraction of GNP. Eventually this would be encapsulated in the Roth-Kemp tax cut proposal and become an important part of the platform of Ronald Reagan.

Heinz was well suited to helping, because his quantitative bent gave him an expertise in economic matters that most of his colleagues lacked. Nothing interested him more than the occasional memos I would prepare on such topics as the relationship of higher personal income to the rebuilding of inventories. So when the Carter administration's economic triumvirate—Office of Management and Budget director Bert Lance, Secretary of the Treasury Michael Blumenthal, Council of Economic Advisers chairman Charles Shultze—came before the Budget Committee to testify, he could hardly contain his glee and pursued them with both political and intellectual vengeance. For their part, they could hardly contain their embarrassment at the president's decision. Democrats on the committee joined in, railing at the administration's alleged disregard for the congressional budget process. Deep fissures in White House relations even with members of its own party on Capitol Hill were breaking into the open, and Republicans were not about to prevent them.

Soon I got caught up in the spirit; Carter's actions and inactions threatened fiscal disaster. I suggested pugilistic debating tactics to my boss, wrote tart-tongued speeches, and even made the poor attempt at humor to propose that he say Carter had misunderstood one of his advisers who had a thick northern accent and thought he recommended a "fickle" policy rather than a "fiscal" policy. Sometimes it took massive discipline to endure marathon committee sessions, which often looked at issues in a disembodied numerical way; this was before Ronald Reagan and David Stockman made federal budgetary matters dramatic front-page news. (Indeed one of my last acts for Heinz was to recommend that he switch from the Budget Committee to the higher-profile Finance Committee—which he did, just before the Budget Committee became popular.) But at times like this it seemed possible to do important work and, at the same time, enjoy the satisfactions of raw politics.

15

PERSONAL AGENDAS, PUBLIC BENEFITS

It seemed to me a staffer's highest calling to suggest initiatives that would not only serve his employer's interests and provide a measure of excitement but have the added reward of contributing (in the staffer's view) to good public policy. Two such episodes during my time with Heinz stood out as satisfying this objective: once when we opposed President Carter's "neutron bomb" and another time when we battled powerful Senator Russell Long over tax breaks for well-heeled national bus companies. In both cases I promoted the issues to Heinz, he gave me the green light to proceed, and our side triumphed. In both cases I think what we did was right, and I think the public benefited. But in both cases it was sobering to reflect on how the personal predilections of a young, unelected staffer could influence congressional action.

The neutron bomb mushroomed suddenly into public consciousness with the publication of a single newspaper story. In mid-1977 the *Washington Post* revealed that development funds for an exotic new weapons system were buried in a public-works bill pending before the Senate; so secret was the program that reportedly even the president had not known about it. Although technically the debate concerned enhanced radiation warheads, colloquially everyone soon came to be talking about the neutron bomb, a more colorful designation that gave the issue a greater dramatic flair conducive to emotional public debate.

The bomb worked by means of emitting radiation; it would annihilate hostile forces without destroying their property, making it easier to move in afterward and occupy enemy territory. The underlying strategy seemed crude and lent itself to the simplification, which many (including myself) were quick to seize upon, that advocates placed a higher value on material possessions than human life. I argued to my boss the sacrilege of such philosophy but, in an effort to persuade, did not restrict myself to mere moral certitudes. I also suggested that opposing the bomb would present us an opportunity to criticize the general ineptness of administration policy and to burnish Heinz's credentials in the national-security area (the mark, it seemed, of a civilized senator). Luckily the merit of my arguments was reinforced by Heinz's workaday political imperatives. He was a busy U.S. senator who nonetheless was expected to keep abreast of all the major issues; taking occasional high-profile positions symbolized to colleagues and constituents that his watchfulness had not slackened. Moreover he enjoyed his job and tried to embrace as much as he could; once persuaded of a good cause, his inclination was to act, not ponder. To the delight of his staff, he generally approved our recommendations.

I prepared a neutron-bomb rebuttal with relish. Naturally I recognized that humanitarian appeals would be insufficient: Although Carter himself had helped usher in a more self-consciously moral era in foreign policy, congressmen remained defensive about taking positions, at least publicly, on other than the basis of hard-headed calculation of national interest. Sam Goldberg, our AA, expressed concern that the wrong approach could stigmatize Heinz as a "bleeding-heart liberal," permanently discrediting his ventures into defense policy. Accepting this wisdom, I made sure to couch our position in pragmatic terms as I went about drafting his statements. Rather than asserting categorical opposition, for example, I emphasized unresolved issues and the desirability of further debate. Although I might have preferred a less tentative position myself, I remembered that I was writing in someone else's name; "raising questions" was a favored means in Congress of leaving oneself an escape hatch depending on the eventual resolution of public opinion.

Advocating a postponement of the decision actually made some sense.

Carter admitted that he had not yet decided what to do, and Congress had barely examined the subject. We could claim that we were pursuing the fiscally prudent course of preventing an appropriation of funds that might not be needed. Still I could not avoid slipping in my own criticism on the merits. Nuclear deterrence, I wrote, was likelier to be achieved when larger and more unacceptable weapons had to be used rather than those of less destructive quality, since the greater willingness of officials to use lesser weapons could ironically lower the threshold of nuclear exchange. Almost as an afterthought, I returned to my original concern: that the weapon—as I wrote in too cute a phrase—was "literally dehumanizing," singling out people for destruction and choosing to preserve buildings instead.

Heinz delivered these remarks on the Senate floor, and they were picked up fleetingly in press accounts of the growing debate. Not surprisingly, it was the "literally dehumanizing" line that reporters found most quotable. Few citizens have the time to peruse the *Congressional Record* and read entire speeches in context; to the world at large (even now, despite gavel-to-gavel cable TV coverage) it is only the heavily filtered news stories that give Congress its reality. Unfortunately these news accounts also appeared to be the source of information for conservative columnist George Will, who shortly produced a compelling piece that cited my phrase and rebuked Heinz for his guileless views. Will was an icon among Republicans, and I shuddered to see him taking us on. With other staffers I debated the appropriate response. Geoff proposed ignoring him rather than calling attention to the fact that he had attacked us. Sam and Larry (the press secretary) argued for answering him head-on to clear Heinz's good name.

Finally we compromised and prepared articles for Pennsylvania papers—the *Pittsburgh Post-Gazette* and the *Philadelphia Inquirer*—where Heinz's position might evoke more support and we could avoid prolonging an unseemly squabble before Washington opinion makers. I consulted a friend, Forrest Frank, an expert on the esoterica of nuclear weapons strategy, for help in making elegant military arguments—such as the idea that hilly terrain and wet weather are neutron absorbers, which might counteract the bomb's radiation—so as to make our position seem worthy of the Joint Chiefs of Staff. The articles were published and probably useful in preempting local criticism. At the same time our original rhetoric had helped rouse liberals within the Democratic party, and in time President Carter, who had decided to go forward with a request for funding, changed his mind and abandoned it. This was our good fortune, for the immense criticism he took for his wavering policy allowed our own role quickly to be forgotten.

What lingered was an uneasiness on my part about the manner in which congressional debate could be conducted. It was a startling fact that a staff aide who barely knew the background of a matter, had only recently become acquainted with an employer and his philosophy, and who could not begin to recite pertinent data about the state constituency that he theoretically served, could exert serious influence on his boss's position in a major controversy, which in turn could have a demonstrable impact on public debate. It would continue to surprise me how much credibility attaches to a senator's most forcefully stated positions, as though they derive from access to vast resources and expertise and are the product of mature and systematic reflection. Here was a senator, possessed of a critical intelligence and attention to detail unusual among his colleagues, relying on the ideas and using the words of an anonymous staff assistant for whose purposes and wisdom he could not himself vouch. Yet his colleagues could be forgiven for listening closely to his words on the thought that, to show such passion, he must have known something they didn't.

Of course a staff member need not dwell on doubts; he will soon be overcome by the thrill of exploits in a new area. Our next issue came along quickly. John Heinz not only enjoyed his job; he wanted to be a good senator. Usually he measured this by the esteem his performance earned him in Pennsylvania, but he also had a generalized devotion to good government, which, in the absence of conflicting constituent interests, he was only too happy to express. In late 1977 he had a perfect opportunity. An assistant director of the Congressional Budget Office, Ray Sheppach, spotted an exceptional special-interest provision in a pending energy-tax bill and sought to enlist a senator to help strike it. The CBO prided itself on political neutrality and was sworn to act as servant of Congress. But this did not prevent individuals from acting in their personal capacities. Ray was able and conscientious and asked his colleague Terry Finn, a Senate Budget Committee analyst, which member he might recommend for the task; Terry, who knew Heinz to be diligent and activist, contacted me. Those were the concentric staff circles around a typical senator: CBO, as an auxiliary research institution, reported to committee staffs, which in turn worked through personal staffs to get to senators. I was expected to act as a final gatekeeper to my boss's time and attentions. In this case, having heard the others out, I became enthusiastic, embraced the cause as my own, and quickly arranged access.

The provision at issue, sponsored by Democratic senator Russell Long of Louisiana, provided a refundable tax credit to the intercity bus industry. That industry consisted essentially of two well-known companies, Greyhound and Trailways, and the credit represented a cost to the Treasury of $1 billion over a five-year period. Because these companies paid minimal federal income taxes, the "credit" would actually take the form of a payment to them from the government. Ray thought such a proposal completely without merit and guessed that Long was promoting it to cultivate the bus industry as the new chairman of the Surface Transportation Subcommittee of the Senate Commerce Committee. Indeed, as we looked at it, the justification did seem tenuous: The profit margin of the industry, although in decline, was still high relative to other regulated industries. While billed as a fuel-conservation measure, the proposal embodied a formula that rewarded only past performance. And it seemed difficult to ensure that benefits would accrue to the bus lines rather than to their more prosperous holding companies; Greyhound was owned by a diversified conglomerate, and Trailways by Holiday Inn. To alleviate any doubt, Ray suggested that we request an official CBO study—which, he assumed, would conveniently arrive at these precise conclusions.

Heinz listened intently to his briefings and agreed almost instantly to pursue an amendment. His major hesitation, not surprisingly, was the prospect of tangling with Senator Long, who was legendary for his parliamentary skills, political influence, and long memory for real and imagined slights. Heinz wisely had me research what legislation Long controlled in the transportation subcommittee that could be held over us; fortunately there was none. Pennsylvania was interested, for example, in rebuilding Conrail, but a major appropriation had already been made. The state also supported development of a high-speed passenger rail corridor between Washington and Boston, but this had already been authorized; moreover, Senator Lowell Weicker of Connecticut, the ranking Republican on Long's subcommittee, could be counted on to get the Northeast what it needed. Heinz himself had introduced a "rail jobs" bill, which was jointly referred to both the Human Resources Committee and Long's Commerce Committee, but the former had already agreed to hold hearings.

Then the question became how to advocate the amendment most effectively. We informed Long of our intentions as a courtesy but knew he would not give in; we were pleased enough not to be threatened, probably a sign that he assumed we had no chance of success. As I surveyed aides in other offices, we realized our best shot might be to frame an "institutional" argument, designed to appeal regardless of political persuasion. We could point out that because the tax credit functioned as a positive subsidy in this case, the appropriations and authorization committees—not simply the tax-writing committee—deserved more time to consider it. In fact only one hearing had been held in those committees, and on that occasion official witnesses from the Department of Transportation and the Interstate Commerce Commission had voiced strong objections. Senators were legendary for their determination to preserve procedural prerogatives; many would view dimly any short-circuiting of traditional process. We also believed the amendment had potential bipartisan appeal even on an ideological basis. To Democrats we could argue that it was just another handout to big business; to Republicans we could say it represented a dangerous new precedent for government intervention in the marketplace.

I worked the phones making these points. Often I did not know which particular LAs in other Senate offices would handle the matter—nor always did the offices themselves. Would it be the tax LA, the transportation LA, the energy LA, or the one who covered the Commerce or Finance Committee? The assignment (typically by the chief LA) would not be made until the issue arose. The easiest approach in these circumstances was to send around a "Dear Colleague" letter, the official early-warning system on proposed legislative activity in which senators stated intentions, outlined arguments, and solicited support. We composed it in our punchiest style (the letter would not be read unless kept brief and interesting) and listed in the last paragraph, as a source of further information, my name and telephone extension, a tip-off to experienced readers which Heinz staffer was behind the exercise and might soon be calling. After a couple of days I canvassed again. The technique worked, having put the matter on at least one LA's radar screen in each office. That hardly meant that senators themselves were aware of the issue, let alone that they had decided on a position. But that was not our purpose, because we did not expect many to endorse an amendment outright that took on both Russell Long and such all-American companies as Greyhound and Trailways. Our more limited objective was to stimulate thinking for the moment when a vote would be cast. If the amendment received a serious hearing on the floor and showed a genuine chance of passage, a quick word by LAs to their senators (departing for the vote) might be enough to carry the day.

The floor debate was dramatic, featuring spirited rhetorical appeals from both sides, vigorous buttonholing in the well of the chamber, and a surprise ending that drew gasps from the galleries. Unlike the House, which had converted to modern electronic voting, the Senate maintained the colorful tradition of fifteen-minute oral roll calls. "Mr. Abourezk," the clerk would call out, awaiting a "Yea" or "Nay" response, and going on like this alphabetically through all one hundred names until he had reached "Mr. Zorinsky." The suspense built until a tally was announced at the end. We had not done preliminary vote counts, nor exacted firm commitments, and the large number of affirmative votes for our amendment gave us great encouragement. At last, time was called, and we had our result: The Heinz amendment was defeated by a single vote. The elation we had felt on receiving so much support was crushed by the outcome.

As the majority leader moved on to other business, however, Senator Stennis approached us to say that his vote had been misrecorded: He had wanted to support us. Usually such votes are final and cannot be reopened, and my disappointment became all the more acute for knowing that we had been cheated by the rules. But Heinz was more collected and suddenly discerned that the rules in this case could assist us. Traditionally a vote is followed by a motion to reconsider, which, by unanimous consent, is laid on the table, sealing the result; it is all in the nature of a perfunctory observance of parliamentary procedure. But Heinz realized that, for some reason, no one had made such a motion; through quick action he was able to call another vote. As the Senate murmured again, the votes were cast, tallied, and announced. The previous result was reversed—by one vote. We won!

Russell Long was not pleased, but in his own way was forgiving. He walked up to Heinz and said, "Your speech was one of the most demagogic I've ever heard." Then he smiled. "I really admired it." John Heinz was floating up toward the chandeliers, and I was not far below. I should have used the opportunity to request a raise, but it never occurred to me. I was still operating largely on the motivation of psychic income. At this moment I was terribly proud to be associated with Heinz. It was a rare senator who would take the time to fight a dogged legislative battle without prior expertise in a complicated area nor with any obvious political benefit to be gained from the pursuit. The entire episode seemed to me the height of good government and the stuff of a staffer's dreams.

16

CONSTITUENT GROUPS AND THE FINE ART OF ACCOMMODATION

We made up for such national perspectives by an otherwise unrelenting determination to please the voters of Pennsylvania. This approach was fully expected of us; to do otherwise would have been to court ridicule and defeat, to defy high congressional tradition and even the purposes of representative democracy. And yet, much as I accepted the convention, there was something about it that rang hollow at times, as though we were simply going through motions. It wasn't enough, for example, to cast a vote and offer an explanation on the merits. Instead every position had to be justified for local consumption, even if the underlying rationale were in fact broader and nobler.

The issue of funding for veterans programs was typical. Heinz supported modest restraint because he took seriously his charge to help close the budget deficit. This was not, however, a sufficient explanation for the state's organized veterans groups, which could be counted on to impugn the human sensitivity, if not the patriotic devotion, of congressmen who did not automatically support all possible increases. We went to great lengths to preempt such criticism. Through press releases, floor statements, and targeted mailings we called attention to our overall record of support and waxed rhetorical about the gratitude the nation owed its men in uniform. If the funding levels Heinz supported in the Budget Committee were somewhat lower than those recommended by the Veterans Affairs Committee, we would point out that they exceeded administration requests as well as previous years' spending. Not to take chances, I would be detailed as the senator's representative to American Legion breakfasts and Veterans of Foreign Wars dinners, the burden of my presence being to convince as many Pennsylvania delegates as I could collar that Senator Heinz, like no other, had their interests at heart.

Agricultural issues were somewhat more complicated because our farming constituency was largely in the dairy business. This presented us with an opportunity to proclaim our concern about the federal budget by denouncing the level of support prices for wheat, corn, and other non-Pennsylvanian commodities. In the "supplemental" and "dissenting" views sections of Budget Committee reports, senators were invited to explain what they might have done differently from those who signed the majority view; Republicans always vied to show how they would have been tougher on spending. Since Heinz, as a moderate, did not generally care to slash social or defense spending, it was always a challenge to find something about which he could boast showing a special skepticism, and the agriculture function beckoned as our obvious candidate. State milk producers, however, were treated differently; there we did whatever we could to help. (We were hardly unique. Senator William Proxmire, otherwise a penny-pincher with federal dollars, backed the dairy price supports his Wisconsin constituents had come to expect.) For my part I learned what I could about the milk-marketing system and other dairy matters, although I never attained more than the most primitive knowledge of the distinctions among "fluid-eligible" milk, "manufacturing grade," and others. But this did not prevent me from trying eagerly to promote the interests of a constituency whose purposes and methods I barely understood. At the time it simply seemed to me that this was the classic purpose of a senator: to fight for his constituents, like one's country, whether right or wrong.

My attitude crystallized as I began writing speeches. Often I had written statements for use on the House or Senate floor, but rarely had I been a speechwriter for purposes of a local political event. Another chance was bestowed on me one week when Heinz agreed to one of his first appearances before a farm group, the Interstate Co-op of Lancaster, Pennsylvania. Had I treated the assignment in academic fashion, the approach would have been obvious: Identify the salient issues of interest to the group, present a careful analysis of the arguments, and render a forthright statement of our positions. But a young aide receives, rather than invents, his wisdom, and it was my clear impression that this was anything but the time-honored method. Instead it seemed that the purpose of speaking to such a group was not to engage it in a frank and educational exchange but to announce whatever views were thought necessary to win it over, earning acclaim and support. Accordingly the speechwriter's function was not to research or analyze the issues but to find out the audience's predisposition about them. From my desk I would call the sponsors of an event, ask what was on their minds, and, most crucially, request to know where the members of their group stood. My informants may have imagined that I was only collecting general background information, but in fact I was scribbling furiously because they were providing me my very lines.

Speeches by politicians to large groups tend to be heavily rhetorical, the sort where paragraphs are one sentence long and pauses between them are obligatory for dramatic effect; premium is given not to subtle exposition but to potential applause lines. The point is to touch upon all matters that will excite an audience's attention and to recite a politician's conveniently favorable attitudes about each one of them. Of course an audience needs a little warming up first, much as a rock concert crowd may require a preliminary act to find the right mood; not everyone looks forward to political speeches. Experienced politicians know that a light touch will put an audience in a receptive frame of mind. A friend then working as a speechwriter for Vice President Walter Mondale once lamented to me the fate of even his most brilliant work: Mondale would send speech drafts back to him with the notation scrawled across the top, "Where are the jokes?" I geared my efforts accordingly, but the quality of my humor left something to be desired. "Perhaps you've heard about chic Georgetown cocktail parties," I had Heinz saying to the farmers of Lancaster, "but I want you to know that I serve only *milk* at mine." Undeterred by the prospect of a thundering groan, I went on to suggest that this was because milk is not only as American as apple pie but even *goes* with apple pie!

The rest of the text read even more miserably because the pandering got worse, and it was phrased very seriously. Dairy farmers, I had learned, were upset about the importation of something called casein because it competed with domestically produced nonfat dry milk. Since casein imports were technically classified as chemicals, I asserted that it was only a matter of time before Americans would be eating chemicals in their ice-cream cones, ruining the taste and texture of America's favorite dessert. At this point I quoted fellow Pennsylvanian Gus Yatron, the ice-cream maker turned congressman, who, relying on the same impeccable evidence, had once opined that ice cream could eventually taste like a combination of air and glue. (Citing Yatron on dairy science was roughly equivalent to quoting Yogi Berra on philosophy.)

I had on other occasions accompanied Heinz to speeches and should have anticipated that he would use my prepared words only as a springboard; like so many other politicians, his inclination was to speak extemporaneously. Once I had ridden with him by helicopter from Washington to another state event, and the entire way he had read and reread my proffered text, underscoring various words as a guide to proper inflection and emphasis. I sat watching this exercise, beaming with pride that my words carried such weight and expecting soon to hear them echo throughout a hall, disturbed in their poetic cadence only by repeated interruptions for applause. In the actual event he skipped quickly over my lines and composed his own. Speechwriters sometimes seemed to serve the purpose merely of putting their bosses in the right mood. (These same speechwriters, I can attest, like to imagine that Ronald Reagan's secret of success as the "great communicator" was simply his willingness to read faithfully, with expression, from staff-prepared scripts.)

In the case of the farmers Heinz used more of my lines than usual, but gave them even greater drama. Where I had concluded that the Food and Drug Administration should be taken to court over the casein issue, he ad-libbed that it should be taken "directly to jail." His remarks earned him an ovation from his immediate audience but had the misfortune to be quoted in the newspapers. Readers divorced from the narrow emotions of the dairy farmers wondered about his judgment. For my part I felt I had incited him. Altogether the speech was not my proudest moment, and in later years I found myself recalling the episode and trying to repent by writing texts of greater integrity.

Our concern about constituencies sometimes focused on more than organized groups; all the state's voters were presumed to have certain shared interests, which we would be expected to advocate. A recurring example was the issue of federal defense spending in Pennsylvania. In the latter part of the 1970s, the northeastern United States found itself in decline as a manufacturing region, increasingly forfeiting jobs to

Sun Belt states and threatened by new competitors abroad. While the country as a whole was staging economic recovery, Pennsylvania continued to be plagued by recession, especially in coal-mining areas such as Scranton and Wilkes-Barre. To aggravate the situation, the Pentagon was closing a number of local military installations. The loss of thousands of jobs at Philadelphia's Frankfort arsenal and army electronics command, as well as at Fort Indiantown Gap and New Cumberland army depot, became important causes among local voters and politicians.

Elected representatives were expected to fight for every available government penny, and our complaints assumed the character of political catechism. Repeatedly we cited statistics, for example, showing that although the state comprised 5.5 percent of the national population, it received only 3.3 percent of defense-contract spending, drawing the conclusion from this that Pennslvania had, in effect, sacrificed an estimated $2.6 billion annually that was "rightfully" ours. Similarly we argued that because only 2.7 percent of U.S.-based military and civilian employees of the Defense Department worked in the state, Pennsylvania had been denied 66,000 federal jobs. Such a purely arithmetic approach to defense issues might have seemed illogical to the rest of the country, but we had little compunction about any argument that suited constituent interests. Pennsylvanians whose jobs were jeopardized did not care particularly which military facilities in the country were, by some abstract Pentagon standard, most entitled to be preserved; they wanted *theirs* preserved.

The irony was that, in pleading for special privilege, we felt compelled to place our arguments on the elevated plane of national interest; there was an etiquette about argumentation in the United States Senate. So we claimed to be fighting not for Pennsylvania per se but for justice—and we became vigilantes on this score. At one point, for example, we learned of something called "Defense Manpower Policy Four," which in theory allowed defense contracts to be targeted to areas of high unemployment. Unfortunately its intended execution had been stymied over the years by southern senators, who did not wish to cede preference in textile contracts to New England states. It was hard to argue principle against adversaries whose position mirrored our own; we were all trying to get a bigger slice of the pie. But we fought anyway, asserting that DMP-4 represented a test of fidelity to national values: Those who opposed its use were reneging on commitments to the unemployed and to the national defense. (This included the administration, which had failed to enforce it.) The problem with using such rhetorical overkill, of course, is that it cheapens the message. Members of Congress become so accustomed to hearing, and themselves using, such bombast that it also becomes quite easy to disregard it. Our battles over DMP-4, while glorious, were predictably futile.

In addition, I became practically a pleading agency for narrow private interests. When the Boeing-Vertol company of Pennsylvania failed to win a $700 million defense contract to produce helicopters, I joined a small delegation led by Congressman Bob Edgar of Philadelphia to meet with Deputy Secretary of Defense Charles Duncan and argue its case. The fact that Edgar was a sincere liberal Democrat and former Drexel University chaplain did not make him a pacifist when it came to the issue of defense spending for his district. We piled into his car and for a moment had no political party but the state of Pennsylvania; arriving at the Pentagon, all of us did our best to look aggrieved as we were ushered into Duncan's spacious office. Of course the Pentagon brass was accustomed to continual congressional pressure in procurement decisions and probably discounted it as perfunctory. Duncan did acknowledge that the Boeing-Vertol proposal had not been "significantly less acceptable" than a winning design by the competing Sikorsky firm, but ultimately he would not be budged. We huffed that this was unsatisfactory and warned that we had not exhausted our appeals. Thereafter Edgar crusaded for a joint meeting on the matter between the entire Pennsylvania congressional delegation and the president himself. Eventually the meeting materialized, but the atmosphere was in reality too cordial to make headway. At this point it hardly mattered. The fact that the congressmen could say that they had pursued the matter to the very top was satisfaction enough. Constituents would be impressed that we had waged a vigorous though losing battle against a hard-hearted administration. The real problem was that, having been seen as so willing to help, we had created our own monster. Soon Boeing-Vertol expected assistance in other matters as well: a $24 million sale to Argentina, a $45 million transaction with Korea. We were as useful as a battery of Washington lawyers and public-relations agents, except that we worked for free.

Was it not possible for local and national interests to overlap? Senator Muskie appeared to be of this mind, and at one point urged members of the Budget Committee to hold hearings "in the field" to gather perspective about national problems; as an incentive he offered the committee's financing and imprimatur. This meant that each senator would be able to convene the august Senate Budget Committee on his home turf (although he might be the only member to attend), garnering all the publicity that such an important-sounding proceeding would command. That the hearings were referred to by staff as Muskie's "present" to members indicated a more candid (if only partial) assessment of their purpose: public relations.

We snapped up the offer, and our immediate concern was to select a location and topic that would serve us best. Philadelphia seemed an obvious venue, since we were weaker there politically than in the western part of the state; we could use greater publicity. But there was a compelling synergy of interests. Philadelphia, too, could use the attention; it was an older city of classic urban problems. We arrived at the topic of "youth unemployment" in part because it was a timely and important one. Three million young Americans were estimated to be looking for work without success; black teenagers in particular had an unemployment rate of 50 percent. President Carter was proposing to spend $2 billion in fiscal 1979 for training and employment programs directed at youth. Was this the right amount? How could it best be spent? Again substantive and political purpose overlapped. The topic also happened to be one that could justify involving all sorts of local VIPs who would appreciate the platform—and give us credit for providing it. I spent much time identifying a cross-section of useful constituencies and then composing a Who's Who of their local representatives for our panel: a councilwoman, a chamber of commerce official, the regional AFL-CIO president, a developer, employment and educational specialists, black leaders, a Wharton School professor, and even a teenager to lend the discussion an aura of authenticity. And I devised a roundtable format, both because I thought it would encourage more animated conversation and because I knew people would be likelier to attend if they didn't have to prepare formal remarks.

The hearing lasted several hours and was acclaimed a great success, but probably it did not serve its stated purpose of giving Congress a better understanding of how programs worked at the local level. After all, only Heinz attended, even though the hearing was in the guise of an official committee proceeding, complete with stenographer and the oft-repeated comment that it was being conducted for the benefit of the U.S. Senate, as if other senators would shortly be sitting down to ponder the transcript of the event. (There was little chance of that.) Heinz himself may have learned something, but he already knew a great deal about the operation of federal programs in Philadelphia, and in any case he had only one vote in Congress to do anything about it.

But the discussion had been interesting, and our constituents had been given an opportunity to vent their grievances and feel as though someone was listening. In turn we would hope to reap their gratitude, gaining favorable public attention for both ourselves *and* their plight. And Heinz, as dynamic as he was, might well use the information he had gleaned to offer a better argument or amendment when the issue arose in the Senate. So was it pandering—or admirable democratic responsiveness? Subsequently the Budget Committee published a 136-page hearing report, including both a transcript and supplemental written submissions, and although it is doubtful that many ever read it, the effort did stand as a testimonial to congressional interest in the subject. It may have been a bit of a gimmick, but it was not a very expensive one and may have produced limited benefits. And if the voters appreciated it, who was entitled to object?

17

INVESTIGATORY INTRIGUE

Nothing becomes Congress quite so much as the confirmation hearing of a high official. Senators represent an essential check on potential executive abuse, and because confirmations partly concern the moral fitness of nominees to hold office, they present a ready-made opportunity to confront an administration over stark issues of character and virtue. At the same time Congress, in the final analysis, is often a hesitant institution, concerned about placing restraints on presidential prerogatives for fear it will be held responsible for consequent malfunctions of government. Confirmations allow Congress to do what it does best: raise questions, demonstrate concern, and hold issues up to the spotlight of public opinion. It may get carried away, seeing more than is there, and yet in the end often shrug and fail in its nerve to carry its exhortations to their logical conclusion. The rejection of John Tower's nomination as secretary of defense in 1989 was notable in large part for the rarity of such action. No cabinet member of an incoming administration had ever before been defeated.

A more normal instance occurred in the spring of 1978 when President Carter nominated G. William Miller, head of multinational

Textron, Inc., as chairman of the Federal Reserve Board. Miller was by all accounts a capable business executive eager to serve in high government office. His confirmation was expected to be routine because he was embroiled in no known controversies and lacked even a provocative ideology. Moreover he had the fortune to be nominated while the travails of Carter's embattled budget director, Bert Lance, were still fresh in memory. The issues of the hearings that forced Lance from office had not been black-and-white, and in their aftermath congressional committees seemed reluctant to stage what the public might see as another undeserved political inquisition. Concern was rising that Congress had overreacted to the Watergate experience and become hypercritical in its investigations to the point of deterring public-spirited citizens from considering government service.

Miller was to be reviewed for his position by the Senate Banking Committee, where the stewardship of Chairman William Proxmire of Wisconsin promised to enliven the proceedings. In an institution full of colorful figures, Proxmire was one of the most unusual and impressive. He was a man of almost eccentric discipline, known for jogging many miles into work each day well into his sixties. At one time I had come across his autobiographical tract on personal health, *You Can Do It!*, which appeared to be an appeal for the almost total ordering of one's life down to the minute. He held the record for never having missed a vote and, even more unheard of in the Congress, insisted on delivering in-person speeches on the floor of the Senate—no fictionalized "as if read" texts for him—every day it was in session. In his home state he had established practically a cult following and needed to spend literally only a few dollars every six years to win reelection.

As a result Senator Proxmire had the luxury to practice an iconoclasm that involved an unpredictability of position and a startlingly forthright manner of presentation. Watching him over the years, I coined a new verb—"to Proxmire"—meaning to heap initial praise on a witness only to let the air out in the last sentence. "Secretary Smith," he would intone, "You are a brilliant man with a superb background, and you are most articulate and well informed." His quarry would smile. "So why is it," Proxmire would continue, "that you have done the worst job of anyone in your position in the entire postwar era?"

When Miller appeared before the committee, Proxmire followed the same pattern, first hailing him as an outstanding businessman and civic leader and then severely questioning his lack of relevant experience to be a central banker. Toward the end of the hearing, he moved in for the kill. Proxmire disclosed that a Textron subsidiary, Bell Helicopters, had years before paid a $2.9 million fee to Air Taxi of Iran for help in procuring a contract there, and that General Mohammed Khatemi, a close adviser of the shah's, had held a silent interest in the facilitating agency. Miller had been at the helm of Bell's parent company at the time. Did he, Proxmire wanted to know, approve of bribes?

Miller of course denied knowing anything of it, and Proxmire seemed to lack further information to pursue the subject. Perhaps he had only wanted to shake the witness to test his intellectual or ethical reflexes. But the audience had been titillated by the exchange, and there was a sense of disappointment that this was as far as it went. As it happened, Heinz had absented himself for a vote during these few minutes (senators left at staggered times to avoid disruption) and on returning found that he had another turn to question the witness; the committee was small enough that senators enjoyed several rounds. As usual I was expected, from my position immediately behind him on the rostrum, to provide a whispered summary of what he had missed, and a suggestion about what he could say to sound, despite his absence, fully informed. Nothing particularly novel struck me, and I was reduced to recommending the obvious: that he propose having the staff check a little more into the Bell Helicopter matter before a final vote on confirmation. Heinz made the suggestion, and it was roundly endorsed as a sensible precaution; no one imagined that it would involve a delay of more than a couple of days.

Instead it became a protracted inquiry, giving rise to more questions and producing public agony for both Miller and the Carter administration as they waited to fill one of the government's most important positions. Proxmire continually referred to it as the "Heinz investigation," both in recognition of its origins and perhaps because he felt that an aura of bipartisanship would imbue it with added credibility. (The harsh Germanic pronunciation he insisted on giving Heinz's name, however, sometimes made the inquiry sound as if it were a military court-martial.) Committee staff played its classic role in expanding the investigation. Such staffs are employed to give concrete form to members' sometimes vague sentiments and are accordingly provided wide latitude to research and advise. They can, to an extent the delegating officials are reluctant to acknowledge, devise the charter of their own operations, but in the end they face the same limitations as those who would lead a horse to water: They can't make congressmen drink.

In this case the staff pursued allegations about Miller's role with great fervor. It was an engaging cloak-and-dagger mystery, enjoyable to unravel, and committee investigators knew that their success would be judged in part by the number of revelations they produced. They learned, for example, that General Khatemi had a reputation as one of the most corrupt officials in Iran and that it had been widely known there that he maintained a close association with both Air Taxi and the shah. Miller had twice visited Iran and functioned as de facto group vice president for aerospace, technically overseeing Bell activities; the $500 million contract at issue represented one of Textron's most important business deals. Ultimately the staff came to question the veracity of high Bell officials and, although lacking hard evidence, remained skeptical about Miller's personal involvement.

This research and analysis was performed almost entirely without senatorial instruction or supervision; fortunately the staff was one of the Hill's best. Lindy Marinaccio, Bruce Freed, and John Collins, the committee's resourceful sleuths, deftly assembled the facts and followed the trail. Ken McLean, the astute staff director, had a naturally protective regard for the committee's reputation and was determined not to compromise the quality of its work; he knew in addition that Senator Proxmire would have no aversion to its winning headlines for heroic muckraking. His counterpart on the Republican side, Jerry Buckley, was similarly disposed: The ranking Republican of the committee, Senator Brooke of Massachusetts, tried when he could to work in tandem with Proxmire and certainly held no brief for a Democratic nominee. Although hardly intentional, the upshot of all this was that the country's economic policy took a backseat for five or six weeks to a small staff research project in the Senate. As Heinz's representative, I also bore responsibility for prolonging it. For one thing, I sought to encourage an aggressive investigation because I assumed my boss wouldn't mind a conclusion that showed that his suggestion of an inquiry had merit. At the same time it was my duty in return to explain to him, on behalf of harried committee aides, why the investigation was proceeding so slowly and to counsel patience.

In the end the staff findings made clear the existence of important unanswered questions, but implied that confident conclusions could not be reached without considerably more work. At this point the senators were back in the game. Several Democratic members of the committee, most notably Don Riegle of Michigan, defended Miller and branded the investigation a fishing expedition; it was not clear how carefully they had examined the staff findings. But most senators were in Heinz's position: They recognized that further investigation might be justified, but had mixed political feelings about pursuing it. Miller was bright, likable, and well respected; the evidence was, at best, inconclusive; the Federal Reserve Board needed a chairman. There seemed to be almost a sense of satiety: that Miller had been harangued enough to pay for any possible misdeeds and that it was not legitimate to hold a company's behavior in one era to the more rigid standards of another. In addition the committee's proceedings had prompted a separate investigation by the Securities and Exchange Commission, and there was a concern that if the SEC found insufficient reason to prosecute (as ultimately it did), senators would look as though they allowed wild rumors to drive good men from Washington. Finally there was a mundane logistical hesitation: Putting up a fight would require learning massive detail about the case, which might be worth the effort if a truly important principle were at stake or if the issue had the potential to become Watergate-level news that could catapult diligent senators to national glory. There were no such prospects here. Thus even skeptical members ultimately announced they were satisfied with the results of the investigation, glad they had undertaken it, and prepared now to wish Miller well in his new job. Proxmire cast the only negative vote.

Looking back, I understand this denouement far better than I did at the time. Then it disappointed me that senators didn't treat the affair more gravely, but now I recognize the hypocrisy that doing so would have involved. Congress can be sanctimonious about the ethics of others, but its own standards are hardly above reproach. More than one senator who served on the Watergate committee later stood accused of improprieties himself. Senators are sometimes quick to criticize the character of those who come before them, but they must wonder at times how they would fare on the witness stand themselves. In the Iran-Contra hearings of 1988, presidential assistants were harshly accused of doctoring chronologies and otherwise distorting the record by senators who themselves indulge in not dissimilar practices: The Congressional Record no less is a highly, and deliberately, inaccurate journal of official proceedings. Congressmen adroitly use parliamentary techniques to document support of both sides of an issue; the sensitive issue of self-bestowed pay raises is a classic example. On occasion one senses that Capitol Hill politicians entertain subliminal guilt and are reluctant to throw stones from their glass houses—unless a large crowd has gathered and is egging them on, as the press and public sometimes do.

There was a silver lining in Miller's ordeal, at least for me: Against this quintessential Capitol Hill backdrop I met my future wife. The hearing room had been swamped with staff. Aides to committee members, such as myself, squeezed behind their respective senators on the rostrum; staff members from other parts of the Capitol, simply observing, packed themselves into the audience. The television klieg lights facing the senators and their aides prevented me from seeing beyond the witness table. A woman named Margot Machol swears that, from her vantage point in the audience looking in the other direction, she saw me clearly.

I talked to her for the first time months after the hearing when I had occasion to call the House Banking Committee, where she worked. Alan Meltzer, a noted economist at Pittsburgh's Carnegie-Mellon University, had called Heinz to suggest a candidate for a vacant Federal Reserve seat; naturally the inquiry was channeled to staff. His candidate was Margot's able colleague, Bob Weintraub, and I needed background information to draft a letter from Heinz to the president that would recommend him. Bob was not there, but Margot was. "I know who you are," she said, when I identified myself as a Heinz aide who did Banking Committee work. "You're the one who sat up there smirking at everything Miller said." Volunteering such direct comments to a stranger turned out to have been utterly uncharacteristic for her. Rejecting the allegation (I found Miller most amiable), I replied equally uncharacteristically: "We'll just have to see about that. Let's meet for lunch." I was in fact the person she thought, but I continued to deny the smirking. Years later, when we had a baby who appeared to smirk during his first days of life, she said, "See, it was you." And also, years later, we were still celebrating our first date by returning to the Dirksen Senate Office Building cafeteria and having lunch, Dutch treat, just the way we had done it originally.

My last duty on Banking Committee matters had to do with saving New York City. America's great metropolis was teetering on the brink of bankruptcy, and Congress was being called to the rescue. I suggested to Heinz that I phone prominent Pennsylvania businessmen, whose views I knew he would value, to see what they thought. Invoking only my status as Heinz's aide, I gaped as everyone without question took my calls: the CEO's of Westinghouse, Alcoa, United States Steel, and others. These were executives of a sophistication to know that busy U.S. senators vitally depend on the legwork of staff. To a man they warned of the need to stave off fiscal crisis: otherwise, they predicted, the municipal bond markets would collapse, preventing other cities from borrowing; the life-support services of a major community would fail its people; and inevitably the federal government would be forced to come in and clean up anyway, but at a far greater cost.

Heinz would hardly have hesitated in any case: Such support was consistent with his crusade to enlist federal assistance in revitalizing the Northeast. Neither was he immune to concerns about Republican prospects in New York in the next round of elections. The committee had started out quite divided, and at one point he appeared to be a potential swing vote; at the least he would not prevent the full Senate from voting on the issue. Proxmire, ever the tough negotiator, claimed that New York didn't need the money: Another of his talented staffers, Elinor Bachrach, had calculated that New York banks could provide sufficient lines of credit and pointed out that state pension funds could invest in short-term notes. The advocates for New York proved a match and took nothing for granted: Financier Felix Rohatyn, Deputy Treasury Secretary Robert Carswell, and others did not hesitate to call me or even pull up a chair at my cramped desk to plead their cases. In the end senators were unwilling to have it said that they had "lost New York," as other officials, in a previous generation, had been tagged with "losing" China. The committee again held back and simply confirmed what was probably foreordained: By a wide margin it favorably reported a large package of bond guarantees. Both houses soon enacted it into law.

18

SEEING THE WORLD

Ali Moertopo, the military strongman of Indonesia, a Southeast Asian nation of over 100 million, smiled broadly at the arrival in Bali of his awaited American visitor. A conference on "the Future of Southeast Asia" would begin that afternoon at the Sanur Beach Hotel on this fabled island, and Ali, who had just welcomed Malaysian home minister Ghazali bin Shafie, *Washington Post* columnist Joseph Kraft, and former California governor Pat Brown, now turned his attention to an emissary of the U.S. Congress. From an assistant's tray in the hotel's open-air reception room, he took a tall glass, shaded by a miniature *Kon-Tiki* umbrella, and offered the weary traveler a tropical drink. "President Suharto wishes you a successful conference," he said, "and looks forward to receiving you later this week in Jakarta." "Happy to be here," I replied.

Global travel is one of the highlights of congressional staff life, and at age twenty-four I was by now a veteran. For the next several days I would be engrossed in vivid discussions about a region that—as of 1977, two years after the fall of Vietnam—was on the verge of developing an important new relationship with the United States. The sponsor of the event, a Jakarta-based think tank, would have preferred elected representatives, but only Senator Bill Roth and Congressmen John Anderson and Jim Jeffords could attend, so staff were invited to fill the breach. Together with Roth aide Charlie Morrison, Jeffords aide Dick D'Amato, and House Republican Conference research director Harlan Strauss, I came halfway around the world at the institute's expense, and it is only a pity that I was not married at the time, for our hosts volunteered to underwrite spouses as well. With the approval of the Senate Ethics Committee Senator Heinz had granted me three weeks' official leave to take the trip. Following the conference I would join Harlan and noted Asian scholar Robert Scalapino on an exotic river tour of Borneo as guests of the provincial governor, and en route home have time for sightseeing in Singapore and India.

During my years on the Hill I took trips to almost every continent, gathered immense amounts of new knowledge and perspective, and had equal amounts of fun; it is no use pretending everything is serious work. Staffers who deal in international affairs have an edge in getting invitations, but by no means a monopoly. Committee aides studying comparative desalination technologies, LAs accompanying their bosses to interparliamentary conferences, and AAs coveted for their general influence are all candidates for overseas travel. Obviously there can be abuse; some aides view trips as an income entitlement and regard recesses as wasted unless they can find somewhere (preferably warm) to visit. Others treat the opportunities very seriously and come back enriched in ways that demonstrably enhance their job performance.

There are many modes of traveling. One is to attend a scholarly conference, as I have described. Perhaps more traditional is as part of a "CODEL," jargon for congressional delegation, and an expression that can strike terror in the hearts of junior Foreign Service Officers typically assigned escort duty in host countries. It is true that CODELs are known for their fun-loving spirit—congressmen requesting embassy cars to take them to nightspots and then showing up late the next morning to meetings with high foreign officials—but that is more the reputation than the reality. In fact most congressmen take their missions seriously, and if they leave time for shopping or sightseeing, it would be odd if they went to foreign lands and *didn't* have the interest to do so. Indeed such travel may be most useful for those congressmen who lack previous overseas exposure; it engages their attention and introduces them to facts and other views in a way that stateside hearings and briefings would not.

My initiation to CODELs came in November 1976, on a five-country, ten-day trip through Africa. (Covering much ground quickly is typical; trips are scheduled in as businesslike a way as possible, if only to avoid charges of frivolity.) The official delegation consisted of nine representatives and one senator, but each was allowed to bring an aide (I accompanied Congressman Bonker) and a spouse or, if unavailable, another relative: Thus, there were also a daughter, father, and brother aboard. It was a convenient time to go; the travelers had just been reelected to new terms, did not begin a new session until after the first of the year, and, fatigued from campaigning, were ready for a change of pace. Andrews Air Force Base is the staging ground for such missions. In addition to the better known Air Force One and Two, which fly the president and vice president, a wing of military aircraft is available to transport congressmen, cabinet secretaries, and an occasional multistar general.

It costs several thousand dollars an hour to put such planes up in the air, so trips were to be authorized only if at least ten congressmen agreed to participate, on the theory that this was the point at which a charter would become economical compared with separate commercial bookings. But the rule sometimes was observed only in fiction. If a congressman wished to arrange a trip, he might seek tentative agreement from nine others to join him. At that point a plane could be requisitioned and the State Department would arrange the details of an itinerary. If at the last minute it happened that some of the other congressmen could not go, the ones who remained would not be expected to cancel. Thus there were instances where a large plane took off with only one or two congressmen aboard, although they would invariably be thoughtful enough to bring along relatives, staff, and friends to help fill the seats. Several years ago one representative took his daughter and six aides to Rio aboard a forty-two-seat military plane at a cost of $56,000; disclosure of this fact became a major campaign issue. Costs on the ground can be equally embarrassing; Senator Tower reportedly billed the government $2,074 for use of a Jaguar on one visit to England. In 1987 overseas congressional trips cost $6.7 million in addition to unpublished charges for planes and embassy support services. Not surprisingly congressmen have become defensive. In inviting other colleagues to join him on a trip to Europe in 1988, Senator Daniel Inouye wrote them that it would not be a "junket," but urged nonetheless that they bring spouses and pointed out that there would be ample time to visit museums and galleries.

In our case about twenty congressmen originally signed up, and ten ultimately came. The trip was led by Congressman Charles Diggs, a former undertaker from Detroit, in tribute to his congressional seniority. This meant that the official designation of the trip was CODEL DIGGS, a name displayed on a placard in the front window of our buses in the conspicuous way that sightseeing doubledeckers in London might identify themselves as MARBLE ARCH TOURS. Diggs was a man of few words and an often pained and dour look; you could almost see him escorting bereaved relatives around his previous place of business. But he had a reputation as a champion congressional traveler, famed for trips that lasted a month and for surly demands on hosts. This left us ambivalent: we were all a bit embarrassed to be associated with his party and yet, at the same time, deeply gratified that we were being led by someone who would ensure us the proper style of travel.

We were not disappointed. In Dakar, on the west coast of Africa, we stopped for our first night, greeted by the U.S. ambassador, who hosted us at his home for an elegant dinner with interesting local guests. The next day we crossed the continent to Nairobi, positioning us the following morning to take in an exotic game park on the outskirts of the city. At each of our hotels the State Department set up its traditional "control room" to change money, provide decks of cards, and offer free alcoholic and other refreshments around the clock. On the third day we flew into Bloemfontein, South Africa, and were bused in from there to our ultimate destination: a conference in Lesotho, a landlocked but independent sliver of a nation in the middle of South Africa. (The circuitous routing was necessary because Angola, with whom the United States had severed relations, did not permit overflight.) Our airborne accommodations included a first-class seating configuration and the presence of military stewards, who cooked fresh meals, incongruously billing the passengers for the cost of the ingredients—the only unreimbursed expense of the trip.

Our mere arrival instantly deepened our knowledge of foreign-policy. Although most of us had not known it in advance, Lesotho wanted us to travel by bus to help assert its claimed right of free transit through South Africa; we encountered curious looks but no resistance from local officials. Other congressmen joining us by way of Johannesburg had a different experience. Unable to obtain transit visas, they were prevented from using scheduled flights; this delayed them forty-eight hours until they could charter a plane. One of them, Republican Silvio Conte, said he now understood much better the vulnerability of neighboring countries to South African pressure.

Was the trip useful from the public's point of view? Delegates to the conference (sponsored by the respected African-American Institute of New York) did little to hide their aversion to the South African government; they included members of the banned African National Congress and outspoken officials of black African states. For some congressmen, not used to hearing such views, this was an educational revelation. For others, critics themselves of South Africa, the occasion presented exciting opportunities. Jimmy Carter had just been elected president, having promised to improve U.S. relations with the Third World. Several U.S. participants, including Congressman Andy Young (one of Carter's closest Georgian backers) and Senator Dick Clark (activist chairman of the Subcommittee on Africa), could be expected to wield large new influence in regional policy. Here was a chance to begin extending American goodwill. Thus Clark expressed strong support of majority rule in South Africa, proposing to bring pressure by a withdrawal of tax credits for American companies there and a mandatory United Nations arms embargo. He and Young also used the occasion to bring greetings to imprisoned South African dissidents Steven Biko and Robert Sobukwe; Diggs, for his part, went to Namibia to express backing for the SWAPO rebel group. The incoming administration viewed such initiatives as helpful.

My most memorable adventures were extracurricular. One day I joined Don and his wife on a side trip to the lovely South African city of Durban on the Indian Ocean. On the return our small propeller plane lost a wheel, bells began to ring on board, the pilot told us we had a problem, and we braced for a crash landing at a small and isolated airport. Although we skidded off the runway into a field and tipped over, miraculously we were able to jump out and race safely from the plane; unlike a movie version it did not blow up behind us. The local mayor, who had seen a disabled plane circling, rushed to the airport and, impressed with the exotic quality of his visitors, offered us automotive transport back to Lesotho. We had never felt more patriotic than when, days later, we were back aboard our big Air Force jet.

CODEL Diggs, after some sightseeing in Capetown, traversed the continent again to Sierra Leone, where we had an audience with President Siaka Stevens; he expressed gratitude that the United States had recently resumed its bilateral aid program to his desperately poor nation. Waiting for an early-morning ferry to the airport, I snapped last pictures of our group, including one of Andy Young balancing a large and colorful basket on his head. Back in the States the next week, President Carter announced Andy's appointment as U.N. ambassador. I showed my picture proudly around the office and then, on a dare, to *Time* magazine—which promptly offered five hundred dollars for exclusive rights. I called Don, who was out in the district; staffers are used to getting approvals. Understandably he proposed clearing it with Andy; unfortunately Andy was in Plains, Georgia, all week. This was in the days before either Federal Express or fax machines, and I could not even get my phone calls through, so that was that. Subsequently Andy and Don both saw the picture, requested copies, and Don for many years prominently displayed an autographed enlargement in his office. Meanwhile, I was out $500.

Another common means of travel is with a group of aides under-written by philanthropic or self-interested outside organizations. Sponsors range from foundations that bring together young people of different nations for wholesome cultural purposes (for example, the American Council on Germany, which sent me to conferences in Berlin in 1977 and Hamburg in 1982; or the American Council of Young Political Leaders, which sent me around eastern Canada in 1986) to foreign governments, especially those with controversial diplomatic objectives, making bids at better public relations.

Typical of the latter was a trip I took to Taiwan in 1976 with about a dozen other staffers from a wide variety of congressional offices. The purpose of its sponsors was unconcealed: to show us Taiwan in a sym-pathetic light so we would use what influence we had to support its continued close relations with the United States. This was, of course, not as innocent as it seemed, considering that shortly the People's Re-public of China would be demanding an end to our recognition of Taiwan in return for restored relations with the mainland. On the other hand, Taiwan was traditionally a close U.S. friend, and lobbying on its behalf hardly seemed nefarious.

Taiwanese officials were said to be behind the trip, but U.S. laws prevented the financing of congressional travel by foreign govern-ments, so something called the Pacific Cultural Foundation was cre-ated in Taiwan to help channel funding. The State Department was required to investigate the financial sources for such trips and to certify that the sponsoring entity was independent of a foreign government. When I called the department to ask its opinion, I was told that while there were grounds for suspecting that the foundation was not truly independent, so many congressional aides had taken the trip, and wanted to take it in the future, that the department had decided it was enough merely to meet minimal technical specifications; the veil would not be pierced. I checked a long list of previous congressional participants and for a second opinion called Dick Moe, administrative assistant to then-senator Mondale. Although I did not know him, Moe seemed to me an authoritative adviser on the subject because he worked for a legislator who carried a reputation for high integrity. "Go," Moe instructed. "If it's wrong, a lot of us are in trouble." Still I had qualms and finally decided as a compromise to remove myself from the congressional payroll for the three-week duration of the trip. Such an action may seem quaint and excessive in retrospect, but this was not long after Watergate, and I remembered it well.

Soon I was flying off first-class on China Airlines and being escorted through Taiwan in the highest style. Multicourse feasts were such regular events that meals began to seem spare without shark's fin soup or pickled octopus. Although our hosts rarely missed an opportunity to proselytize for their point of view—the military on the island of Quemoy lectured us with maps and pointers about the danger of "imminent invasion" from the mainland, which we could see across the strait—the mere feeling of indebtedness for a paid vacation was doubtless expected to do the trick. Yet in my own case the exercise backfired. Although impressed with Taiwan and its people, I was so determined to show I had not been improperly influenced that, when a local reporter later called to interview me about the trip, I made a point of saying that I still thought normalization of relations with the People's Republic was appropriate. This was reported, and rather than impressing readers with my objectivity in the face of foreign blandishments, it antagonized conservatives, who then lambasted Don in letters to the editor about his liberal adviser who wanted to sell out Taiwan.

Eleven years later, in 1987, I was invited on a similar trip, this time to the People's Republic. A dozen aides went over under the sponsorship of the "U.S.-Asia Institute," which although located in its own charming townhouse on the Hill, seemed to have a close working relationship with the Chinese People's Institute of Foreign Affairs. Like the Taiwan trip, the one to the mainland was well organized and informative. We met trade officials and defense scholars, saw classic tourist sights such as the Great Wall and out-of-the-way curiosities like the Shanghai stock exchange, sailed the picturesque Li River outside Guilin, and walked the bustling streets of Guangzhou. Did we become experts on China or blind defenders of its policies? Of course not. Did we gain sensitivity to a different culture and a new interest in the issues between us? Just as surely. We were uniformly impressed, for example, at how favorably disposed to Americans ordinary Chinese seemed to be, probably making us less surprised by their massive pro-democracy demonstrations two years later. Admittedly it was not all work, but there are certainly less edifying ways to spend twelve days.

Even domestic travel opportunities presented themselves. Once I joined a group of aides that the air force ushered around to supersecret defense installations that looked like the backdrop of *Seven Days in May*: the subterranean headquarters of the North American Air Defense Command, buried deep in the side of a Colorado mountain, and that of the Strategic Air Command in Omaha, where rows of military dispatchers sat behind radar scopes in an eerily darkened room ready, it seemed, to order planes scrambling for nuclear war. It only added to our sense of cinematic drama that our mode of transportation was a borrowed vice-presidential jet complete with wall clocks representing different time zones and airphones (this was long before such things were commercialized) that we were allowed to use midflight to surprise and impress our earthbound colleagues. On another occasion, I joined in a staff mission to inspect aircraft carriers in Norfolk, guided by a navy liaison officer, John McCain. A functionary posted in the Senate to assist staffers, he was of humbler station, in a sense, than congressional staff itself. But he was unusually articulate and as a former POW had an understandable zest about his opportunities. Within several years he had resurfaced as a congressman, then senator, from Arizona, even touted in 1988 for second spot on the GOP ticket. Presumably he desired to perform public service upon a larger stage, but I suppose it is possible he simply wanted to escape having to lead another staff tour that featured as many elementary questions as I seem to remember asking him.

There is, of course, one offbeat way for staffers to travel: at their own expense, something I did in the early days, before I began receiving invitations for trips financed by others. Still, my congressional status conferred advantages. In 1976, for example, I took three weeks' vacation to tour Latin America, and the State Department volunteered to help arrange embassy briefings and other events in the seven capitals I would visit. Thus in Panama I had meetings with officials of the Panama Canal Company and the U.S. Southern Command and joined a nighttime police patrol of the Canal Zone; the information I gathered would be helpful in persuading my boss to support the prospective treaty changing the status of the U.S. presence there. In Rio I talked to economists and urban planners about the usefulness of U.S. development aid; in Santiago, to dissidents of the Christian Democratic party about their concerns for human rights. Everywhere embassies would lend me a car, driver, and translator to see "nontourist" areas; I may be the only visitor in the history of Peru who spent his entire time inspecting the dusty environs of Lima without also going to see the Inca ruins of Machu Picchu.

All of this intellectual curiosity reflects not my virtue but my youth; today my priorities might be more conventional. I took things a little too seriously and possessed a self-importance about my mission. In Lisbon, on another trip, U.S. ambassador Frank Carlucci, alerted to the presence of a congressional visitor at the embassy, came down the hall to offer his time in helping me understand the dramatic and unfolding events there; he believed that the United States needed to support socialist Mario Soares in his attempts to revive Portugal's fledgling democracy. Carlucci was soft-spoken and unassuming; in return, I pressed my view on the need for congressional supremacy in foreign affairs. Carlucci, a Foreign Service Officer by training, must have been taken aback to hear the role of Congress not only depicted in such terms but especially by a staffer. Yet his effort was worthwhile; I returned to Washington and promoted his point of view among congressmen and aides, even at a time when his own administration was expressing doubt.

Certain committee aides—for example, those in the foreign affairs and intelligence areas—need not rely on their bosses' plans, the largesse of organizations, or their own pocketbooks to take them abroad, for a part of their very job description is to travel the world to make firsthand assessments. Some may be duplicative—the State Department, CIA, and numerous newspapers and magazines gather similar information—but Congress has come to insist on independent sources. Thus some staffers can virtually select their own topics and itineraries and travel several times a year. Today I have a friend on the Senate Foreign Relations Committee staff, Peter Galbraith, who challenges me to "country counts," so often does he go abroad. I am of course no match; his is in the mid-seventies, not including airport stops. I criticize Peter mercilessly, but he knows that underneath it all I am full of envy.

Yet Peter, who has been a Democratic staffer on the committee for over ten years, takes his trips seriously and has adeptly used them to advance important causes. One example may serve as a testament both to his abilities and to the influence of congressional staffers. Pakistan has been the object of much of Peter's professional interest. He and Benazir Bhutto, now the youthful prime minister of that nation, met each other on their first day as freshmen at Harvard, continued their acquaintance in graduate school at Oxford, and over the years have remained close friends. When Benazir's father, the country's first elected prime minister, was overthrown in 1977 and later executed, Benazir became the heir to his political legacy but, as an often-jailed opponent of the new Pakistani regime, was widely treated as persona non grata by U.S. policymakers. In 1981 Peter traveled to Pakistan to assess President Reagan's proposed $3.2 billion aid program there and, in the process, to locate his old friend. Through her mother he confirmed that Benazir was serving solitary confinement in an unventilated cell; he smuggled a note to her expressing his concern, and months later she smuggled one back graphically describing her incarceration.

Peter worked assiduously to stir congressional action. At his urging, Senator Pell, the committee's ranking Democrat, introduced legislation tying aid to a restoration of civil liberties and representative government; Peter clued in Congressman Solarz, and the House agreed to Senate language. Although watered down to a mainly rhetorical injunction, it was enacted into law as part of the Foreign Assistance Act of 1981 and signaled heightened U.S. concern about human rights— doubtless derailing any plans the regime had, as some supposed, to place Benazir on trial or even set her execution. In addition Peter persuaded other committee members—such senators as John Glenn, Alan Cranston, and Paul Tsongas—to raise the issue whenever possible in speeches as well as meetings with U.S. and foreign officials.

When Pakistani president Ul-haq Mohammed Zia paid a state visit to Washington in 1982, Peter saw his opening. The Foreign Relations Committee traditionally hosts a coffee for such dignitaries behind the louvered doors of its ceremonial offices in Room S-116 of the Capitol. As a staffer involved in the relevant issues, Peter joined his senatorial employers around an oval mahogany table beneath the room's mammoth chandelier and decorative maps of the world. Senator Pell, normally the mildest-mannered of men, turned to Zia and asked pointedly about Benazir's condition. Zia, who had been a model of diplomatic comportment until now, exploded. She had been transferred from jail to "house arrest," he shot back. "She lives in her own home, bigger than any of yours. She has servants, she can see friends, she can use the telephone." Skeptical, Peter placed a phone call to Benazir moments after the meeting ended. The police answered, explaining that her house had been redesignated as a prison and that she could not use the phone. "But I've just spoken with your president," Peter declared; the phone clicked dead.

A standoff continued until December 1983, when visiting foreign minister Yaqub Khan reiterated Zia's contention that Benazir's friends were free to see her. Peter decided again to test the official claim. He traveled in January to Pakistan, armed with a letter cosigned by Pell and committee chairman Percy, requesting permission for him to see Benazir. This time he also had embassy assistance, having persuaded key senators to allow ambassador-designate Deane Hinton to assume his position without a committee hearing in return for help in the case. After a week of traveling elsewhere in Pakistan to survey other committee concerns, Peter arrived in Karachi on the last full day of his visit, still lacking official authorization to see his former classmate. The next morning he learned that, two hours after his arrival in the city, the government had placed her on a plane to Switzerland. Days later Peter met her in London and they celebrated her freedom by resolving to engineer her victorious return to Pakistan.

In April Benazir came to Washington from London to see Peter and to press her case with members of Congress. (I had a bit part in the drama; on this and a future occasion Benazir took lodging in my wife's old apartment.) Peter realized that it would not advance Benazir's cause to be seen in the United States as a political firebrand; rather he wanted opinion makers to see her as the warm and civilized young person she was. While he counseled that Congress could hardly help overthrow Zia, he pointed out that individual members *could* be useful in bringing pressure on Pakistan to hold elections and then abide by the results. Thus he arranged for her to meet widely with congressmen, journalists, and the foreign-policy community, and on return visits in 1985 and 1986 she became increasingly better known and admired. In April 1986 she returned to Pakistan, where she was greeted by the largest crowds in its political history. There she campaigned for national elections, and when Zia died in a plane crash two years later and the United States raised its voice in support of Pakistani democracy, elections were allowed to go forward; Benazir would be the principal opposition candidate. In November 1988 Peter joined her in her living room as they awaited the stunning results: She had won.

Two months later Peter was again in Pakistan, this time in the prime minister's residence for a dinner that Benazir hosted in his honor, seating him for dramatic effect across from Yaqub Khan, still the foreign minister, whom Peter had pleaded to all the years of Benazir's captivity. It was a moment of great sentiment and satisfaction. And what of the consequences of this aggressive staff activity for the American public? Democratic government had been restored to a nation of 100 million, and U.S. relations with a strategically important country had been placed on a much improved footing. In theory it is possible to wonder whether Congress—and, more specifically, its aides—should supplant an administration in the conduct of sensitive foreign policy, traditionally a preserve of the executive branch. But it is harder, in this case, to question the concrete result.

PART IV

CAMPAIGN

Cairo, 1980. Fact finding with presidential candidate John Anderson was a dirty job, but somebody had to do it. COURTESY OF THE AUTHOR

19

ELECTIONEERING

It may seem a departure to tell about a presidential campaign in a book about Capitol Hill, but the dividing line between these subjects is far from clear. Visions of higher office dance in the heads of many an incumbent, and even the staffs of those running only for reelection often dedicate their energies to electoral rather than legislative goals. Some have described the typical congressional office as a permanent campaign machine. For an LA, rolling up one's sleeves to help out can be not just a refreshing diversion but an opportunity to gain a more authentic feel for the roots and imperatives of one's boss and, indeed, the larger political system out of which legislation arises.

But presidential politics? That's not so uncommon either. In 1988, for example, six presidential candidates served at the time in Congress (Democrats Biden, Gore, Simon, and Gephardt; and Republicans Dole and Kemp), and three others had served previously (Democrat Hart and Republicans Bush and DuPont). Both vice-presidential candidates in the general election—Dan Quayle and Lloyd Bentsen—were sitting senators. The situation resembled previous campaigns. In 1984 Democratic candidates included Senators Hart, Glenn, Cranston, and

Hollings; and in 1980 Republicans included Senators Dole and Baker and Congressmen Crane and Anderson. That was also the year that Senator Ted Kennedy challenged President Carter. Senators John Kennedy, Lyndon Johnson, Barry Goldwater, Hubert Humphrey, and George McGovern also came from an institution that House Speaker Sam Rayburn once derided as an ongoing presidential primary. Rayburn was wrong in at least one respect: Running from the House of Representatives would also become accustomed behavior.

I worked in the 1980 campaign—and for two years preceding it— for John Anderson, the Illinois congressman who ran first as a Republican and later an Independent. I had met him on my trips to Africa and Southeast Asia and kept in occasional touch. One day in 1978 he phoned me at my desk in Heinz's office, inviting me to meet him in the House dining room. It was mid-afternoon, few tables were occupied, and it was easy to have a private conversation. But the subject was hard to broach; in a sense, it was preposterous. "I'm thinking of running for president," he said with understandable self-consciousness. Although the papers had reported the rumor, few had noticed. Anderson, a nine-term Republican, was well known on the Hill but otherwise obscure to the world. Fortunately for him I was a political junkie, not only aware of his interest but greatly intrigued about joining such a journey. I had enjoyed working for Heinz and coming to know the Senate better, but ironically the experience had so broadened my interests beyond foreign affairs that I found myself hungering for further discovery. On the spot I accepted Anderson's exciting offer to join his staff; elsewhere I have chronicled in detail the fantastic two-and-a-half-year period that followed.* My intention here is to relate that experience to congressional life and political campaigns in general.

My new boss was an impressive figure in the Congress, a man of rare intellect, moral character, and devotion to public issues. He represented Rockford—we would not, during the campaign, eschew parallels to another Republican congressman from Illinois who won election as the sixteenth president—and also held a significant elective post among his peers: chairman of his party's "conference" in the House, the third-ranked GOP leadership position in the chamber, after the minority leader and whip. Anderson's seniority made my tenure with him fundamentally different from my previous congressional tours. Bonker and Heinz had been freshmen in their respective chambers,

---

* *Diary of a Dark Horse: The 1980 Anderson Presidential Campaign* (Carbondale: Southern Illinois University Press, 1983).

inexperienced in the legislative process, low in the pecking order, and brimming with the enthusiasm and dreams of political ingenues. Anderson had already reached great heights of achievement and was, if anything, in the autumn of his congressional service, a little saddened perhaps that the best years of his life might be behind him. But at age fifty-seven he was vigorous and looked most distinguished: regular Scandinavian features, thick white hair, and scholarly horn-rimmed glasses. Once, before he became recognizable to the world at large, he was surprised when a tourist stopped him and said, "I know who you are." Beaming, he began to shake her hand, but she was determined to prove her knowledge. "You're Cary Grant!"

Anderson was also among the Congress's most respected members. Originally a rock-ribbed conservative, he had become progressively more moderate over the years and regularly showed a willingness to buck political pressure when principle was at stake. In 1968 he cast a key committee vote in favor of controversial fair-housing legislation; similarly he was among the first of his party to call for President Nixon's resignation during Watergate. Most of all he was renowned as an orator, someone who could, even under the constrained five-minute rule for speeches on the House floor, rivet the attention of colleagues with a stentorian voice and silver-tongued eloquence. To some he seemed at times almost too sober and righteous. But perhaps because my first impressions of him had been formed in such places as a gambling casino in Lesotho and on the beach in Bali, I knew him to be a man of abundant warmth and unpretentiousness (and I came to know his wife, Keke, too, a zestful and quick-witted woman who readily supplied any plainspokenness her husband may have lacked). In my own experience Hubert Humphrey had no equal as a legislative dynamo; Don Bonker had a surpassing sense of morality; and John Heinz was sharp as a tack. But Anderson possessed an intellectual curiosity, a depth of knowledge, and an ability to make broad judgments, take stands, and communicate messages that stood out among politicians. He was, I thought, the very model of a public leader.

And so it was odd, if understandable, that there could be a certain melancholy aspect to this period of his life, as if he, like others nearing the end of a career, were suddenly overcome with thoughts about roads not taken. He had been thwarted in his ambitions to attain greater influence within Congress (as a Republican, consigned to seemingly perpetual minority status in the House; as a moderate Republican, to further minority status within his own increasingly conservative party) and was beyond the point of changing careers. Perhaps to lay his motivations, even in part, to midlife crisis is extreme, but clearly the frustrations of his limited power as a congressman helped prompt his bid for the presidency. A national campaign beckoned as better suited to his temperament: more receptive to someone of his moderation, oriented to larger issues than often occupied congressional attention, composed of wider audiences looking for something different.

As a result I found myself working for a congressman who essentially felt he had outgrown his job and might now use it as a springboard to greater things; I fully shared the perspective. Our concerns became almost otherworldly; Congress provided only the immediate stage props. My job was to help Anderson create the foundation for a presidential bid, to do the things that might have been performed more naturally in a separate campaign office located off the Hill. Why didn't we open one? For us the preliminary phase of the presidential mating process went beyond mere ritual; Anderson was genuinely unsure whether to proceed. Not until a year later would he formally declare, only after we had toured the country prospecting for financial and political backing. (We didn't find much, but we did convince ourselves there was potential.) Until then, expenses for a campaign would seem a luxury.

At the time I joined him, Anderson had only two other political aides, both of whom worked out of the House Republican Conference; as chairman, Anderson was entitled to name its staff and use them as he saw fit. The executive director of the conference, Mike MacLeod, functioned as a senior adviser; fortunately his confident manner and thinning hair helped camouflage his admitted inexperience. In addition he delegated to one of his own junior assistants, Kirk Walder, some of the thankless mechanical tasks of organization. Others on Anderson's various staffs—such highly capable aides as Bob Walker, also of the conference, and Don Wolfensberger, of the House Rules Committee, on which Anderson served as ranking Republican—continued to be relied on for legislative rather than campaign expertise. All of this left something of a vacuum, and if Anderson now admitted me to his innermost political cabinet, it was mainly by a process of elimination.

The position to which I was appointed carried a prestigious but thoroughly misleading title: Republican staff director of the House Ad Hoc Committee on Energy. Like the Holy Roman Empire, it was fallacious in all respects: I was not yet registered as a Republican; I had no staff to direct; and I did not work principally on energy matters. The slot was available to Anderson as ranking Republican on the committee, a temporary panel created to consider President Carter's energy proposals. By the end of the first year, it had completed the bulk of its work, and Dave Swanson, the conscientious staffer Anderson had previously employed, accepted an invitation to serve the Senate energy committee, where more was happening. But the Ad Hoc Committee had authority to continue until the end of the session (there were still some loose ends), and Anderson did not wish to forfeit a valuable staff vacancy. Neither did I suggest that he do so, when I learned that it came with the eye-popping salary of $36,000 a year, so much in my view that I was embarrassed for quite a long time to admit to anyone how much I made.

In theory a large staff worked under me, but this was pure illusion. The whole reason for an ad hoc arrangement was that House rivalries prevented the establishment of a permanent committee with consolidated energy jurisdiction; too many other committees wanted a piece of the action. Speaker O'Neill's inventive solution was to refer the administration's proposals to those other committees, set strict deadlines for action, then charge our specially created body with reviewing their work and stitching together a coherent overall package. Most of our staff was supplied through provisional designation from other committees; the fact that ours was a blue-ribbon panel consisting of committee chairmen and other senior congressmen meant that members generally had enough of their own aides to tap for assistance.

My duties were performed in the committee's utilitarian quarters in the Cannon House Office Building, one large and boxy room where our small core staff sat at neatly arranged desks facing the door, as if we were telephone operators ready to take calls during a telethon. My Democratic counterpart, Dick Krolik, worked a few feet away and made life most pleasant. He was a debonair sixty years of age and an old pal of the committee chairman, Lud Ashley of Ohio. His wry humor and relaxed manner helped preserve a proper perspective on the activities of the committee, which was one of amused detachment. Most of the negotiations over Carter's energy program had already taken place, and the legislation remained only to be passed, signed, and ballyhooed.

Fortunately for us, much of my job description—writing speeches, advising on issues, accompanying Anderson to local events—occupied a gray area between campaign and congressional activity. Anderson had a well-developed sense of ethics, but congressional strictures were imprecise. The institution by its nature is so intensely political that it becomes a practical impossibility to say in many instances where the discharge of official duties leaves off and aspirations to higher office (or reelection) begin. A congressman and his staff, for example, are not supposed to use office typewriters, photocopy machines, and phone lines to solicit financial contributions for election campaigns, but who is to judge their ulterior motives in taking positions, proposing bills and amendments, giving speeches, or issuing press releases that happen to be of value in both legislative and campaign contexts? Being responsive to important constituencies confers obvious electoral benefit, but it also happens to be an essential obligation of the conscientious congressman. In the House, where the two-year election cycle means another contest is nearly always around the corner, a staffer's thoughts rarely stray from how something will "play" in the district. A deeply internalized—and perfectly legitimate—objective of staff is to make the boss look good, and there can hardly be a more obvious reason to do so than to assure his (and his aides') continuance in office. Some staffers go off the payroll for a month or two as the election approaches in order to assist on the campaign trail, but for most, simply doing their ordinary job is a large contribution in itself.

In-house resources can mean a great advantage to incumbents; that congressional newsletters pour out of offices more in election years than off-years suggests their underlying purpose. (The Congress now allocates well over $100 million annually to cover its "franking" privilege.) Internal House and Senate rules address even the most explicit campaign work only gingerly: Staffers may engage in it on office premises so long as during the course of a day they perform their official duties for a "normal" number of hours. The circumscription is modest, for seven or eight hours could probably be considered a normal day's work, even though congressional staffs routinely work much longer. Moreover the authority to classify the nature of the work and log the hours rests with the very parties who have the incentive to transgress, and higher enforcement is almost nonexistent. As a result, when Anderson's longtime aide, David Stockman, decided to run for Congress himself in 1976, Anderson graciously allowed him to remain on the office payroll even though he would devote time to his own campaign planning. And when it came to Anderson's own intentions in 1978 to explore a bid for the presidency, it seemed perfectly natural to build a staff from within for the effort.

At the beginning I spent much time drafting speeches. Anderson liked to have a set of prepared remarks for every major event and more skeletal "talking points" for the minor ones. Schedules changed constantly—unexpected congressional votes, for example, could cause us to cancel appearances at the last minute—and he had such abundant obligations that a sense of priorities allowed him to focus only on those that immediately loomed. Preparations for an event therefore took place often only a day or two in advance. I would call the organizers, learning sponsors' names (for an introductory paragraph expressing gratitude for the invitation to speak) and seeking facts with local color to work into a joke or two, practical information such as the desired arrival time and length of remarks, and, most important, directions from the airport.

But with Anderson's encouragement, I made an effort not to let anticipated crowd reaction dictate the substance of what I wrote. Instead I would simply choose a timely national news topic and try to weave in our evolving campaign themes. For the Chase Manhattan board of directors it seemed to me Anderson might want to review the latest economic data and argue how it confirmed the need for the Kemp-Roth tax cut, which he supported. (Now that I was in the House, it was proper to reverse the billing order of Representative Kemp and Senator Roth.) Before the Edison Electric Institute he might want to describe progress on energy legislation and use the opportunity to stress the need for a balanced program of oil exploration and conservation. To Northwestern University students, or the Radio Relay League, he might want to give more of a "stump speech" about the need for shared sacrifice to reduce the budget deficit and American dependence on overseas energy sources. Armed with my ideas, I would insert the appropriate typeface element into my IBM Selectric and spend the next several hours composing a speech that, in almost the same motion, I would hand to my boss as he left for his event.

Another duty in my early days with Anderson was to accompany him to Washington receptions. More accurately I cajoled him to go, guided him around to as many guests as possible, and, by making exaggerated public motions toward my watch, prevented him from lingering so long that he would refuse to go on rounds again the next night. We drove around in his big, clunky Buick, which was useful if only because its congressional license plate—ILLINOIS 20—allowed us to park at otherwise forbidden curbs in the crowded downtown area. He did not enjoy the party circuit but admitted that it might be of campaign utility; I scribbled names on a notepad of anyone who sounded like a potential supporter.

Occasionally I would travel with him out of town—when our campaign coffers grew larger, I was on the road nearly full-time—and we took what events we could get. We were honored when an invitation came to address the National Governors Conference in Boston, particularly when we learned that Anderson would speak immediately after Ted Kennedy. The press coverage that attended an appearance of this much more famous politician, we assumed, would remain in place for us. Our logic was flawed; the entire press contingent quickly packed up at the beginning of Anderson's speech in order to follow Kennedy out. Governors who had made sure to find their seats for Kennedy's speech treated Anderson's as an intermission, using the time to socialize and return phone calls.

In the fall of 1978, during the congressional election campaign, we took advantage of invitations Anderson received as a GOP leader to stump on behalf of party candidates around the country; our hope was to earn chits for his own presidential contest. One weekend we headed for Davenport, Iowa, to campaign for the reelection of Congressman Jim Leach, a fellow Republican moderate. A local television interviewer took Anderson aside, and as the camera lights went on and he seemed the center of all attention, delusions rushed to our heads that he would be asked about his presidential intentions in this important early caucus state. Of course the interviewer wanted to know only about congressional issues. Even Leach was not stirred. After the event he and his wife invited us to the coach house where they lived on his father's riverside estate. "John," he said, "I hope you're considering a *vice*-presidential strategy," implying his assumption that our intended objective was futile. We sighed, as we would do many times more.

In Pittsburgh we made an appearance to help a struggling contender named Stan Thomas, a low-key and likable mechanical engineer making his first bid for office. His obscurity gave him no chance of winning, but this did not prevent a campaign aide from speaking only in the most optimistic of terms. We succumbed to the temptation to think positively as well, lest we admit to ourselves that this detour was not the most prudent use of our time. The aide drove us from the airport to the Golden Triangle area downtown for a joint press conference. One reporter showed up. "It's Sunday," the aide explained, leaving us only to wonder why the event had been scheduled. From there we drove to a nearby country club where Anderson would join Thomas at a luncheon. We had been given a grandiose guest list—CEOs of the biggest corporations, presidents of the unions—but of course it turned out that these were only the names of invitees, not of the minor functionaries who actually attended. Finally we went off to a suburban picnic, where several dozen local Republicans, almost uniformly dressed in flowery Bermuda shorts, did double takes when Anderson introduced himself as a prospective candidate for president. "What's your name again?" they would ask in disbelief, certain that if someone were running for president, they would know it. Having verified that it *was* someone they had never heard of, one of them took me aside and whispered, "President of the *United States?*"

Anderson had a sense of disbelief, too. Was this really the way he would have to run for president for the next two years? Perhaps candidates like Nixon, Carter, or Bush had the patience to travel the countryside, picking up support vote-by-vote, but Anderson determined practically on the spot that this would not be his way. He would have to figure out some other method—or give up his ambition.

It might have been predictable that this approach would not suit him; even in his own district, politicking did not come naturally. Once I was with him in Galena, Illinois, a picturesque town he represented. We pulled into a small diner to use the phone, and a few customers, scattered at tables, looked up quizzically. They didn't recognize their congressman and stared only because we were overdressed and looked out of place. Other politicians might have seized the opportunity to shake hands and collect votes, but the look on Anderson's face suggested that the thought did not enter his mind. Indeed I had the sense he was glad *not* to be recognized. Even at obligatory events he made little effort to adapt. That evening he spoke to a GOP gathering in Jo Daviess County, at the southern end of the district, launching into a tub-thumping lament on the parlous condition of the nation. Several times he seemed to reach a natural climax, and the audience breathed relief. But like a Wagnerian opera, the speech never seemed to end. It was nearly an hour before he finally sat down. The audience applauded the feat of his endurance more than the substance of his remarks, which had sailed over their heads. Anderson was interested in large national issues, and he assumed that everyone else would be too.

Back in the Congress, I remained responsible for watching Anderson's interests on the energy committee. Fortunately for my preoccupied boss, I was able to discharge many responsibilities without his active involvement. The disembodied nature of a committee operation became clear one day as the year was drawing to a close. Dick Krolik, my Democratic counterpart, turned to me from his desk and said,

"Well, it's about time my boss thanked your boss for his efforts." With that he typed a letter in Congressman Ashley's name addressed to Anderson and full of lofty sentiments, which he composed aloud with my approval. The letter was then sent on dutifully to Ashley's personal office. Whether Ashley actually saw and signed it or simply left that to a secretary, as other members sometimes did, I cannot say; but within a couple of days the letter had come full circle and arrived on my own desk, just a few feet from Dick's. It had, of course, gone to Anderson's personal office first, but our practice was to channel correspondence to the relevant aide in anticipation that Anderson would request a suitable reply. Thus I turned to Dick and announced that his letter had arrived safely, asked him what effusive compliments Ashley might enjoy hearing from Anderson in return, and drafted the appropriate response. The cycle was repeated, and a couple of days later Dick received my letter.

At the very end of the legislative session serious committee activity momentarily resumed. Natural-gas legislation finally emerged from a House-Senate conference and came to the floor, in tandem with other components of a National Energy Act, whose consideration had been deliberately delayed. The intention of the Democratic leadership, seeking to aid President Carter in enacting a centerpiece of his legislative program, was to submerge the controversial natural-gas provisions in the more popular overall package. Those who opposed the natural-gas bill would be placed in the predicament of either supporting it or otherwise having to tell constituents that they had voted against an entire national energy policy that had been nearly two years in the making. Congress had in large measure gutted Carter's original proposals, but the president, having declared the energy crisis to be the nation's most urgent business, would not freely admit failure. Instead he clung to his enfeebled program, and congressional debate assumed a significance more symbolic than real.

The climax of that debate was fitting (given the bill's already protracted legislative history): thirty-one hours of ponderous floor debate beginning on a Saturday morning, continuing all through the night, and not finally concluding until six forty-five Sunday evening. At times like this—and such collegiate "all-nighters" occurred regularly at year-end as congressmen struggled to complete business they had too long postponed—the scene on the House floor bore an eerie resemblance to a dance marathon of the 1920s. Members vied to outspeak each other, and even to stay awake. Appropriately music drifted onto the floor around three o'clock in the morning as a group of congressmen, determined to pick up the pace of things, staged an impromptu jam session in the cloakroom, complete with the wail of a plaintive saxophone.

Anderson had the responsibility of managing Republican opposition to the bill, so I sat on the floor during these hours sandwiched between him and a core group of hardy GOP souls who, notwithstanding the prospect of certain defeat, vigorously denounced the follies of the bill as though they had a chance. Bud Brown of Ohio was deeply learned on this as on other subjects, but some felt he had too pontifical an air, and undeservingly he was somewhat tuned out. Dave Stockman, now a congressman from Michigan, similarly specialized in speeches of great substance, but they were usually so clever and forcefully stated as to command even the attention of arch-opponents. In this case he parodied the endless new oil classifications the energy bill would introduce, describing the minute categories and subcategories that might determine the price at which producers could sell. The presentation was his usual tour de force, setting him apart from more ordinary colleagues: It was evident he had actually read the legislation on which he pronounced. Nearby, Jack Kemp of New York sat stoically, listening carefully to the many speeches and, when the sentiments expressed did not suit him, making snappy asides, which helped keep us awake. A former professional football player, Kemp had a raspy voice and occasional locker-room deportment, which cloaked impressive intellectual dedication.

When it came Anderson's turn to speak, he complained most about the procedure, adopted the previous day, that prevented a vote on the natural-gas bill alone; his service on the House Rules Committee gave him a special interest in such matters, which, since they set the parameters of debate, could be as important as legislative substance itself. In addition he lambasted the energy scheme at issue as a typical Democratic marvel of tangled regulation and bureaucracy. Notwithstanding Anderson's brilliant text—he was fatigued enough to read large parts of my work, simulating such emotion as he could given the hour— the Republicans got clobbered on the vote. As poetic justice for my ineffectual efforts, I found myself seated the following morning at breakfast in the House dining room next to Doc Long of Maryland, an aged Democratic congressman who had a reputation for being crotchety and unreasonable; I cringed in the expectation that he would complain all during the meal about the Republican position. For some reason the great energy crisis failed to stir his passions that moment, and I found him instead most interesting and pleasant.

Perhaps the Democrats were simply being charitable in victory. Indeed within weeks I was invited to the White House bill-signing ceremony, even though I had technically led the Republican staff forces of the House in opposing it. Many other foes of the bill stayed away, but the chance to witness history, in my view, transcended partisan considerations. Not to disappoint, President Carter signed the legislation with fanfare in the East Room, congressional leaders arrayed around him, and chief aide Hamilton Jordan watching with unaccustomed satisfaction from the back of the room this commemoration of a rare congressional success.

As the crowd filed out afterward, the president stood by the door and shook hands, enabling the White House photographer to snap pictures as though each guest had just emerged from a private audience. A couple of weeks later we were to receive these as a memento of the occasion. I never became a Carter booster, but had the picture been a better one, I wouldn't have hesitated to tack it up on the wall. Even an administration so roundly ridiculed for the quality of its legislative relations knew the value of flattering congressional aides. I resolved to carry the lesson into the White House of President Anderson.

20

PROTÉGÉS AND PRESS SECRETARIES

When the Ad Hoc Committee dissolved with the Ninety-fifth Congress in January 1979, my habitat changed to Anderson's personal office. I had not been certain of this transition—the positions there were few and appeared to be filled—and therefore I considered other possibilities which happened to come my way, such as serving either of two freshmen senators as chief legislative assistant. Only six months before I would have found the prospect of such work too thrilling to pass up, but now it seemed almost ordinary compared with the heady prospects of presidential campaigning.

But a new year brought changes in Anderson's office. Mike Masterson, the efficient AA, had been invited to help run the state of Illinois' Washington office, and this was more to his taste than becoming involved in a quixotic political quest. Steve Anderson, the low-key press secretary (no relation to the congressman), seemed to think that public confusion over names might be useful and began to contemplate a congressional race himself if his boss announced he would not seek another term. Anderson, of course, did make such an announcement, and Steve ran, but in the end his effort to portray himself as more conservative than his longtime boss backfired when he failed to gain Anderson's endorsement. He placed fifth in a field of five and eventually returned to Washington as a representative of the frozen-food industry.

When Steve left, I became Anderson's press secretary. I had no experience in journalism, but I was a newspaper junkie, one of those classic Washingtonians known for their fanaticism of reading half a dozen papers before nine in the morning and flipping incessantly among every broadcast of the nightly news to be sure they didn't miss a story. We were a subspecies of humanity whose greatest peeve was that some people couldn't differentiate between network news and local news or couldn't remember which columnists wrote for which papers. Such knowledge was, after all, fundamental to our daily lives, since we were expected to pepper our conversations with appropriate learned references: "Did you see the story Mudd did last night on TV?" or, "Broder's column this morning is all wrong." After several years on the Hill I was familiar with the major national policy debates of the day, as well as the long cast of Washington politicians and journalists who dramatized them. I imagined that nearly everything I did was important, and I would not have traded my work for anything. Washington observers will recognize symptoms here of the noted scourge of Potomac Fever, which the public sometimes erroneously assumes to afflict only politicians: the ones, after all, who are elected to all the power and perquisites. But it turns out that congressional staffers—who spend their lives bathing in these reflected experiences—are almost equally susceptible.

Indeed, my fever was as acute as Anderson's. We shared many of the same obsessive perspectives, which to normal human beings might have seemed evidence of maladjustment. Nothing interested us more than the news, and we felt almost nothing to be more significant in life than matters of public policy. We were both, in addition, naïfs at national politics. Despite decades of running for office, Anderson had a disdain for glad-handing and back-slapping, which gave him an occasional blind spot to their importance. The difference between us was Anderson's more intellectual character: He would have taken it as a compliment to be called a political theorist or dreamer. I had more of a fascination with individual personalities, the wacky details of the process, the chemistry among press, voter, and politician. In close proximity over the next two years—a press secretary needs to be at his boss's side—we reinforced each other's eccentricities.

The tradition of mentor and protégé is much alive in Washington: older politicians adopting much younger aides as virtual surrogate members of their family. Jimmy Carter had his press secretary, Jody Powell; Ronald Reagan had longtime public-relations aide Mike Deaver; Howard Baker had a homegrown reporter-turned-adviser named Tommy Griscom; George Bush has his (albeit comparably aged) Secretary of State, Jim Baker. Such intimates perform functions often quite different from their titular responsibilities. They are expected to advise, console, and, as necessary, talk back. They are alter egos in whom confidences are freely reposed and on whose recommendation actions are readily taken, in return for their assuming the mentor's interests and even personality as their own; perhaps it is not surprising that the protégé is often a fervent political strategist, quite literally the politician's politician. The aspects of the role are not always visible, since it is performed most successfully when the privacy of the relationship is closely guarded. Yet its influence is extraordinary, since the adviser is to a large extent merged into the principal.

Remarkably enough this is the status that I came to occupy with Anderson. From the beginning he and his wife treated both Margot and me familiarly, having us often to their home and visiting us frequently as well. In part this had to do with the circumstances of our original acquaintance, but the tradition of complete informality continued in his employment. Almost the first week I worked for him, Anderson phoned one Sunday morning to invite me to discuss campaign strategy over breakfast. Within the hour, he had driven from his home in suburban Maryland the many miles to my apartment in Washington and, having picked me up, through the city until we found a McDonald's (to which we both were partial) on K Street downtown. Over Egg McMuffins, he asked my views on the coming presidential race. I was abysmally inexpert, but he didn't seem to care. The fact that I was a novice meant I would not laugh at his ambitions, which so many others regarded as fanciful. Those who had known Anderson long had a fixed idea of him as a congressman; in my eyes he began with a clean slate.

This, I think, goes a long way toward explaining how someone of such stature and ability could have accepted someone so different as a close confidant and adviser. I was, after all, twenty-five years old when I began working for him; he was fifty-seven. And the role I assumed was startlingly influential. Outsiders to campaigns assume that serious candidates know their positions and their minds soundly; one hears of "handlers" but assumes that they work mainly with inexperienced or unintelligent office seekers. Anderson was deeply knowledgeable, strongly opinionated, and fiercely independent. Yet his intellectual curiosity made him eager for new and specific things to say, and the hectic character of a campaign and congressional schedule gave him precious little time to devise them himself. Much of the time, as a result, I hovered in his shadow, slipping him notes for press conferences and speeches, which he would often utter verbatim. While he was busy reading briefing papers or granting interviews, I would be combing newspapers for current topics on which to pronounce, assembling pungent comments, and scribbling speech drafts on yellow legal pads as neatly as a plane or limousine ride would allow. Of course I knew Anderson's philosophy and positions, and if I were useful, it was because I could anticipate what my boss would have wanted to say if he had possessed the time to do his own work. Indeed, if ever I began to lose sight of that fact, I could count on Anderson to find a moment to rest, think his own thoughts, discard my own, and deflate my sense of self-importance.

Evidently my most immediate predecessor in a protégé's role had been Dave Stockman, an Anderson staffer for five years in the early 1970s. Stockman had been a Harvard divinity student who enrolled in a politics seminar taught by visiting *Washington Post* reporter David Broder. One day Anderson asked Broder whether he had encountered any promising young people who might enjoy working on the Hill, and Stockman was recommended. Years later—but before Stockman's fall from grace in the Reagan era—Broder evidently remained so impressed with him that veteran Anderson staff members recalled his saying, "When Stockman becomes president, don't forget who discovered him." Anderson felt the same and promoted Stockman rapidly through the ranks of his office during the next five years until Stockman entered Congress.

By the time I arrived in 1978, however, the two were estranged. Though they had been intimately associated at one time and continued to cross paths in the close quarters of the Congress, they rarely spoke. Anderson was surprised by Stockman's aggressive conservatism, which Stockman displayed more as a congressman than he had as an aide. The enmity was sealed when Stockman early on endorsed John Connally for president instead of Anderson. Withholding his support from Anderson was disappointing enough; but awarding it to Connally, whose positions and style were so utterly antithetical, seemed to

Anderson almost a calculated insult. The final act of treason, in Anderson's view, occurred during the general election campaign, when Stockman volunteered an impersonation of his former boss to help prepare Ronald Reagan for his debate with Anderson. (Stockman's performance in the mock debate so impressed Reagan that it is said to have been the reason he was willing to grant Stockman, age thirty-four, the coveted post of budget director.)

Stockman's falling out with Anderson suggested the potential complications of a combined personal and professional relationship. Often I would participate in heated political discussions with the Andersons, and my quasi-family status encouraged a mutual candor not otherwise brooked among aides. Yet while it acted to excuse the exuberance of my arguments, it also gave me a discomfiting ability to reach them on an emotional level. This was at times an awkward position for someone who was still expected to serve them the next day on a subordinate and businesslike basis. In addition too visible a display of my relationship had the potential for arousing office jealousies. Already there was a divide among Anderson's staff between those who performed daily legislative chores and those who were admitted into his confidence on politics. In part it was a matter of self-selection—most of his congressional staff felt out of their depth in the campaign area or simply lacked interest—but as his presidential quest assumed greater importance in Anderson's own world, those who were left out of these activities began to feel a sense of neglect.

All of this chastened me to act quietly in my role, yet there was still another reason. Perhaps there are others who, thrust into such positions in their mid-twenties, are capable of taking a high profile with gusto and self-assurance, but I simply felt too young to do so. I had no compunction about making brash suggestions to Anderson in private and actively seeking to influence his actions, but it seemed to me that our campaign was already having enough trouble gaining public credibility to flaunt such youthful advisers. My personal ambitions were not difficult to contain, in any case, since I had by now fully developed a staffer's expected passion for anonymity. Aides were supposed to toil for the glory of the elected official whose nameplate hung on the front door; if they sought personal visibility and acclaim, they were free to run for office. (Not all staffers abide by such traditional etiquette anymore, and increasingly some have gained a status and recognized influence almost independent of their employers. In recent years, for example, at least two House press secretaries—John Buckley with Jack Kemp, and Christopher Matthews with Tip O'Neill—became sought after for their own colorful comments, not simply those of their bosses.) Playing as invisible a role as possible, I would arrange for Anderson to have lunch with this columnist or that reporter, sometimes absenting myself from the event to avoid its looking staged. And I would write belligerent statements for Anderson to deliver, or casually urge him to take controversial positions, knowing that I myself as a candidate might tremble to do so.

The relationship, as such, was synergistic. Working in the shadows, I felt less inhibited about taking initiatives; Anderson's shock of white hair would endow them with suitable authority, reassuring the world (and myself) that they could not be entirely reckless. And Anderson himself needed the staff prodding, for left to his own he was sometimes merely rhetorical; and yet he was far more willing than most politicians, when proposals came his way, to take action. He was delighted when someone suggested strong (presumably sensible) statements or, best of all, "new ideas." We were, in consequence, an effective one-two punch. He served as an outlet for my own intellectual reveries, and I as an *agent provocateur* who spurred him to express his inherent nonconformity.

The story of Anderson's famous fifty-cent gasoline-tax proposal epitomized the process. Once when President Carter was expected to announce major energy proposals, Anderson felt challenged to do so too. On a Saturday morning, when others might have been golfing or sleeping, he rose early and, in longhand, drafted his own lengthy statement, then phoned, inviting me to join him in the office, where I might perform appropriate editorial, secretarial, and press chores. As my boss he knew I didn't have much of a choice, but as usual he generously offered to make it easier by giving me a ride in. His proposals were more general than concrete, but toward the end he did make one that stood out: To reduce the level of imported oil consumption, Anderson urged an "emergency excise tax" at the pump. "I would suggest," he wrote, "twenty-five cents a gallon." Although such an idea was not unheard of on editorial pages, it almost certainly had not been uttered before by a serious politician. Even so, my own reaction was that it still lacked the severity to change ingrained consumer habits; fifty cents was more to my liking.

By now Anderson had gone off to the House gymnasium for his habitual midday swim and was unavailable for consultation. As typist I had considerable prerogative. Word processors were not standard equipment for Hill aides then as they are now, and I did not look forward to realigning the paper to make subsequent changes. I typed in "fifty cents" in place of "twenty-five cents" and simply hoped to convince Anderson of my judgment when he returned. He proved initially skeptical but ultimately accepting. "Let's go with it," he said after brief debate, instructing that I make copies of the statement and circulate it to colleagues and press. Largely it went unnoticed; no one particularly cared what an unseeded presidential candidate said. But now we were on the record with our gas-tax proposal and, fortunately, as time went on, grew increasingly confident of its merit.

At the same time we recognized the reflexive public opposition that efforts to raise a tax might encounter and wondered how we could make the idea more palatable. *The New York Times* inadvertently answered our quandary one day when it published a letter to the editor that proposed coupling a gasoline tax with repeal of state sales taxes. Here was a way, in theory, to reduce consumption by raising one tax but to offset new burdens by offering relief from another. Excitedly I brought the idea to Anderson's attention, but we soon realized its limitations: Not all states had sales taxes, and repeal would involve action at the state level rather than in Congress. But Bob Walker, our creative staff economist, suggested a twist: using the proceeds of a gas tax to reduce *Social Security* taxes, whose scheduled increase was the object of widespread criticism. Anderson was delighted with the idea, and I dubbed it the "Fifty-Fifty Plan," in reference to the fact that the fifty-cent gas tax would be combined with an equivalent 50 percent reduction in Social Security payroll taxes. The name helped remind audiences that the proposal had twin features, but of course the gas tax was the dramatic one on which they fastened. There were still other provisions—protecting truckers, traveling salesmen, and the elderly—but few listened to the details. In fact interest in any part of the proposal picked up only when the administration was rumored to be considering a gas tax of its own.

Our efforts to gain recognition on the issue were deeply frustrating, but they taught us a great deal about the dynamics of the press. Four thousand news correspondents are credentialed to the Capitol press gallery, a measure of the extensive coverage that is available to congressional activities. It is not equitably apportioned. The press, as its readers and listeners might expect, focus largely on topical or entertaining news or on well-known personalities. An ordinary politician tends to be quoted only when his comments are relevant to a larger breaking story or are waggish and colorful. As a result we were often forced to ride the coattails of other candidates and issues. Daily conversations with reporters and assignment editors gave me a hint of what would "lead" the news the next day, and accordingly I would draft statements and press releases to capture the anticipated interest. The stronger our comment, the more likely it was to be used. When we debated a reaction to John Connally's "peace plan" for the Mideast, for example, we knew we had a choice: We could say, diplomatically, that it "concerned" us, or we could say, more theatrically, that it "displayed a shocking insensitivity to history and a cavalier disregard for true peace." We said the latter, and news organizations eagerly seized upon it.

In these respects the media obviously influenced our timing and tone, but we said nothing we did not believe. It is certainly possible to have qualms about press secretaries—their role often involves blatant political propagandizing rather than mere communication—but they do provide an essential service brokering "buyers" and "sellers" of information. They make their bosses available in the galleries, encourage them to provide quotable comment, and otherwise disperse their opinions to the public. On occasion they may overstep their functions and seek to muzzle, rather than unleash, their clients. For my own part, I channeled Anderson to any reporter who would listen. He enjoyed speaking his mind, and interviewers rarely failed to be impressed by his intelligence; in the end he proved to be his own best advertisement.

In my desperation to publicize him, I even opened our doors uncritically to photographers. Once a young woman presented herself at our office saying she wanted to take pictures for *Time* and *Newsweek*. Ecstatic, I allowed her to accompany Anderson for the next several hours, surprisingly inexperienced though she seemed to be. That day I joined Anderson for lunch with *Washington Post* columnist Meg Greenfield. "Who *is* that?" Greenfield asked, as the photographer hovered obtrusively near our table. "That," I replied proudly, "is a photographer for *Time* and *Newsweek*." Greenfield shook her head. "I don't think so," she said. "Oh, you're wrong," I corrected her. It turned out of course that *I* was wrong. The photographer was a freelancer and had meant only that she hoped to *submit* her pictures to those magazines. She had no actual assignment, and no pictures were ever published. She was new to the business, but I was even newer. (She honed her skills, however, and was later hired by Vice President Bush as his official White House photographer.)

Friendly critics often suggested to us that the way to boost our fledg-ling campaign was to "get an issue" or "come up with an idea." They were often unaware of our gasoline-tax proposal, as well as numerous others, and rarely did they have their own specific suggestions. As we would learn time and again, often it was not *what* was said but *who* said it that made something newsworthy. When famine occurred in Cambodia, Anderson gave speech after speech about it, but it became "news" only when Ted Kennedy appropriated the issue, and a front-page headline only when President Carter, locked at the time in battle with Kennedy, responded. Remarkably Anderson's most widely quoted comments in the early days were mere humorous asides, as when he finally achieved a percentage point of recognition in national polls and proudly proclaimed that he was "no longer an asterisk," or when our campaign office was robbed of small electrical appliances and he called it a "third-rate burglary" (invoking the famous phrase used by the Nixon White House to dismiss the Watergate break-in), or when reporters pressed him on how long he could last in the race, and he replied that it would be "as long as I have clean laundry." These comments were the perfect light touch for "people" columns and the last story of news broadcasts, and voters in the early days were to hear more of them than almost anything Anderson uttered on grand national policy.

For practical purposes, the field of Republican candidates had two tiers. The first one—consisting of Reagan, Bush, Howard Baker, and John Connally—was reported on constantly. The second—Dole, An-derson, and Congressman Phil Crane—seemed an afterthought. I spent much time reminding Anderson how Jimmy Carter and Walter Mon-dale had been, at one time, equally obscure; but he would then re-mind me of others—such as former Pennsylvania governor Milton Shapp—who had run for president and were never heard from again. Too, I consoled him with the thought that front-runners often fal-tered—Ed Muskie, Scoop Jackson, George Romney, among them—and that little could be predicted in advance. (In 1978 my wife had lunch with her friend Jim Brady, later to be Reagan's press secretary. Jim was a canny political observer. His vision of the 1980 general election: "It's going to be Kennedy versus Connally—and you heard it here first!") Anderson accepted that conventional wisdom could be flawed; his problem was that it would take arduous years of campaign-ing to disprove it.

In the meantime our outward signs of progress were discouraging. We set up a small office on Eighth Street, Southeast, tucked above the Metropolis Bike Shop. In the first several months of its operation (following Anderson's formal declaration of candidacy in June 1979), even its few rooms seemed vacant. We employed at the time only two or three paid staffers, and volunteers drifted in sporadically. Our initial campaign manager, Bill Bradford, was pleasant and competent, but it was a tribute more to the intellectuality of our effort than its political seasoning that he was a retired diplomat fresh from assignment as United States ambassador to Chad. (The director of the preceding "exploratory" phase had declined to stay on, questioning whether Anderson had sufficient "fire in his belly" to wage an effective campaign.)

By the end of the year we would have raised only $500,000. Months before, I had attended Connally's announcement and gasped to hear him say he might reject federal matching funds because otherwise he would be limited by law to spending $14 million; we could not conceive such numbers. Then on a visit to New York, we were hosted by one of our supporters at a small dinner in the elegant University Club. It was purely a get-acquainted affair, with no money involved. By coincidence George Bush was holding a fundraiser in an adjoining room. Curious to see the activities of a rival, I walked over and encountered his brother. On learning my affiliation, he was happy to disclose not only that the event had raised $50,000 but that George had needed to leave early to attend *another* dinner. I heaved a sigh, but shouldn't have been surprised. I had also been to Bush's announcement, which filled up the entire National Press Club ballroom (ours had been held in the much smaller Rayburn Room of the Capitol). He had released breathtaking state-by-state lists of supporters and introduced a campaign chairman, Congressman Barber Conable, who, as a friendly colleague of Anderson's, we had until then imagined might join *us*.

Regularly we debated whether to continue. Earlier in the year Anderson had considered shifting gears and running instead for the Senate from Illinois (Adlai Stevenson III was contemplating retirement). One afternoon, on a trip to Chicago, we borrowed Senator Percy's downtown office to pass the time between appointments. Anderson sat in these commodious quarters gazing out on the panoramic view of Lake Michigan and took the measure of a senator's station; it was inviting. Yet in a way it was easier to run for president, where a candidate could do well simply on the basis of early success in a small state like New Hampshire; Illinois had many times the population and much higher media costs. (Anderson was known in only one corner of the state.) Moreover the issues of interest in a statewide campaign were, in

Anderson's view, narrow and mundane: local public-works projects and wheat prices, not the M-X missile and national health insurance. To Anderson, unlike traditional politicians, all politics was not local but national. Even at this point, I suspect, he might have been willing to leave the race for something less than the presidency—had Jimmy Carter, for example, reached out to moderate Republicans and invited him to become ambassador to the United Nations. Anderson's fundamental objective was to transcend congressional service. He admired several congressmen—Tom Rees, Gilbert Gude, Pete Biester—who had recently opted to retire in their prime to resume other careers rather than waiting for the onset of old age or the humiliation of electoral defeat. Running for president was a means of accomplishing the same end.

We discussed his hesitations, but always concluded with a resolution to wait things out; one of my roles, it seemed, was to discourage precipitous decisions. Even on a limited budget, it would be possible to keep going until the first primary returns. Any embarrassment of withdrawing would not be much greater then than now; and maybe fortuitous things would happen in between. In the meantime I would try patiently to get Anderson better known. I shuttled him among the numerous national and out-of-town news organizations based in Washington, many of which, then or later, would write obligatory profiles, tending to suspend critical judgment out of compassion for his seemingly hopeless plight. We did much the same among the local newspapers in New Hampshire, Vermont, and Massachusetts, the earliest primary states. None of this would bring Anderson instant renown, but the cumulative effect was to promote his reputation among voters who tuned in early. If a match were struck, things might be ready to ignite.

21

CHARACTER AND CONSULTANTS

The kindling we were looking for came in the Iowa candidate debate of January 1980. In two weeks Iowa would be the nation's first site for the selection of convention delegates, but the form this would take—countless living-room caucuses across the state—made it seem poorly suited to a campaign like ours, which lacked serious grass-roots organization. As a result our young political director decided we should apply no effort there, not even Anderson's own brief appearance in a debate. One day I saw a small item in the paper noting that only Reagan and Anderson had declined to participate. I knew Reagan's strategy: He was the front-runner, who didn't want to tamper with his fragile status. But Anderson needed any exposure he could get. The debate was not purely a state event; it would be televised nationally. I suggested to Anderson that he reconsider. "What debate?" Anderson asked; he had not been consulted.

Off we went to Des Moines for the first face-off of the season; such exchanges were not so plentiful then as they were to become in subsequent campaigns, and great excitement filled the air. Anderson was a skilled debater, and although the campaign staff presented him with volumes of thick briefing books, he arrived early not to study but to take a swim and clear his head. He had often participated in "cattle shows," where one candidate followed another in delivering formal remarks to large audiences, but this was the first instance where the rivals would gather on stage together. The opportunity seemed a breakthrough; at last he would be seen, literally, on the same level as the others. He took full advantage of it, presenting himself as only few outside Washington already knew him: forceful, rational, and direct.

It was an approach that stood out. The others replied to questions with safe and predictable positions; everyone had the immediate Iowa audience in mind and its particular constituency groups, such as farmers. Anderson was different, supporting President Carter's unpopular grain embargo, describing his own controversial gasoline-tax proposal, and rejecting the Republican orthodoxy that taxes could be lowered, defense spending raised, and the budget balanced all at the same time. In the end he even had the chance to offer a stirring statement of philosophy. Everyone claimed they wanted to tackle tough national problems, Anderson said, but no one was prepared to take political risks. He gripped the table and let his voice rise. When he had proposed hard choices, he said, the other candidates had only ridiculed him, but if Americans were serious about their future, they would have to sacrifice. The hall burst into applause, giving Anderson's closing statement by far the greatest reception. Viewers at home, we were to learn, sat up too. Anderson had been noticed.

It may be that John Anderson was the original standard bearer of yuppie political philosophy: conservative in his economics and more liberal on social and foreign-policy issues. The combination had long typified moderate Republicanism—in 1980 this also seemed to encompass Howard Baker and perhaps George Bush—and in later years defined "new Democrats," such as Gary Hart and Bill Bradley. But Anderson had an even more salient attribute, which appealed to younger voters like myself: a rare candor that caused commentators to label him a "nonpolitician." He didn't seem to be suppressing unpleasant truths nor pandering for votes. He valued moral courage; he wanted to be a statesman. True he could go to excess at times, prophesying doom like a Cassandra or demanding repentance like a Jonathan Edwards; he admitted he might make a "hairshirt" president. His positions were often so frank and outspoken that some observers, accustomed to the failings of ordinary politicians, felt compelled to ascribe his behavior to perverse personal needs, such as covetousness of editorial acclaim or a fundamentalist religious upbringing. (His pulpit style of speaking suggested to some that his chosen profession was really only a sublimation of his original ambition to become a preacher.) Anderson may have had a certain self-righteousness, but in my own view it was simply a reflection of an extraordinary, and wholly secular, strength of personal character. Symbolically Anderson activists in the beginning had included many League of Women Voters and Common Cause types, exponents of good government who seemed to admire their candidate most for his moderation and integrity.

Now the Iowa debate added a new element: disaffected Democrats who happened to tune in to a GOP debate and suddenly confronted the possibility that they could be comfortable with a Republican. Jimmy Carter at the time was widely unpopular in his own party, and Ted Kennedy, following a disastrous TV interview with Roger Mudd, deeply disappointing even to many liberals assumed to be his natural supporters. All at once Anderson became a source of interest to Hollywood movie moguls, Manhattan literati, Cambridge professors, and college students everywhere. One memorable weekend I accompanied him to Los Angeles for a command performance at the Bel Air home of Stanley Sheinbaum, an impresario of liberal causes who seemed to host a floating salon for celebrities and intellectuals. An intimate dinner party offered the beginnings of a West Coast Anderson Mafia, which for the rest of the campaign would help shake trees for money and moral support: producers Norman Lear and Grant Tinker, Warner Brothers chairman Ted Ashley, author Irving Wallace. Lear led off the question period by asking Anderson the same question that Ted Kennedy had fumbled in his interview with Mudd: "Why do you want to be president?" Anderson's answer—that he had been "front row and center" for nearly twenty years, had a lot of ideas, and felt impelled now to make a larger contribution—was not particularly stellar by his own standards but seemed to satisfy his inquisitors, who the rest of the evening seemed perceptibly relieved that they had at last found a candidate.

The national press fed the excitement. Sally Quinn, a *Washington Post* social columnist otherwise known for her vitriolic pen, wrote a touching profile that jolted the city awake one day when it appeared together with a nearly life-size picture of the Andersons on the front page of the paper's much-read "Style" section. Bob Scheer, whose previous interviews with candidates had elicited the famous "lust in my heart" remarks from Jimmy Carter, produced a warm and wholesome campaign piece for *Playboy*. (And a good thing, too. Although we found Bob most likable, Anderson had nearly lost patience with his unceasing requests for interview time as we drove about New Hampshire enclosed in the same small van.) At an elegant but jammed fund-raiser on East End Avenue in New York City, the crowd momentarily quieted as I turned up the volume of a TV for an expected *CBS Evening News* story on how the once obscure Anderson campaign had "taken off." To see Walter Cronkite say it instantly transformed dreams into reality—and increased our take of contributions that very evening.

Meanwhile I had been in conversations for some months with *Saturday Night Live* about the possibility of Anderson's making a cameo appearance on the late-night comedy show; I knew that virtually everyone in America under age thirty watched it. Sensing that we were close to a deal, I prevailed on Keke to add her voice. She phoned actress Jane Curtin and took it brilliantly from there, describing her husband's extensive oratorical experience on Capitol Hill and the fact that, as a senior in high school, he had even played the part of Abraham Lincoln. Keke's charm was perfect, and the next day producer Lorne Michaels called me to arrange Anderson's screen debut. It turned out to be a nonspeaking appearance—this avoided potential demands of other candidates for equal time—but proved enough to solidify his status as radical chic.

The evidence came as we returned to the campaign trail, pulling up to the student lounge at MIT one evening for a scheduled speech, which we expected to attract a characteristically ragtag assembly of thirty or so young people. We had trouble finding a parking place nearby—a large event in the area seemed to be clogging the streets with traffic—and finally in our impatience drove into a restricted area and parked illegally. We studied our map to be sure we were in the right place (doing all the navigating ourselves, we always had doubt). We did seem to be, and all of us had the same thought: Why couldn't our schedulers have made elementary inquiries about competing events that evening? Who would come to Anderson's speech if something else so interesting was going on?

Of course it turned out that everyone was coming to see *Anderson*. Jerome Wiesner, the university president, found us and provided an escort through the throng, exclaiming that he had not seen such a large student crowd since the administration building had been taken over twelve years earlier. All through New England we would find similar crowds in the next several days. Anderson's celebrity was capped by a series in the *Doonesbury* comic strip romanticizing the unsophisticated character of our intimate little campaign and its unexpected brush with success.

These were indeed the *Doonesbury* days, alternately exhilarating and comical. By now I was on the campaign payroll (happily accepting a reduced salary for the privilege), away from home much longer than expected and, as a result, traveling in the same suit, carrying only a briefcase jammed with papers and underwear, and wearing galoshes permanently over my shoes because they had developed holes and I had no time to buy new ones. Occasionally prominent supporters guided us around, such as Congressmen Jim Jeffords in Vermont and David Emery in Maine, but more often we were left to our own devices, relying on dedicated campaign staffers like Tom Wartowski, a onetime Rockford reporter who had covered Anderson and now tendered his services as an uncomplaining driver, a description that would not have fit any of the rest of us. (Tom also had a sturdy and clean-cut appearance that, when he donned sunglasses, made him a dead ringer for a Secret Service agent; this delighted us, suffering as we did from an inferiority complex every time the Reagan and Kennedy battalions swept by.)

Beyond my duties as press secretary and speechwriter I, too, shared responsibilities for reading road maps, checking our party into hotels, and coordinating such as we did with our Washington headquarters. Much of the time we were effectively incommunicado (this was in the days before cellular car telephones) and made tactical decisions on the spot. Indeed our communications were so imperfect that one evening, when the phone rang in the wrong "holding room" of a high school gymnasium where the Republican candidates had gathered to speak, Nancy Reagan answered and graciously went out into the crowd to ask people who I was and where she could find me. In future months the campaign became far better organized but, as a result, more bureaucratic. The advantage at least of our original status was that we had a sense of spontaneity and adventure.

One night in New Hampshire, for example, Anderson learned that all the other candidates were headed to the Highway Hotel in Concord to participate in a "gun owners' forum." As with the Iowa debate, our political director had declined an invitation to the event without consulting the candidate; he had decided that the subject matter was too controversial. But Anderson enjoyed speaking out on sensitive issues; it seemed to him a high duty of running for office. Straightaway we went to the forum, where he made an extemporaneous plea to license owners of handguns; the other candidates uniformly vied to denounce any form of gun control. The crowd booed Anderson loudly, a reaction that caused him genuine surprise; he thought it would content itself with tepid applause. But TV footage of the exchange was perfect for the next day's news, serving to confirm Anderson's growing reputation as a politician eager to enter the den of lions. By now we had signed a media consultant, Bob Sann, to produce our first commercials, and he evoked the sentiment nicely in his tagline: "The Anderson difference." It may have reminded some of an aspirin commercial, but it was catchy and memorable, and everyone got the point.

For all the interest that had begun to build, Anderson placed only fourth in New Hampshire, distantly behind Reagan and Bush. Still we found cause for delight, coming in just a couple of points behind the much better known Howard Baker and well ahead of John Connally and Bob Dole. As such, the performance was much better than expected, making each hour electric as primary day approached one week later in Massachusetts and Vermont. There was still a sense of improvisation to our campaign—I slept on a couch in the Andersons' suite at the Copley Plaza Hotel in Boston—but the crowds that greeted us were of a size and enthusiasm usually reserved for front-runners. An election-eve finale at Quincy Market in Boston at last made us think we had a chance. In an atmosphere reminiscent of a rock concert, screaming fans besieged Anderson on his way to the podium and then gave deafening approval to his every utterance.

The setting was equaled the next night in the ballroom of the Sheraton Boston when he appeared to claim victory. Moments before, we had sat nervously upstairs watching returns and nearly fainting in shock when networks projected Anderson wins in both primaries. The candidate tried now to explain the reason for his success by quoting Emerson: "Nothing astonishes men so much as common sense and plain dealing." Our supporters roared their agreement, and Anderson would invoke the line many months more, but in fact I had found it only hours earlier in a book of quotations that I had scoured in desperate need of new material. Anderson was handed an earpiece so that Walter Cronkite, broadcasting from New York, could interview him live, then we jumped into a police car for a dizzying ride to an interview with rival anchorman John Chancellor. He gave us the bad news— that Anderson had been nosed out slightly by Reagan in Vermont and by Bush in Massachusetts. It didn't matter; even a pair of second-place finishes was the stuff of fantasy.

More than once I had mused with Anderson about whether success could ever spoil us, and of course we had resolved to keep campaigning the same way no matter what; we shared a belief that elections presented an exciting opportunity for public education. For the time being, we kept our pledge, and it was in this spirit that Anderson appeared before a jammed press conference the morning after his "victory." In the past he had criticized other candidates for dwelling excessively on the horse-race aspects of the campaign: who was higher in the polls, who had raised the most money, what tactical efforts would be necessary in the next state. Now that the world was listening to *us*, he had authorized me to prepare something of a different nature. In the early-morning darkness, as we toured the network television shows in whirlwind fashion, I raced through the newspapers looking for the right subject; now Anderson pulled my notes from his coat. "I want to make a comment on the election held yesterday . . ." he paused for effect, "in Zimbabwe." And so, when others might have been talking about delegates and momentum, Anderson was addressing U.S. policy toward Africa.

But we carried the "new politics" a little too far for primaries that would be conducted under old traditions. Anderson's departures from GOP orthodoxy became so pronounced that, in the pivotal Illinois candidates' debate, Reagan was able to lean over avuncularly and ask him, "Now, John, you wouldn't really prefer Teddy [Kennedy] to me, would you?" As I sat in the audience at Chicago's Continental Plaza Hotel, my heart sank; Anderson's loyalty had come into question. Reagan surged ahead, taking the primary with 48 percent, although Anderson at 37 percent still far outflanked Bush at 11 percent. But momentum, as Bush often pointed out, could be everything, and Anderson began to tumble; by Wisconsin, once considered our most fertile terrain, he was an also-ran. We were now in the strange predicament that Anderson's popularity among voters in general was far greater than among those who would cast votes in Republican primaries. Although he had not given the matter serious thought before, at every press conference the drumbeat rose: Would he consider running as an independent?

We went out to California to rest and contemplate. Walking along the beach in Malibu one fine April morning, Anderson confided that his Republican race was over. Yet he was inclined somehow to keep running; in his view many otherwise "disenfranchised" voters wanted the choice. Students jammed Ackerman Union at UCLA and Memorial Auditorium at Stanford. At Berkeley, which not long before would have hooted a politician off campus, two thousand students squeezed into Zellerbach Auditorium to see him and another fifteen hundred listened over loudspeakers outside. In a score of limousine rides among events, we debated what to do. The most prominent pollsters privately told us we had a chance; they had never seen such volatility in their data. Carter remained massively unpopular; the electorate was nervous about Reagan. It seemed an historic moment; Anderson felt he was making a difference, and it was hard to let go.

Once the decision was cast to run, he gave the reins of authority to David Garth, a New York political consultant. I had taken Anderson to meet Garth in his Fifth Avenue offices months before: Garth had been Heinz's campaign guru, and I had always heard him described in legendary terms, as though he could win anything for anybody. To an extent he had, having helped groom politicians such as New York mayors John Lindsay and later Ed Koch, Los Angeles mayor Tom Bradley, and assorted senators and governors. But we were the darkest of dark horses, and he showed little interest in us; he quoted prices we could not begin to afford. Now that money was rolling in and we were preparing to do something so adventurous, I urged Anderson to link up again. We needed the best help we could get.

We knew nothing about consultants, but our baptism was quick. Anderson acknowledged to a *Washington Post* interviewer that he was definitely going to run as an independent, and the moment the story hit the newspaper, Garth phoned me, shouting furiously that Anderson had "blown it." Candidates, it seemed, were not to act on their own but to follow instructions from their strategists. In the future, he ordered, Anderson's statements would be cleared in New York. Initially I found my encounters with Garth disconcerting, but after a point they became amusing. His vocabulary was largely limited to the unprintable and generally expressed at high volume. Even the most minor incidents set him off, and he rarely failed to predict catastrophic consequences of any event he had not scripted. He was a short, stout man who, despite his obvious intellect, might have considered it a compliment to be likened to a street tough. Reporters said he belonged to the "shin-kicking" school of politics; if one of them wrote a distasteful story, he did not hesitate to call threateningly at any hour to vent his hyperbolic displeasure.

It was not for me to be squeamish if Garth delivered on his magic. Unfortunately his tactics turned out not only to change the character of the campaign but, in so doing, to jeopardize its appeal. Garth was the consummate political packager, and he seemed to treat Anderson as he did his typical clients, immediately curbing his spontaneity (to avoid creating controversy) and reducing his visibility (to avoid "peaking too soon"). A new press secretary was instructed to keep the media at a distance and dispense comment sparingly; at one point Garth told me we should try to squelch news magazine interest in cover stories. Anderson, meantime, was sent around the country to assist in state-by-state "ballot access" drives (a major hurdle for an independent) and avoided articulating new positions.

Such tactics may have been effective in fighting previous political wars, but Anderson had made it this far by being different. To the extent that he became a conventional candidate, supporters lost the sense of excitement about him that they needed as motivation to buck the two-party tradition. The press, which had reported so sympatheti-cally on his openness and candor, began to change its views. (Media analyst Jeff Greenfield later wrote that the proof the press was not as important as some believed was that although they liked Anderson, he didn't do so well in the end. I saw the evidence differently. Reporters *had* liked him early on, but later changed their minds.) To make things worse, Anderson's loss of support tended to snowball, because others defected as they decided he had no chance. Neither an Anderson-Reagan debate in October nor eleventh-hour advertising efforts were enough to stanch the decline; Anderson had peaked (at about 25 per-cent) almost at the point of his independent announcement in late April and slipped thereafter about one point every week and a half until, when the vote came in November, he was left with only 6 per-cent.

My time with Anderson had an impact on me that was larger than the campaign experience: It fundamentally altered my ideas about what politics should be. Perhaps it would be more precise to say that it restored a conception that a few years of Hill experience had caused me to abandon as hopelessly naive. I had come to Capitol Hill to find expression for youthful idealism but had quickly learned that change occurs only slowly and incrementally. The vehicles for progress were not always, it turned out, ideas and logic but often things known as coalition building and interest-group politics. Soon I became proud, not of my idealism so much as of my newly developed sense of prag-matism. I felt highly sophisticated to be able to say, "Oh, no, you *can't* do that" or, "Oh, yes, we *have* to say this." I accepted the idea, common in congressional as well as presidential contests, that the win-ning candidate was likely to be the one with the best pollster and po-litical consultant—not necessarily the best character or ideas.

But eventually such cynicism made me uncomfortable. During every campaign season one reads in the newspaper candid acknowledgments by aides of the insincerity of some of their candidates' positions, together with an explanation of their political necessity, as though the ones to whom the deception is directed will never see these confessions. And they may not: The readership of in-depth political articles is an elite; but still there is something troubling about such an open charade. My early Hill experiences had awakened me to the gamesmanship of politics, and I became as fascinated and engaged as anyone else in the constant calculations of political self-interest. But my subsequent time with Anderson reminded me of the higher purpose of politics, which had initially motivated my involvement. What, then, was the revelation of the campaign? In *The Candidate*, a movie of ten years before, a media pro (whom the screenwriter modeled on Garth) trims Robert Redford's outspoken qualities and makes him a winner. Now came a twist. As I saw it, the "professional" approach in Anderson's case helped the candidate to *lose*. Saddened though I was by the outcome, it was possible to be heartened by the message. Character may at times matter as much as consultants.

I remained in touch with Anderson in the years following the election, and it gave me some sense of why he would consider a presidential run again, as he did briefly in 1984. Occasionally Margot and I would go out with him and his wife for dinner—to Houlihan's in Georgetown, Fio's on Sixteenth Street, and other favorite cheap eateries—and invariably he would be recognized and stopped. It seems to be an instinct of human nature in such circumstances to proffer encouraging words. "We voted for you," strangers would say. "You were right," "You should have been elected," "You should run again," they would chorus. If such comments were taken even half seriously, it would have turned anyone's head. Anderson, in particular, still had a passion for public affairs. He had spurned lucrative law firm offers to spend time teaching and speaking; and as the budget deficit widened, he felt vindicated in the prophecies he had delivered during the campaign.

Of course politicians are not alone in contracting presidential fever. Many staffers and volunteers can't wait to join up every four years, not only out of interest in the candidates and the process, but also because the experience can be—if the right side wins—materially rewarding. One person who applied unsuccessfully to be Anderson's campaign manager went on canvassing the field, finally joining Bush's effort and achieving considerable prominence there and in the White House. A number of headquarters workers during Anderson's independent phase had campaigned in 1976 for Morris Udall and would be back with Walter Mondale in 1984. Others would join Reagan in 1984, and (myself included) Bush or Dole in 1988. Washingtonians have it easy: They live in a city that tends to be the site of presidential campaign offices because that's where the candidates so often reside. But the benefit is mutual: Campaigns know it to be the source of many enthusiastic staffers.

Presidents gracefully retire to other areas outside Washington, often their hometowns: Johnson went back to the LBJ Ranch, Nixon to San Clemente, Ford to Palm Springs (admittedly not Grand Rapids), Carter to Plains, and Reagan to Bel Air. But many unsuccessful presidential candidates remain in the capital, perhaps to keep them in better touch should they decide to go again. John Anderson, Eugene McCarthy, and George McGovern, for example, took up permanent residence in Washington even when they no longer served in the Congress; they did not return to Illinois, Minnesota, or South Dakota. Each of them either ran again or thought actively about it. Howard Baker, after leaving the Senate in 1984 but letting it be known that he was thinking of a presidential race in 1988, signed on with a law firm in Washington (although he simultaneously affiliated with one in Tennessee). Gary Hart attempted to set up shop back in Troublesome Gulch, Colorado, perhaps to emphasize his western roots, but he retained—as Donna Rice's visit to a Capitol Hill townhouse would demonstrate—an occasional Washington presence. Others could conveniently remain in the capital because they had official capacities there: senators like Bob Dole, John Glenn, and Fritz Hollings, and of course Vice President Bush.

But ex-candidates do eventually fade. One day in 1986 I went with Anderson to lunch at the popular Duke Zeibert's restaurant on Connecticut Avenue. The Duke himself escorted us through a large luncheon crowd to a table at a far end of the restaurant. For a moment we felt a satisfaction that Anderson's enduring celebrity had entitled him to a reserved corner table where he could enjoy privacy.

Five minutes later, however, the Duke came running back, evidently prompted by another patron. "Mr. Anderson, Mr. Anderson," apologized this preeminent arbiter of social status in Washington, "I didn't recognize you." He invited us to exchange our table for one up front, where the restaurant showcased its most prominent guests. Anderson declined, but whispered to me wryly, "Maybe we'll get a free bottle of wine out of it." We didn't. It was obvious the world no longer considered him presidential material. But Anderson, recently back from Florida and looking very healthy, at that moment may have been just as glad.

22

WHAT PARTY AM I, ANYWAY?

Following the 1980 campaign no one was quite sure how to label me. In terms of party registration and several years of previous employment, I was a Republican. To many in the GOP, however, Anderson's defection had been a form of political regicide. (Ironically some of these critics had urged Ronald Reagan to bolt the party in 1976 after his primary loss to Gerald Ford.) In addition Anderson had become progressively more liberal in his independent phase—and this was now the hour of conservatives. Democrats were more charitable. Many of their own had been dissatisfied with Jimmy Carter, and as for concern about keeping the presidency in their party, Reagan's "landslide" comforted them that the votes drained off by Anderson would not have made a difference. (I always wondered. My impression was that Anderson stirred many negative feelings about Carter that were expressed—since Anderson didn't seem to have a chance at the end—in votes for Reagan.)

I myself had trouble figuring out where I belonged. I shared Anderson's original schizophrenia on the issues: conservative on economics and more moderate on foreign and social policy. This was a classic burden of my generation; in some way we needed to reconcile the moral consciousness of the 1960s with our more immediate pocket-book concerns as adults entering the 1980s.

Seeing politicians at close range was not much help in sorting things out. When I first came to Washington, I imagined that there was some correlation between personality types and political disposition. Weren't Democrats supposed to be compassionate and Republicans hard-headed? Personal demeanor turned out to be no gauge. Phil Burton and Bella Abzug, two of the most liberal House members, seemed among the most calculating and strident; and Jesse Helms, notoriously conservative in philosophy, was so courtly in manner that he might have won a staff members' poll for personal likability. If there was any group that seemed almost uniformly pleasant, it was moderate Republicans, but their numbers were too limited to provide a scientific sample.

Symbolic of my political ambivalence was the admiration I had for a part of the program of the new president, whom I had recently tried hard to defeat. Anderson had been my candidate of choice, but I agreed with Reagan that government had become too large and inefficient; even for Anderson I had written countless speeches denouncing Carter's economic policies and touting (at least during the initial primaries) GOP alternatives. Non-Washington friends, who knew my disposition on economics, asked me whether I might be taking an appropriate position in the new administration. This was, of course, out of the question. True, it had thousands of jobs to fill, but it also faced the claims of many times that number who could cite original support of the president's candidacy. Political appointments are fundamentally a spoils system, not a talent search; they are intended to reward demonstrated loyalty and philosophical commitment. And why not? These are the attributes that help assure implementation of a president's presumed mandate. At the same time, there are bound to be some positions for which active campaign aides do not possess requisite qualifications. As a result, the newcomers did make occasional compromises, and it was startling to see how many "Reagan supporters" of only tangential political involvement were suddenly catapulted into interesting and reasonably high-level executive positions. But there would certainly be no prominent ex-Anderson aides among them.

It is a paradoxical fact that one sometimes has a better chance of administration appointment by remaining aloof from the political process than by becoming actively involved. Backing a particular horse is a high-stakes gamble. If it succeeds, the payoff can be immense; if not, the result can be exile. I found this a painful irony. I had pursued my Capitol Hill career because I enjoyed politics, and by now I shared a dream of many Hill aides that one day I might have a chance to contribute something in the executive branch. There were clearly parts of the Reagan agenda that I would have been glad to advance. But my Anderson credentials, I knew, would be a permanent bar. This is not to say that exceptions are *never* made, but they tend to be at the highest levels where other factors come into play. Frank Carlucci, for example, who had served as Carter's deputy CIA director, was appointed deputy defense secretary under Reagan—mainly because he had a close relationship with defense secretary Caspar Weinberger, who in turn had a close relationship with the president. Even so he would have been unlikely to advance any further except that the Iran-Contra scandal rocked the administration in 1987 and caused a scramble for high officials of bipartisan reputation. Thus he was made national security adviser and then defense secretary. Bob Hormats was not so lucky. He had served as a deputy trade representative and then as assistant secretary of state under Carter. Reagan's secretary of state, Al Haig, wanted to promote him to undersecretary, but Haig's influence was not as great as Weinberger's. Hormats was stalled by Hill conservatives, and Reagan declined to pull out the stops.

Perhaps it is not surprising that there are few political "independents" in official Washington. Elected representatives have strong party affiliation—it provides access to primaries, organized support and financing, and reserves of traditional voters—and the rest of the federal city takes its cues accordingly. This includes Hill staffers, even if they work for employers of a different party who never ask their registration. It is simply the way the world, as they know it, is divided: There are Democrats, and there are Republicans. And for those who seek plum jobs in the administration, a record of party loyalty makes claims much easier to establish.

This is quite different from the way the rest of the country sees it. A third of American voters typically describe themselves as independents, and many who assert a party tie often display only a tenuous allegiance; that is what makes elections as unpredictable as they often are. In 1988, "Bush and Bentsen" bumper stickers became common in Texas, meaning that voters were supporting a Republican for president and a Democrat for the Senate; it was hardly thought to be promiscuous. Ticket splitting in Washington, however, could raise eyebrows. If you cannot state to a near certainty which party you will support in the next election, or should you exhibit a pattern of working for politicians of both parties, you may arouse suspicions of either opportunism or indecision.

In a way this attitude is mystifying. Shouldn't it be the height of principle to consider politicians on their individual merit? Shouldn't it be the proposition of blind loyalty which raises questions: a commitment to support or oppose *anyone* simply on the basis of party label? I have chosen my employers because I admired them and liked the jobs they had to offer; it should be painfully evident that I did not choose according to prevailing political winds. I went to work for Hubert Humphrey and Don Bonker, Democrats, during the Republican Ford administration. When Democrat Carter arrived in town, I went to work for John Heinz, a Republican. I continued working for John Anderson long after it had become clear that he would lose. And (as I explain below), I went back to a Democrat at the beginning of the Reagan era.

On the other hand, while umpires are supposed to be neutral, players are not. It may be that voters are entitled to shift allegiance more readily than political operatives. My wife, a Republican diehard, agrees. She thinks you can make a switch once (Reagan, after all, was a one-time Democrat), but feels that after that your political trustworthiness comes into question. This may not be of concern if you are just an ordinary voter; but if you wish to pursue politics for a living, it is something else. That is why I eventually decided to become an independent. I believe strongly in loyalty to individual candidates (I stayed with Anderson to the end, despite misgivings), and I tend to support moderate Republicans, but I don't want to feel guilty if I take the opportunity at each election to choose the better man or woman. I didn't happen to support Ronald Reagan in 1980, so that was that.

My friend Joel Perwin, who had seen administrations in Washington come and go, assured me that political time flew by quickly and that before I knew it there would be another campaign and another chance. (He himself, a Mondale aide in the late 1970s, fled to Miami at the advent of the Reagan years, there to practice law until his team came back to power; fortunately he enjoyed it, for the Democrats were to remain in the wilderness longer than many expected.) In the meantime the Hill was full of interesting opportunities, so perhaps I would just wait.

I decided it was time to pursue my long-standing ambition to work as a committee staffer on foreign policy. At last I would stop diverting myself into other transitory adventures. The Republicans had taken the Senate, and Charles Percy of Illinois was ascending to the chairmanship of the Foreign Relations Committee. Foolishly I expected that his friendship with Anderson would give me an edge for a position. But they were not close friends, and he had few slots to fill. Moreover, Percy was looking for experts who boasted credentials in the field—academics, think-tankers, State Department types—and after several weeks the answer came back: Would I be interested in serving as press secretary in his personal office? No, I said, that wasn't what I had in mind. I was surprised and disappointed and in the meantime had failed to look into other possibilities. I became anxious; I would be working in Anderson's office only until a new Congress came to town on January 3 and his term ran out.

But now the old-boy network swung into action. A friend from the House Banking Committee, Jamie Galbraith, had been tapped to be the new staff director of the Joint Economic Committee (the *joint* in the title meant that it had both House and Senate members) and invited me to join him. He had worked closely for the incoming chairman, Congressman Henry Reuss of Wisconsin, and thought my press skills might be useful in publicizing the work of the committee. Neither economics nor press relations were areas where I intended to dedicate my career, and I especially hesitated about being hired by partisan Democrats when my own predilections in the area tended toward, if not Reaganomics, at least traditional Republican views. But when one is strapped for a job, rationalizations come easy. Jamie had a brilliant mind and the warmest of personalities; on meeting Reuss, I found that he did too. The chance to work with them would be a joy. Economics would be an exciting area to work in, forming as it did a central part of the new Reagan agenda. My job would be simply a way station as I evaluated other options. It came with a fat salary ($46,000 as of 1981). And I could begin the day after I left Anderson. Still I wondered. When I asked friends about my quandary, more than one said I was being too picky: Most of the world, they pointed out, didn't love their jobs. I had become spoiled if I expected always to find a perfect position.

Finally Jamie assuaged my concern about working for the Democrats by pointing out that the press position in which I would be hired was technically a nonpartisan "administrative" slot that served the entire committee rather than Republicans or Democrats per se. I might have expected otherwise, however, when he began to refer to the two of us and Richard Kaufman (the committee's general counsel) as a "triumvirate" that would run the staff on Chairman Reuss's behalf. Accurately or not, one is assumed on the Hill to subscribe to the views of one's employer, although even modest reflection would suggest that positions and philosophies are bound on occasion to diverge. But the excitement of resuming active Hill life at the beginning of a new political era overcame my squeamishness about precise arrangements.

PART V

JOINT COMMITTEE

Democrats on the Joint Economic Committee hear testimony. Left to right, Senator Paul Sarbanes, Representative Parren Mitchell, Representative Henry Reuss (chairman), Senator Ted Kennedy. Reuss's portrait, a perquisite of retiring committee chairmen, hangs above Senator Kennedy. AZAR HAMMOND

23

A SCHOLARLY SIDE OF CONGRESS

Budget Director David Stockman made his first appearance before the Joint Economic Committee in February 1981, and Henry Reuss couldn't wait. It was only one month into the Reagan administration, and the new president was still on a honeymoon with Congress. Talk was in the air that the recent election might presage permanent realignment in the politics of American voters, and congressmen acutely sensed the trends. Despite a fifty-seat Democratic margin in the House, conservative "Boll Weevils" would soon help muster majorities for Reaganomics, and future Democratic presidential aspirants such as John Glenn and Dick Gephardt would be voting for tax-cut programs they would later renounce. Speaker O'Neill, rather than fighting, would by April simply arrange to take a trip to Australia and New Zealand.

Not Henry Reuss. Armed only with his usual grace and humor, he was eager to engage his former House colleague in intellectual battle. Everyone knew Stockman proposed to eliminate school-lunch subsidies and zero-interest student loans that served the middle class. But Reuss remembered him from his congressional days as an exponent of broader cuts. When Stockman appeared, Reuss asked why he had stopped there; weren't there some *"rich* oxen that can stand a little goring"? Stockman said he had looked, but found everything he could. Reuss, the lawyer, sought to refresh the witness's recollection. What about "general aviation"? he asked, referring to government-funded services for private planes owned by wealthy hobbyists and corporations. What about interest deductions for the purchase of second and third homes? What about continued financing of the Clinch River Breeder Reactor? Reuss said he had heard Stockman raise his "stronger voice" against these in years past, while he was raising his own "weaker one." Alternately Stockman squirmed and smiled; he knew he had been caught. These were programs he would have liked to cut, but ones with constituencies he knew even he couldn't beat.

It was one of the many entertaining, even edifying, moments I would enjoy watching Reuss produce over the next twenty months. Yet little ever came of it, a fact that was also typical. Reuss wanted to establish the committee as the congressional counterpoint to the Reagan economic revolution, and he and Jamie supplied immense creativity and grit to that end. They also had a talented staff and a high tradition. But the committee faced basic hurdles that were beyond their control: Its politics was out of sync and its mission was out of date.

The JEC, as it is universally known, was set up under the Full Employment Act of 1946 and designed as the congressional equivalent of the President's Council of Economic Advisers: a place for detached, academic analysis of broad economic policy. As such it was a product of good intentions, but over time it had outlived its original purpose. For one thing other institutions in the Congress had supplanted its role. The Congressional Research Service, the Congressional Budget Office, and the House and Senate budget committees each employed economists and others who collected data and produced regular economic studies.

The CRS and CBO were in a sense the apotheosis of congressional staff: staffs without congressmen, reports without committees. They were a testament to the belief that issues ran deeper than congressmen alone could fathom and that permanent bodies of researchers could invest legislative decisions with objective rationality. Their staffs were of high caliber, but the idea that scholarship is politically neutral was refuted in the factional battles that occurred over appointment of CBO officials, and in complaints about whether the institution gave equal time to competing schools of economic thought. Even its purest academic product would be filtered: Congressmen might have more information at their disposal (for example, they now knew the budget impact of laws they proposed), but they still had their ideologies, and they would still listen to constituencies. For all of these limitations, the development of such new resources represented a noble effort to improve the quality of congressional debate. The implication for the JEC, however, was that others were now performing on a larger scale much of its intended function.

Another problem for the JEC was a committee structure that encouraged political deadlock. Its membership consisted in equal numbers of Democrats and Republicans, evenly supplied from the House and the Senate. In theory such symmetry ensured balanced perspective, but in practice it meant either that the members agreed on points that were so unobjectionable as to be meaningless or fought along strict party lines over real differences—and produced no majority result. Reuss's position as chairman (under the committee's complex rules, the post alternated between House and Senate and was awarded to the senior committee member of the majority party in the designated chamber) was largely titular in character. He could gavel the committee to order, appoint some of its staff, select some of its hearing topics, and speak on behalf of the Democrats. But he was deprived of the power of typical committee chairmen, who could claim to represent a majority of votes; having a single additional member on his side would have allowed him to speak for the entire committee. At a time when the Reaganaut message rang loud and clear, the JEC had difficulty finding its voice.

Finally, almost alone in the Congress, the committee lacked legislative power. Its sole purpose was to survey, analyze, and report—but not to deal in actual bills or resolutions. It had a proud history, having been chaired at one time or another by Senators Hubert Humphrey, Paul Douglas, and William Proxmire. Even the immediate past chairman, Lloyd Bentsen of Texas, had taken credit for major accomplishments: He claimed to have introduced supply-side economics to the world at large, by way of recommendations in a JEC report (even if he spent 1988, as a vice-presidential candidate, denouncing the Republican version of the theory). But the committee's essential role was hortatory, and that was the problem.

This meant that one of the great imperatives of the modern Congress—the search for "visibility" through media exposure—was even stronger on our committee than usual. In large measure we existed only to the extent that we were seen, which for me as press secretary translated into pressure. But the potential was limited: The press tends to focus on reports and pronouncements that carry the prospect of concrete legislative action. Most congressmen behaved accordingly; they paid lip service to the importance of having a body in their midst devoted to reflective analysis, but it was clear that, in competition with other activities that could produce more tangible results for themselves and their constituents, the JEC had low priority.

In a sense Henry Reuss was a metaphor for the committee: a sparkling intellectual whose influence in the chamber may have suffered on that account. Despite nearly thirty years in Congress, he retained an aversion to the gamesmanship of Washington. It reflected his priorities that he had chosen to surrender the chairmanship of the House Banking Committee, which was in the thick of daily legislation, to take the reins of the more academic JEC. Nor had he adjusted well to the occasional blow-dried superficiality of a newer era. He wore baggy pants, had an air of European gentility, and possessed an old-world eloquence replete with an unending supply of colorful proverbs and erudite allusions. Once in deriding the flimsiness of Carter anti-inflationary policies, he had reached into his literary repertoire and cut out stick figures of French soldiers to aid in a graphic presentation to colleagues. He explained that, as in the 1920s novel *Beau Geste*, Carter was simply propping up "dead legionnaires" against the economic parapets to give the appearance, not the reality, of defending his outpost.

Some years later, after Congressman Reuss had retired, Margot and I visited him and his wife at a summer residence they had purchased near Figeac, France. As we drove through the winding back roads of the Dordogne Valley, we wondered what eccentric motivations had led them to take up here instead of one of the many scenic, and more convenient, locations in his home state of Wisconsin. But when our little Peugeot made its final twists and turns along the river and up a hill, we looked ahead and understood completely: In the splendor and tranquil greenery of southwestern France, the Reusses had found a small medieval tower, which they converted into a carefree and inviting retreat. Reuss seemed utterly in his element here: a scholar, a gentleman, and, in the best sense, a man out of time.

Keeping in character, his service on the JEC was in the nature of a paean to days past. Reuss was an unreconstructed New Deal liberal who delighted in the opportunity to challenge the new fashions of the Reagan era. The committee's vice chairman was Roger Jepsen, a conservative Republican. The two were an odd couple in more than ideology. Jepsen, from Iowa, was as simple and direct as Reuss was subtle and intellectual; Jepsen came from a farming background, Reuss from an old-line family of Milwaukee bankers. Both, however, had strong ideological beliefs, and this made for strains in their relationship, not to mention the smooth functioning of the committee.

Their key aides were cast perfectly. Reuss and Jamie carried on the tradition of mentor and protégé: They shared political brainwaves and could finish each other's sentences. Jamie, twenty-nine, was big, tall, red-haired, and exuberant—and no one doubted his determination to represent his boss's point of view. One day he encountered Reuss coming out of the credit union. Excitedly Reuss told him he had just caught a glimpse of David Stockman on TV telling a press conference—in the wake of bombshell confessions in the *Atlantic Monthly*—that he was resigning. "Better tell Tip," Reuss said, and before he had uttered another word, Jamie was on his way to the Speaker's office nearby. He burst in on a meeting and whispered his news in the Speaker's ear. "Ah," Tip said, thanking him for the information and then turning to the group in his office. "David Stockman has resigned," the Speaker announced, adding, "just as I had predicted." Jamie, satisfied, walked back and found Reuss, who had resumed listening to the press conference. "I suppose you've heard," Reuss said, "that he didn't resign after all." What Stockman had begun to say was that he had *offered* his resignation—but the president had not accepted. Jamie walked back sheepishly to tell the Speaker. It was all in a day's work as a protégé.

Jamie's Republican counterpart, Bruce Bartlett, was another bright and youthful staffer, whose cherubic countenance belied a dogged advocacy of Reaganomics. He had worked for Congressman Jack Kemp and helped craft his former boss's famous 33 percent tax-cut proposal. It was no doubt a matter of some annoyance that, owing to the Democrats' turn in the chairmanship, he was only "deputy" staff director despite representing as many members as Jamie. Together the two of them went at it, often regarding even small issues as worthy of pitched battle.

In this they were aided by staffs of uniformly high caliber—and partisan inclination. Republican Bob Weintraub, for example, was a lovable former college teacher who—large, mustachioed, and jolly—might have made a natural Santa Claus at an office Christmas party. His professional goal in life was to spread the gospel of monetarism, an economic theory usually espoused by orthodox conservatives. Reuss always found it amusing that Bob had previously worked for a liberal Democrat, Parren Mitchell—a tribute, he thought, to the persuasive powers of staff. Mark Policinski, another GOP aide, had an inventive mind and articulate manner, and it only enhanced his charm that he looked to all the world like the popular "Meathead" character from the television series *All in the Family*. These and other Republicans huddled in twin rows of desks in one narrow staff room, and those who opened the door into their chamber knew they needed to be prepared for intellectual combat.

The Democrats were at least an equal match. Richard Kaufman, the general counsel, had for many years served Senator Proxmire's interests on the committee and seemed in the process to have absorbed the legendary dynamism of his boss. He was a prodigious worker, always on the run between projects, his desk piled high with stacks of research materials to prove it. And Richard had a more literal case of Potomac fever than most; by night, he returned to a houseboat docked on the river in Southwest Washington. Paul Manchester was the soft-spoken and serious statistician, who seemed to have numbers available to document any necessary point. And there were gentle souls like Bill Buechner, Kent Hughes, and Mary Eccles, who had responsibility for various economic topics and quietly prepared hearings and prose contributions for their side all year long.

Although the main battles occurred between Democrats and Republicans, occasionally there were even intraparty complications. One day Senator Jepsen held a press conference to release a study on Social Security, loaded with obvious political implications. It was the first Jamie had heard of it, although he and Bruce had agreed to give each other advance notice of their respective activities. He confronted Bruce, who knew nothing of it himself. It turned out that another JEC Republican staffer, who evidently possessed his own contacts and agenda, had simply commissioned the study on his own, then presented it to Jepsen, who assumed it had run the ordinary course of approvals. Jamie, understanding of Bruce's predicament, was charitable.

One of the JEC's major projects was to produce an annual report analyzing national economic trends. In the past the committee had sometimes managed to bridge differences among its members in the interest of gaining unanimity; this was thought to produce greater public impact. Reuss made an initial effort at such bipartisanship but was not unhappy to entrench when Jepsen rebuffed him. Both sides seemed to prefer the satisfaction of uncompromising rectitude to the prospect of watered-down influence. Even so, each knew that a shift of one vote could confer "majority report" status on their side.

Accordingly Jamie worked hard trying to keep the Democrats in line and, in addition, to win over a Republican. He passed a draft report to an aide of GOP moderate Chalmers Wylie; the aide read it, liked it, and persuaded Wylie to sign. Jamie, perhaps too gleefully, told Mark Policinski of the defection, and Mark turned on the political firehoses. Almost within moments Republican Leader Bob Michel had intercepted Wylie on the House floor to warn him of the potential embarrassment to Republicans. Congresswoman Margaret Heckler, also said to be on the verge of signing, got a similar message. Both backed off quickly. Republican staffers sighed with relief, but told Jamie admiringly, "You didn't do anything we weren't trying."

In the end the committee prepared two separate and contradictory reports signed respectively by Republicans and Democrats: one an encomium to Reaganomics, the other an excoriation. Like the Great Schism of the fourteenth century, there appeared to be dual papacies, both laying claim to the JEC mantle. The press conference at which the reports would be issued took place early in Reagan's term, almost at the height of his popularity. It was held in a hearing room of the Dirksen Building, and at the appointed hour most of the Republicans filed in proudly, where they would wait on their side of the podium for a turn to face the cameras. Meanwhile Reuss stood alone on the other side. It was not a fashionable time to be a Democrat, and not one other colleague had arrived, although this was the committee's biggest moment of the year. At last Dick Bolling walked in, a poignant gesture in more than one respect. Bolling, a longtime House member, was the consummate insider, and over the years had had his differences with Reuss. His appearance now signaled something of a reconciliation. Both no doubt had come to realize that, in the face of the GOP onslaught, Democrats would have to huddle together.

I had joined Jamie for lunch that day at Mel Krupin's restaurant downtown, where we met a friend, Steve Rattner, who would cover the report for *The New York Times*. The point of such background meetings, naturally, was to suggest points for emphasis in a story, and Jamie carefully summarized the substance of the Democratic report. Of course Steve was too savvy not to recognize the more interesting news, which was the fact of two separate but equal committee reports. The next morning the front page of the *Times* carried a piece under a headline emphasizing committee deadlock. Instead of giving the Dem-

ocratic views new voice, the story made them seem weaker for the fact
that they failed to represent a majority.

Reuss, in his own witty way, needled the administration on other
matters, and while his lonely efforts did not always have major impact,
they made a contribution and they gave his staff some fun. One day
in June 1982, Murray Weidenbaum, the president's chief economist,
appeared before the committee. At the time the economy was in the
throes of recession, and Weidenbaum, seeking to portray things as being
under control, stated in prepared testimony that administration economists had in fact anticipated such reverses in their own "unpublished
worksheets." For many in the audience the comment was comforting,
but Reuss sat up; he knew that official administration forecasts of the
time had spoken not of recession but of roaring economic growth. "My
reaction to that is," Reuss said, "*now* you tell us." He asked to see the
worksheets. Weidenbaum, himself an agreeable sort, smiled but declined, citing the confidentiality of internal executive-branch memo-
randa. The worksheets did indicate a recession, as he claimed, but he
hardly wanted to supply Democrats such a smoking political gun.

Tongue firmly in cheek, Reuss's reaction was quick. Could it be
that the president was refusing a reasonable request of the Congress? If
so, he informed Weidenbaum, "you are precipitating a Constitutional
crisis!" The administration could not, he said, come before the Congress, brag about its foresight, dangle the evidence in public, and then
fail, when asked, to exhibit it. He would have to proceed, through the
Freedom of Information Act, to procure it, Reuss concluded. In fact
the matter was pursued during the next several months through extensive correspondence, and Richard Kaufman even prepared formal legal
opinions for the chairman's use. It hardly mattered when we later learned
that the committee had been in possession of the worksheets all along;
administration sources, as a courtesy, routinely supplied them to our
statistician.

Lest the usefulness of the JEC be questioned, we felt a regular if
unspoken obligation to justify our continued existence. Anxiously we
searched for topics that might increase our visibility and relevance. It
was not especially a concern if an issue had been studied several times
over elsewhere in the Congress or if a cabinet secretary had testified
on the same subject to another committee only the day before. The
JEC's attitude in this respect was hardly unique. Each committee, and
even subcommittee, has come to consider it almost a sovereign right
to hear directly from administration officials on almost any subject

(jurisdictions are only loosely observed for purposes of "informational" hearings), and to choose the most newsworthy issues which will reap the most publicity. It has become a common complaint of administration officials, not that they testify on the Hill—that is of course their obligation—but that it is with such frequency and duplication. Often an official will use identical remarks in different appearances the same day, changing only the introductory sentences so as to greet the proper committee.

On a monthly basis we scheduled hearings at which the Bureau of Labor Statistics announced employment and other data to an eager press. Senator Proxmire had established this tradition in 1970 to protect the independence of the BLS at a time when the Nixon White House, deeming the agency politically uncooperative, had tried to suppress its public exposure. Invariably the testimony was presented by Commissioner Janet Norwood, who, although exceptionally competent, spoke in a monotone that reminded me vividly of my junior high school science teacher. One day when she delivered bad news about unemployment, I recall Senator Ted Kennedy, a committee member, making a fruitless effort to induce her denunciation of Reaganomics. She demurred in almost all commentary and stuck strictly to the numbers. Still, in the view of most, such soporifics were a small price to pay for not only ensuring the integrity of economic data but also producing front-page news stories that would, in passing, typically mention the JEC.

Regularly the committee assigned the CRS and others to study issues, presenting their reports to the public on our own letterhead; colorful comments from committee members—who with the possible exception of Reuss and one or two others almost surely had not ·read the material—were contained in accompanying press releases. Sometimes this scholarship could be quite useful. On a three-year rotating cycle, for example, the JEC commissioned unclassified studies on China, the USSR, and Eastern Europe by the Central Intelligence Agency and other official bodies. This gave the academic community access to the work of government specialists without explicitly having to fund it for public use, which might not have been considered appropriate. The resulting work was regarded by sinologists and Sovietologists at the time as the best collection in existence.

Reuss himself was not a press hound. The fact that he convened hearings on such obscure topics as "Incomes Policies in Sweden and Denmark" suggested his more abstruse objectives. Still he felt protective of the committee's historic prestige and did not want JEC contributions to go unnoticed. Often he would mention particular ideas to me and suggest that I "peddle" them to my journalist friends. On one occasion when I saw him in the morning and expected to be complimented on the fact that the committee had been cited in a story on the front page of *The New York Times*, he winked: "It should have been *above* the fold."

The JEC experience provided a pleasant refresher course in economics—I heard reams of testimony in the course of its frequent hearings—but my press duties quickly became routine. Much as I admired Reuss personally, my own views about the economy were much more of the free-market variety, and I could no longer pretend that my role was merely a neutral information-dispensing function. Reuss and Jamie granted my request for a broader assignment, and I became a de facto committee economist, transferring from the JEC's main office on the ground floor of the Dirksen Building to an out-of-the-way cubbyhole in the former Immigration and Naturalization Service Building across the street. The quarters were dilapidated, but their musty odors and frayed electrical wiring were more than offset by their relative spaciousness and tranquillity. From my perspective—sharing office space with a congenial committee economist, Debbie Matz—the hectic pace of Senate life was barely visible. Here I sat in quiet reflection for the first time in my Hill years, dedicated to research and writing on broader topics than the crowded agenda and day-do-day nature of congressional activity usually allowed.

In deference to my political views, Reuss allowed me to pursue topics that would lend themselves to bipartisan committee recommendations; we chose trucking deregulation and coal development. The first issue was suggested by Jamie's wife, Lucy, an astute transportation economist who called our attention to the fact that President Reagan's well-known advocacy of deregulation was being honored only in the breach by his Interstate Commerce Commission. Some observers attributed this to the fact that the Teamsters, who benefited from continued regulation, had provided the president one of his few sources of union support during the campaign; the new ICC chairman, Reese Taylor, had in fact been their recommended candidate for the job.

I was given carte blanche to produce a hearing on the subject, although its preconceived purpose was to build a "record" in support of subsequent recommendations that would favor more aggressive deregulation. This was easy, because most experts outside the ICC seemed to be of one mind on the subject. Thus was I able to bring together an impressive collection of strange bedfellows for the occasion: former ICC members Marcus Alexis (a liberal Carter appointee) and Thomas Trantum (a moderate Republican), and Hoover Institution scholar Thomas Gale Moore (a key Reagan transportation adviser). Seated at the witness table, they vied to denounce the inefficiency and high cost of Taylor's regulatory policies.

Taylor, whom I escorted into the hearing room in the middle of all this for his opportunity at rebuttal, seemed struck by the sight of such an imposing coalition. He turned out to be a pleasant man, and more accommodating than we had expected; he asserted for the record his own belief in deregulation. Afterward I drafted a short list of fairly strong recommendations, circulated it, and had little trouble gaining unanimous support: if both consumer activists and free marketeers could sign off—the two extremes of the spectrum—so could almost any senator. Our action earned notice in the press, adding to an ongoing drumbeat for change, and materially contributed, I think, to eventual trucking reform. It was a classic instance of staffwork. Virtually all that congressmen needed to do was (on the advice of their aides and perhaps even with the help of an automatic pen) sign their names.

My project on coal development originated more directly with Reuss. He had an old friend in a senior position at one of the country's largest mining firms who had argued to him the need for accelerated exploitation of domestic coal resources to conserve petroleum. Reuss asked me to research the subject for possible committee recommendations and, despite my initial skepticism, I came to view his friend's position sympathetically, perhaps because he proved to be a major source of my information. I wrote a long study, which Reuss, with few changes, approved. Moreover, convinced that it could gain broad support, Reuss thought this an opportunity to achieve the bipartisanship that had eluded us in our annual report. Back and forth my document went among offices as aides added and subtracted points and recommendations to suit their individual interests: Some wanted to mention other energy sources important to their states, others wanted to express caveats about environmental impact, and so on. After lengthy delays and continuous compromise, I finally produced a document of sufficient ambiguity to win unanimous approval. In the process, unfortunately, it lost its edges, received scant attention, and had no discernible effect on policy.

The committee's low-key existence did have advantages. Hours were nine to five, except during recesses, when they were even shorter. No one dreamed of working weekends, vacation allowance was nearly six weeks a year, and the committee observed every conceivable holiday. It was, in some sense, a bureaucracy of intellectuals, a place for institutionalized contemplation: quite a different environment from the usual hustle and hubbub of more legislatively oriented offices.

The Congress might barely have noticed had the JEC disappeared, and in fact there were occasional calls for its abolition. The Stevenson committee on Senate reorganization, for example, recommended that course in 1977, but Congress—although it did eliminate joint committees on atomic energy and defense production—decided to keep the JEC, citing its historic role as an analyst of the president's economic program. As long as the president maintained his Council of Economic Advisers, it seemed, the "iron law of emulation" (as Senator Daniel Patrick Moynihan called it) would have its effect. Still, even if the JEC had become redundant, and something of a frill in times of feverish budget cutting, its continued existence did convey a notable symbolism: However coarse and harried the legislative process, there remained a place for reflection.

24

BURNOUT: WHERE DO ALL THE STAFFERS GO?

I knew I was getting old when summer interns started arriving at the JEC with birthdates in the 1960s. I had a faint notion that persons of that vintage would still be in diapers, but outwardly they appeared to be normal adults. One of my eccentric personal habits is to ask people their first memory of a "national" event. (Mine, for example, was seeing President Eisenhower wave from a motorcade traveling down Hollywood Way in Burbank, California, although this event may have been etched in my mind less for its historic significance than because we were let off from nursery school to witness it.)

The youngsters find this a quaint request, confirming in their minds my own doddering age, but they willingly comply. In one case an intern thought a moment and replied proudly, "Kennedy's assassination." I thought about it a moment. "That's impressive," I said. "You must have been only two years old." The intern shrugged modestly. "Wait a minute," I reconsidered. "I bet you're thinking of *Robert* Kennedy's assassination." The intern looked up puzzled: "I don't know," he said, "it was one of them."

It had always struck me that congressional staffers, even in the most senior positions, were disproportionately young people in their twenties and thirties. It took me a while to realize why. In my early days the Hill had seemed such a fast track. Compared with beginning lawyers (the career of choice for so many of my college friends) Hill aides exercised more responsibility, dealt in more exciting issues and advanced more rapidly—and for all this weren't even paid so differently. But within a few years it seemed almost a dead end. Salaries were capped, aides still worked deep in the shadow of others, and the permanence of employment, dependent as it was on the political fortunes of elected patrons, remained ever uncertain.

A lawyer friend once observed to me that Hill staffers don't "build equity." The years a lawyer has toiled tend to be counted in establishing his rank at a law firm; ultimately if he is lucky, he will achieve partnership. Hill staff, on the other hand, rely entirely on the grace of momentary benefactors. No matter how long they serve or how hard they work, they will not be promoted to member of Congress or subcommittee chairman; staff rank is a permanent caste. If they have specialized in a sufficiently narrow and commercially valuable way, the private sector may award them some degree of credit for their experience; if not, they may have little to show for their Hill years other than an interesting life. In the meantime they will always remain subordinate, and Congress can draw the line painfully. Its buildings abound with elevators, dining rooms, and other areas labeled "Members Only." Law firms confer various perks and exclusive rights upon their upper echelons, but none that I have ever seen boasts separate elevators designated "Partners Only."

As these realities unfold, hard-charging staffers are also likely to feel afflicted by mental, even moral, fatigue, usually known under the trendier name of "burnout." It is the flip side of all their years of excitement: a weariness of the battles, the pressures, the long hours, the lagging salaries, the investment of personal psyche in causes that are rarely resolved. The challenges of dealing in such a large institution as Congress, and with such grand matters of national policy, mean that one's impact may ultimately seem quite limited. For a while you feel as though you've accomplished something because your boss sent your letter to four hundred constituents, or read your statement at a hearing, or perhaps even passed your amendment. But then you see that one statement, one amendment, or even one whole law is hardly enough to reform the world as you want it. For all the delicious tactical victories, you begin to sense the gradualness, occasionally the hopelessness, of obtaining your larger objectives—perhaps the sort of revelation that made eventual stockbrokers out of antiestablishment demonstrators of the sixties.

Many of these feelings came over me finally at the JEC. At twenty-eight I began to feel that life might be passing me by. But what does a Hill staffer do at this point? I had never really thought about it. Originally I came to the Hill simply because it seemed like an interesting thing to do, not because I conceived of it as leading elsewhere. If anything, I assumed that either I would stay in government indefinitely or that things somehow would take care of themselves. Now I found myself without a profession, except as a specialist in legislation. As noted earlier, an occasional staffer seeks election to Congress—a homegrown AA can be forgiven for the self-assurance that if he was capable of supervising his boss's life, he can handle the job himself. But I lacked serious roots in a local constituency, and the idea of being a congressman had lost some of its allure. Senior staffers can at times exercise more influence than junior congressmen; they may not have the same status, but neither do they face the extreme demands on finances and family life of representatives essentially required to live in two places.

When they leave the Hill, many congressional aides aim for better-paying and more secure jobs downtown. It is an irony that young people who are attracted to Washington for the most idealistic of reasons become best qualified by their experience to work for special-interest groups (the ones willing to pay for such expertise). It has become commonplace to hear aides today talk about the cleverest ways to climb the government ladder and "cash in," taking jobs not for their inherent interest as much as for their career potential. At one level of course this is perfectly understandable. Jobs are, for most people, a practical affair, and the intelligent job seeker plays to his or her strengths. It is especially enticing to do so in Washington, where two cultures exist side by side: middle-income government workers and monied lawyers and lobbyists, many of them performing work that is very similar except for the interests they represent. But at the same time it is, I think, a distressing development, defeating the philanthropic aspect of government service and raising obvious ethical questions about conflicts of interest. Loose congressional guidelines have made it possible for aides to draft laws and then—moments later and for large fees—offer their services to clients who want to exploit or (in a legal way, naturally) evade them. Indeed if aides pause in between such roles, it may be only to take an executive-branch position that will enhance their value still further.

If I didn't want to do such things (or couldn't, because I lacked the salable expertise), the private sector in Washington gave me few other choices. Law firms? I had, at the time, no appropriate credentials. Think tanks? There was not enough of a scholar in me; the JEC had been about my limit. It had been for a life of action that I had come to town. Consulting? I lacked a useful specialization. Private parties pay for knowledge of defense contracting, not African border disputes. What else did people do in Washington? I had little idea. Among close friends, my wife and I knew only one couple both of whom had private sector occupations outside those I have described (real estate and hotel management).

Perhaps I was unduly impressionable in hearing stories of superlawyers like Clark Clifford and Joe Califano, but it seemed to me that practicing law in Washington gave one the latitude to establish a separate identity and yet remain involved in politics. My friends at law firms were by now beginning to receive substantial responsibility. There, it seemed, they would be set for life and yet, at the same time, have the freedom to transfer in and out of government as the times inspired them. Obviously it might have been a more logical sequence to go to law school at the beginning, but then, I am certain, I never would have come to the Hill and fully discovered the rewards of politics and public policy.

And thus, in the fashion of Detroit, I decided to retool for the eighties. My wife had a favorite admonition: "Don't be a short-term optimizer," by which she meant not to seek immediate gratification in favor of more important long-run interests. My calculations persuaded me that I still had the bulk of an adult career ahead of me and that a temporary detour could be worthwhile. This is the only way I can explain the fact that in September 1982, nine years out of college and having just turned thirty, I enrolled as a full-time student at Harvard Law School, commuting back to Washington on weekends (because my wife, her job, and our home were all still there). The inconvenience of this arrangement was exceeded only by its expense, and it is a wonder that Margot remained married to me through such an eccentric midlife experience.

My legal studies and political hibernation went on for three years, after which I practiced corporate law for a year. I found much of it quite interesting and became so absorbed in the culture that once, when told a colleague was leaving the firm "to go to Scotland and write," I misunderstood and wished him well at "Scotland & Wright." Law firms are hierarchical, however, and I had to begin at the bottom. Traditional legal practice focuses on appellate court opinions, not legislation, and my Hill background was not particularly useful. If anything, employers considered such experience a liability, fearing that older associates might not work uncomplainingly for endless hours in a library checking footnotes on minor legal points. They were only partly right. I hated it, but did not complain.

After a while I began exploring political activities on an extracurricular basis. At one point I was put in touch with former senator Howard Baker, then practicing law, who needed a speech on international trade for a forthcoming appearance at the Chicago Council on Foreign Relations. I did not know him, but admired his moderate brand of politics and thought the assignment might be fun. With Alton Frye, the mutual friend who introduced us, I went to Baker's office at Vinson & Elkins in downtown Washington, and for an hour we visited, discussing both trade and political topics. His quarters were posh, but they did not compare to the ornate reception rooms and crystal chandeliers of the Senate majority leader's offices, which he had previously occupied, and a constant hum of activity no longer surrounded him. Frequently during the conversation he made reference to events of his congressional days. For all the money he was being paid, his heart was elsewhere, and it did not surprise me when, sometime later, he accepted President Reagan's invitation to become White House chief of staff. We had different stations but the same perspective.

My return to Capitol Hill occurred abruptly. One day in the spring of 1986, I found myself sitting in a windowless room at the Communications Satellite Corporation in Germantown, Maryland, performing what in the legal business is euphemistically known as document discovery. It is for good reason that this exercise is considered the bane of litigators, itself a specialty in the law that I had never wanted to practice, which my firm had assured me I would not have to practice, but which, alas, I was now practicing. For purposes of a large and complex lawsuit on behalf of a client, we desired to examine all internal correspondence over many years that might bear on certain issues. Many thousands of documents fit this description. Carton by carton they were brought in to our small conference room, where half a dozen of us pored over each page, eyes glazed over, looking for key words and names. After stoic effort we would complete each carton and feel a momentary sense of satisfaction, only to see another carton wheeled in shortly. The process looked endless, and after several days the same thoughts started obsessing me: What have I done with my life? Is this what I left the Hill for? How am I ever going to get out of this room?

Jarringly the phone rang; I was barely aware that the room had a phone. It was passed to me, and the voice at the other end identified herself as the secretary to Senator Robert Dole of Kansas. "The Leader," she intoned, "wants to see you." Dole had succeeded Baker as Senate majority leader, and the term "Leader," I knew enough to realize, was the title by which the occupant of the position is widely, if somewhat pretentiously, known. "Why would he want to see *me*?" I asked. I did not know him, and the call had been completely unexpected. The secretary did not know but was sure she had the right person. I asked what might be a good day. "Today," she said. I explained that this was impossible, since I was many miles on the outskirts of the city, without my own transportation, and working on this assignment in blue jeans. "The Leader wants to see you *today*," she repeated with a finality that ended debate. I agreed, hung up the phone, and turned to my colleagues, smiling as the beauty of the thought began to register: "I'm afraid I will have to be leaving you," I announced. I opened the door, stepped over several waiting cartons, and was on my way.

By now I realized what might be afoot. I had in fact spoken many months before with Dole's former chief of staff, Rod DeArment, about an interest in volunteering—or conceivably working—for Dole if he pursued his widely reported ambition of running for president; I greatly admired Dole's intelligence and political skill. Perhaps Rod, a very gracious sort, had remembered and raised the possibility. I charged home, changed, and miraculously arrived at the appointed hour. Dole greeted me in the reception room of his Capitol suite and took me around a corner onto a secluded outdoor ledge just a few feet from the Senate chamber. Two patio chairs were set up as though this was an accustomed habitat. From such a vantage point a visitor could gaze clearly down the Washington Mall on this crisp spring day and feel almost like the majority leader himself to see so much of Washington spread out before him.

We talked for over an hour largely about his prospective presidential campaign: who his rivals would be, ideas for potential themes, strategies for the primaries. I had expected him to be coy about his plans, the usual etiquette for this stage, but he was not, and I was impressed by his directness. I suggested a Harry Truman "plain speaking" campaign motif, which seemed well suited to Dole's laconic style and the nostalgia of American voters for the haberdasher from Missouri. Dole nodded, less because he agreed, I realize now, than because he had probably heard the suggestion a hundred times before.

He seemed reluctant to broach the obvious question of what I could do for him. At first I assumed that this was because he was wisely reserved about making any offers until I had passed his oral examination; but later I was to learn that, like many politicians, he was simply uncomfortable discussing personnel matters. The problem was compounded because no one else was present either to stimulate needed discussion or follow it up; I could, at a moment like this, see the value of staff. In fact Dole only elliptically reported our conversation to his chief of staff, Sheila Burke, who was responsible in this matter, as in others, for translating his broad sentiments into concrete action. Immensely competent though she was, even Sheila could not always puzzle out her boss's intentions.

Dole mentioned to me his possible need of advice on international trade; important legislation on that topic was wending its way through the Congress. Now that I had gone to the trouble of becoming a lawyer and had acquired specialized knowledge in trade law, advising him on that subject was of greater professional interest to me than becoming a political operative again. This turned out to be the key: Soon Dole offered me a position in his office as adviser on trade, with an understanding that I might also be asked to render campaign advice. It required little deliberation to accept. I had not planned to reenlist on the Hill, but neither had I bargained for the tedium I encountered in a law firm; I could return to law practice later. For someone so eager to sample Hill experiences, the opportunity to work in the Leader's office was irresistible.

Dole did have some concern about the symbolism of hiring an ex-Anderson aide at a time when he would be trying to impress conservatives who played a strategic role in the Republican nominating process. To me the concern seemed misplaced; it was hard to believe anyone would notice. Moreover it was not as though Bob Dole and I occupied positions of equal stature. The question, it seemed to me, was not whether Dole's colleagues would think he had turned liberal because he hired *me* but whether my friends would think I had turned more conservative because I was going to work for *him*. The solution we reached was to engage me as a consultant under contract. If questioned, it could be explained that I was there only to assist in legislative

248 / IN THE SHADOW OF THE DOME

deliberations on trade, not as a permanent staff addition. I liked the idea myself because I had been thinking of going out on my own to establish a law practice. Dole could be my first client and I could try simultaneously to get more. Of course it turned out that almost every other possible client represented a potential conflict of interest, and that the twelve hours a day I worked for Dole left no time for anything else. In practice the consultant status became blurred, and I was treated identically to the other leadership staff. The office was of such exalted status that there were no LAs; I was now "counsel to the Leader." Four years before, I had felt burned out. Now I felt revived, excited to be back on the Hill, and ready to go one last time.

PART VI

MAJORITY LEADER

Now you can see why Bob Dole is the successful vote-getting politician, and I'm just a backroom aide. U.S. SENATE

25

LIFE AT THE TOP

For the next year and a half I worked in the office of the Senate majority leader, although it was euphemistically renamed the office of the "Republican Leader" when election reverses returned the Senate GOP to minority status at the beginning of 1987. It was located just a few feet down the hall from the Senate chamber and functioned as Dole's legislative nerve center, housing the handful of aides who advised him on the politics, procedures, and substance of daily floor action. (This was in addition to Dole's "personal" office, which was dedicated to home state matters and tucked away in the elephantine Hart Office Building half a mile away; although Dole epitomized the "national" senator oriented to the largest and most visible issues, he did not neglect the local concerns and voters that kept sending him back.)

Bob Dole cut an imposing figure in the Congress. He was tall and athletic and looked younger than his sixty-four years. He had been a senator since 1969 and risen to national prominence when Gerald Ford selected him as his running mate in 1976, only to attain equal notoriety when some blamed Dole's "hatchet man" manner for the ticket's defeat. His badly organized 1980 campaign for president folded after the first primary, and Dole would joke in 1988 that fortunately, because of this, no one remembered it. In 1981 he became Finance Committee chairman and seized the opportunity to rebuild his reputation. Focusing on the deficit issue, he achieved new statesmanlike stature by shepherding through the Congress a bill that closed tax loopholes and gave lobbyists fits, this at a time when neither the Reagan White House nor the Democrats wanted anything to do with raising taxes. In 1984 he became majority leader and continued to enhance his image of strong leadership.

It was Dole's style, as much as his institutional position, that explained his power. In an era when Jimmy Carter, George Bush, and so many others were derided (often unfairly) as "wimps," Dole was seen as "tough." When he made a decision, he stuck with it. He spoke his mind, but always plainly and to the point; his upright mien and hardened gaze caused few to doubt his single-minded determination to win. Even his famous lighthearted quips were delivered with a straight face. One weekend he came to the office in a cardigan sweater; normally he dressed as formally as Richard Nixon, who was known for walking the beach in a suit coat. Someone complimented Dole on his new attire as he strode near my desk. "It's worth ten points in New Hampshire," he said, walking on without cracking a smile. So devoted was he to work that a friend of mine, Roger Sandler, a photographer on assignment to take pictures of VIPs *at play*, found himself stumped. He had snapped cabinet secretaries weightlifting, other senators jogging. A session was arranged with Dole in the hot summer months. At the appointed time Roger was brought to Dole's outdoor ledge. What, Roger wondered, could his extracurricular activity be? Sitting on a chaise in the summer sun, soaking up the sun's rays, it turned out, in a starched French-cuffed shirt.

For all his dignity, Dole was not an intellectual but a man of action. Like General Eisenhower, he liked his memos brief; he wanted to know the bottom line, and he wanted boxes in which he could check off decisions. Over the years he had learned the essence of most issues and seemed to feel now that refined discussions of details were an idle use of time. He relied more on instinct than advice, a mode that has its obvious dangers but at least had the virtue of expeditiousness. He and his wife (then secretary of transportation) were often compared for the similarity of their determined manners, but in this respect they differed: As a lawyer, Elizabeth had been trained to read every last word, to the point that some complained she was *too* thorough. Her husband was more of a strategist and dealmaker, not one to pore over technical material and the fine print of legislation. (When he later explained his delay in endorsing the INF nuclear arms treaty as due to his desire to read it first—rather than because, as Vice President Bush charged, he was "straddling" the issue—those who knew him smiled at the cleverness of the defense. Saying he wanted to read things was not only perfectly sensible but an exquisite jab at those who criticized him for not doing so enough.)

Unlike other presidential candidates, who had to convince voters that they had strong executive abilities, Dole's problem was potentially the opposite: a concern that his style was somewhat authoritarian. Critics charged that he was a "one-man band"; they said his 1980 campaign, for example, had foundered on his insistence on deciding every detail. This was not my experience on the legislative side. In the absence of his own immediate interest in an issue, Dole expected us to become thoroughly conversant in the factual content and political implications of virtually everything in our domain, and intimately involved in relevant negotiations. Dole was himself a workaholic, often the first in and the last out every day, and expected the same feverish activity of his staff. He was subject to quizzing us at any time about our work, and since he seemed to have a near photographic memory for what we told him, we had some incentive to get it right.

Even without asking, we knew he wanted frequent status reports and an opportunity to approve significant action. Usually our communication was by memo, placed on the top of the television in the press room outside his personal office. Continually throughout the day he would pause there and either read the material on the spot or tuck a batch of papers under his arm and take them back inside. The procedure was remarkably efficient, making turnaround sometimes a matter of minutes, and never more than a day. (Rarely, however, would we know his reaction beyond a simple check mark at the top indicating he had read the memo, or one in the Approved/Disapproved boxes at the bottom of the page. This was not surprising; a wartime injury made writing difficult.) Dole's nearly insatiable appetite for political knowledge—What does the White House need? What do the Democrats want? Have we checked with Senator So-and-so?—was his way of identifying points of vulnerability and consensus. In turn this allowed him to put together the packages and compromises that gave him his well-deserved reputation for legislative legerdemain.

Why, then, did I constantly hear that Dole couldn't "delegate"? The reputation, I think, came from his habit of playing things close to the vest, at times frustrating his staff. Once Senator Kennedy came to see him about a bill, bringing along an aide. Dole summoned no aides of his own, nor did he tell any about his meeting until later, when for some reason he asked the name of Kennedy's aide. A colleague of mine replied politely, "I don't know," adding, after Dole left, "If I had been *invited* to the meeting, I might have known who he was talking about." Other legislators operated differently. Once when I approached Senator Bradley about supporting a Dole initiative, he excused himself from the committee dais where I had found him, asked me to stand by, and picked up a nearby phone to find out from an aide whether it conformed to his other positions. Satisfied, he signed my document, then as I walked away, called after me, still thinking solicitously of his aide: "Don't forget to send him a copy."

Dole also had a reputation for a hot temper, confirmed in the public mind after tart-tongued comments to rival George Bush during the 1988 presidential primaries. I can only say that during my tenure I never once saw him raise his voice or utter a profanity. To the contrary, the usual manifestation of his anger was a silence toward people or things that displeased him. One day a key aide said, shrugging, "I've been trying to figure out why he hasn't spoken to me in two weeks." Dole was highly controlled and had an aloofness rare in politicians; as much as he saw of his staff, his personal relationships were distant. He was not one for chitchat and rarely said "good morning"; Jo-Anne Coe, a twenty-year staff veteran, was quoted as saying that she had never heard him say "thank you." Once when he wrote "good" above someone's memo, more than one colleague in the office suggested framing it. He was a strong, silent type and seemed to assume that everyone else was too. Early on, Dole invited me to join him one evening at an event downtown, so naturally I asked if I could ride with him; the majority leader was, after all, supplied with a car and driver. He nodded, and the ride—he sat in the front and I shared the back with his pet schnauzer "Leader"—was quite pleasant, although unaccompanied by elaborate dialogue. But when I recounted the incident later, other staff members were startled to learn of my audacity. Asking for personal accommodation of this nature was just not done.

Perhaps it was this very sense of discipline and occasional sternness that gave him such an impressive presence; one staffer said she felt such respect for him that her instinct was to stand when he entered the room. Indeed we all held our boss in awe, and I found myself admiring him immensely. His succinctness and candor were refreshing, his acerbic tongue a source of constant amusement, and his quick, intuitive grasp of issues and process a strength that inspired confidence in his ability to govern and lead. Even his humor was not to be underestimated. Once I made the mistake of thinking I could write jokes for him. He was giving a speech at a dinner at the Brookings Institution, and I imagined that for such an occasion they would need to be particularly subtle and sophisticated. I wrote out several possibilities, each a paragraph or two long. Dole did me the honor of sitting down and reading them. "Good try," he said charitably, but handing them back. "People won't follow them." Of course I was sure he was wrong, and feared he would turn to his ordinary repertoire. We went to the dinner that evening, and he used the standbys he had relied on in every speech that month. For example, a major highway bill had just passed, and he began by saying, "Elizabeth would have been here but she was busy changing fifty-five-mile-per-hour signs." I braced for silence, but instead heard a roar.

And the quips came constantly. Once he passed the health affairs adviser near me, at a time when "Retin-A" formula was being ballyhooed as a means of erasing facial lines. "Have they got any of that in shaving cream yet?" he asked. Someone at a fundraiser would ask what it was like being part of a Washington power couple, and he would tell an affectionate story about Elizabeth. *People* magazine had come to do a story, he said, and asked that they pose for a photograph making the bed. Laughter. "But they didn't know the half of it," he would add. "Elizabeth was only helping me because they were taking the picture." The audience would convulse. But his one-liners were not always so comical, and sometimes helped to convey the emotion that he clearly possessed but often held back. One day a senior campaign adviser asked Dole why he was taking such a prominent position on AIDS; Dole was trying to put together legislation on the subject at a time when others thought it too politically controversial. "Because people are dying," he said to a group of assembled aides. Then as he turned around and headed to his office, he added, not even looking back, "Sometimes you just have to do what's right."

Dole's leadership staff was headed by Sheila Burke, a woman of extraordinary capability who, although only my own age, had self-possessed interpersonal skills that gave her an air of maturity well beyond her years. She was a onetime nurse who had worked on health issues for Dole during his tenure as Finance Committee chairman, and her natural talent as chief of staff made me wonder whether the best experience for the pressure-cooker environment of the Hill might not be precisely hers: someone used to dealing with the pains and trauma of emergency room cases. Her reserved manner in a way matched Dole's, but she was unfailingly courteous and fair-minded; she brought to her job enormous absorptive capacity for detail, limitless patience and stamina, and almost total unflappability. She would have made a superb staff director for anyone, but seemed an especially perfect fit for such a demanding boss.

Sheila was assisted most closely in her duties by an aide imported from a House leadership office, Jim Whittinghill, whose easygoing and folksy manner was evident in his custom of wearing cowboy boots, talking romantically of places like Montana and Texas, and keeping at his desk, to the horror of the nightly cleaning staff, a glass-encased stuffed rattlesnake. Whit helped monitor floor activities on an almost minute-by-minute basis. Walt Riker, the mustachioed press secretary, parried endless media requests for Dole's time and, often as a substitute, churned out nonstop press releases and other quotable epigrams on Dole's behalf; his deputy, Dale Tate, was a onetime *Congressional Quarterly* reporter who specialized in writing Dole's more formal speech texts. The remainder of the professional staff consisted of accomplished specialists: health advisers Marie Michnich and successor Lynn Drake (a practicing dermatologist); defense expert Tom Carter, an ex-military aide to the president who had been entrusted to carry the black box of nuclear codes; and gurus of tax law, Rich Belas, and foreign policy, Al Lehn. David Taylor operated the computer, diligently punching in form letters and calling up legislative data, when he and Walt were not quizzing each other on Duke basketball statistics.

One special-purpose aide proved particularly valuable. Bob Dove, the previous Senate parliamentarian, served as a consultant on floor procedure. Despite a gentle academic nature, he had been abruptly deposed by Democratic majority leader Robert Byrd with the change in Senate leadership; evidently his sin had been to put his encyclopedic knowledge at the disposal of Dole, which he assumed to be his professional obligation. Byrd had fumed under Dole's regime and perhaps thought Bob's removal would cleanse the chamber of the influences he despised. If so, it had just the opposite effect, for Dole cleverly hired Dove for his personal artillery corps; Byrd had violated the time-honored political principle that writer Chris Matthews has well described: "Hug your enemies." All day long Bob sat at his desk, eyes glued to closed-circuit TV coverage of floor proceedings, ready at an instant to explain the baffling convolutions of Senate procedure and to advise Dole on either extricating the GOP from parliamentary quagmires or helping to mire the Democrats in one of their own. He contributed even to subtle psychological warfare: The very sight of him walking onto the Senate floor sent chills down Democratic spines.

For my part I had charge of international trade and occasional economic issues and, like everyone, pinch-hit when gaps in coverage arose. Dole's work habits dictated our own. I would arrive usually by 7:30, by which time others might already have started the coffee percolating, and Dole might well have convened a breakfast meeting with visitors in an adjoining conference room. Our full forces would be in position by 8:30, entrenched for the rest of the day in the middle of the Senate legislative maelstrom. I made up for my virtuous arrival time by trying to leave "early," at 6:30 or 7:00 in the evening, a necessity if I were to see my small children before they went to bed. Others on the staff remained until late into the evening, sometimes ordering in pizza and almost literally ensuring that the lights of the Senate were turned out, which on occasion did not occur until midnight or later.

Our quarters were cramped in the classic manner of Congress, perhaps even more than usual because we occupied the most prime real estate of Capitol Hill. Many visitors imagine that congressmen and their staffs maintain offices in the main Capitol building, near the Rotunda under the lofty granite dome. Only the leadership staffs do so; they need to be in constant proximity to their bosses, who spend much of their day on the chamber floors. (To be precise, senior senators are granted small, unmarked "hideaways" in the back halls where they can take refuge from the sometimes oppressive demands of their own staffs.) Our offices were far more ornamental than the buildings other senators inhabited on the outskirts of the Capitol. Those who came to see us would get a taste of our status at the appointments desk on the ground floor; while ordinary tourists had relatively unrestricted freedom of movement at that level, only visitors whose names we had cleared in advance were allowed to proceed to our second-floor suite. This had a necessary security purpose—a small bomb had exploded some years before in a hall outside the Senate chamber (no one was injured)—but it also lent our office neighborhood an aura of prestigious exclusivity.

Appearing at the front door of the Leader's enclave, guests would be greeted by attentive receptionists, who seated them in Dole's own elegant reception room while they waited to see us. There they could peruse photo albums of his recent overseas trips, page through large and glossy picture books on Kansas, New Hampshire, and Iowa, which just happened to grace the coffee table, or wonder about the identity and function of an official-looking young man often seated at a rococo desk in the back of the room. (It was Dean Burridge, an aide who accompanied Dole much of the day, holding loose papers, reminding him of impending appointments, coordinating the movements of car and driver, nudging away unwanted visitors, and otherwise providing the aura of a mini-entourage.) The prized moment would be catching a sudden glimpse of Dole himself entering or leaving his adjoining inner office, a reminder that despite the ceremonial appearance of this ornate space, it actually served real-life functions. (In fact the line sometimes blurred: Dole often played host in this room to illustrious visitors, such as baseball greats of yesteryear in town for an old-timers' game, and in the halls nearby I had seen special tours accorded Brooke Shields, Ginger Rogers, and Woody Allen. Was this "real life"?)

Meanwhile our visitors, having beheld such splendor, were in store for disappointment when escorted back into our cozy legislative den. There we would need to find empty chairs to pull up alongside us, making sure to move the wastebaskets so as not to block the well-traveled paths among our desks. The incommodiousness of these circumstances was partially redeemed by vaulted ceilings and imposing chandeliers; at least we could claim our offices had character.

Yet we were to be grateful even for these few square feet. When we went into minority status, Senator Byrd let it be known that he intended to make new allocations of space, cutting us back drastically and even moving our location. On one occasion, perhaps merely as a negotiating tactic, he showed Dole the new quarters he had in mind for a part of the staff: rooms buried deep in the Capitol basement and used in a different era, we learned, as the Senate's coal bin. Thus did Byrd, not for the first time, make the mistake of challenging Dole's mettle; a standoff was to follow for many weeks. We felt particularly affronted because Dole's predecessor, Howard Baker, had been charitable enough to let Byrd keep his offices in 1980 when Byrd had made his own transition from majority to minority ranks. But Byrd argued that the Republicans in the meantime had greatly expanded the majority leader's space and that it was time to restore it to previous dimensions. In the end we agreed to having one room lopped off the suite, and managed to fit in again, albeit more snugly than before. But elections, we realized, can do worse things to people, and soon we had forgotten this particular dogfight as much larger battles beckoned.

The personalities of Bob Dole and Robert Byrd were perfect foils for each other. Both were capable of high statesmanship when crisis required; but both were also accomplished legislative duelists who were not above using every parliamentary weapon to advance a cause. Byrd was alternately charming and ornery. With his pompadour gray hair and a slow, mellifluous voice that pronounced every word ever so precisely, he was a colorful figure as he ambled up and down the center aisle of the Senate floor telling a hushed gallery—usually the senators themselves weren't there—his beloved historical anecdotes. But he could also be a schoolmarm, lecturing colleagues about the need to speed up business, although he himself was sometimes the culprit who consumed the most time. Indeed he had won the Democratic whip's job from Ted Kennedy years before after impressing colleagues with his ability to spend endless hours on the floor performing thankless parliamentary drudgery.

Yet he was the object of much affection for his countrified and personable manner; he was proud of his rural West Virginia background and claimed to like nothing more than playing a fiddle. Once, my brother-in-law in Utah told me that Senator Byrd would be coming out both to speak and play music. A fine fiddler himself, Kennard had been invited to back Byrd up and asked me to find out in advance "if he wants to twin a number." It took some courage on my part to pose the question, having no idea what it meant and concerned about its strange-sounding implications. But I did so, and Byrd, so often dour, broke into a radiant smile, delighted that someone else was familiar with such expressions. Leaving the solemn floor proceedings behind, he motioned me to follow him outside the chamber to his suite down the hall. Without stopping to explain, he brought me past a cordon of secretaries to his innermost office and sat me down, fumbling through the drawers of his desk. After a minute or two he found what he wanted and handed me a wrapped package. "I've recorded my music," he explained proudly. "Promise me you'll play it." I was happy to, although bluegrass is not exactly my thing. But when I opened the gift later, it turned out to be an ancient eight-track cartridge; I found it impossible to locate an appropriate tape player, and I wondered whether Byrd, generous though he was, had known that his tape was technologically obsolete. Some might have considered it a metaphor for his approach to the Senate. He was not a television-age politician, but a sincere and old-fashioned one.

Dole lacked Byrd's eloquence, but was much quicker and sharper-edged; more often than not, he seemed to get the better of their exchanges. On one occasion Byrd took to the floor to complain of Dole's canny parliamentary tactics. "I did not become majority leader to lose," Dole retorted. Even when roles reversed, and Byrd became majority leader again, Dole resourcefully devised new strategies, most notably the threat of procedural filibuster, giving the minority an influence well beyond its electoral proportions. Despite a 54–46 Democratic margin, Byrd saw his agenda stall quickly and squirmed as the world expressed bewilderment at his powerlessness.

The defense-bill debate of 1987 was a classic confrontation between Byrd and Dole, showing the power and continuing evolution of parliamentary technique. The legislation limited testing of President Reagan's Strategic Defense Initiative and, as such, was anathema to loyal Republicans. In older days a filibuster typically consisted of marathon speeches by hoary senators relying on Senate rules that required unanimity among members to proceed with business. Today delays are more often created through procedural devices: roll calls, quorum calls, objections, and appeals. To avoid an expected filibuster on the defense bill, Senator Byrd attempted his own parliamentary gambit. He sought to take up the bill during "morning hour" (a period of routine speeches technically allowed to last up to two hours), during which motions to proceed to bills were, under Senate rules, "nondebatable."

But Byrd did not correctly reckon either the knowledge of Bob Dove, the parliamentary whiz on our staff, or the determination of Bob Dole. An obscure rule, it came to light, allowed senators to ask to be excused from voting, and to interrupt a roll call to explain their request. On the morning that Byrd intended to bring the bill to the floor, GOP senators sprang their attack: During an otherwise ordinary vote to approve the previous day's *Journal*, they took turns asking to be excused from voting and, one by one, to explain why. Byrd objected that such tactics were dilatory, but his point, while legitimate, was self-defeating: Objections were heard to his objection, roll calls were taken, then appeals. The presiding officer (a junior senator, as usual, was assigned such dreary duty) barely understood what was happening, but fortunately could rely on whispered instructions from expert staff. The upshot was that the bill could not be brought up without either a "unanimous consent" order or a "cloture vote" supported by sixty senators to prevent further filibuster. A stalemate on the issue ensued for four months (Byrd allowed the Senate to go on to other things) until the GOP relented when some of its members let it be known they would consider supporting cloture. SDI was at last taken up on its merits, and a compromise was eventually signed into law.

On other matters as well the administration expected its party leader to serve the president's interests, and of course Dole recognized both that obligation and the personal dividends of loyalty. Contributing to the success of a Republican president would inevitably reflect well on the entire party, and even in defeat he could win admiration for political chivalry. Thus did Senator Dole carry water on several prominent and unpopular issues—vetoes of the highway bill and sanctions on South Africa, as well as the Robert Bork and Daniel Manion judicial nominations—where he might sooner have reversed course and cut his losses.

Other Republicans were not so gallant. Thirteen of them refused to back the president in his opposition to the highway bill, even in the aftermath of the Iran-Contra scandal, when a defeat gravely threatened his congressional standing. One afternoon Reagan showed up on the Hill, first for a meeting in Dole's office, then a larger one with recalcitrant senators across the hall in the "old Supreme Court chamber," usually roped off as an historic point of interest for tourists. A personal lobbying mission by the president was virtually unprecedented, and some senators were persuaded to switch their votes if the entire group did so. But still there were holdouts, and the strategy collapsed; the president left the Hill having only magnified his failure. Through it all, Dole's political loyalty stood out.

After the Bork nomination to the Supreme Court was defeated, the administration plunged ahead with another provocative candidate, but Dole again carried on gamely. That he considered Douglas Ginsburg too inexperienced for such high appointment was made clear by his sardonic public references to "this young man," even as he defended him. On the afternoon when the nominee confessed to smoking marijuana as a law school professor, Dole appeared in my part of the office and instructed nearby aides, "Get Ginsburg," who was in the next room. It was a curt manner of expression even for a man of few words; Dole, in his tight-lipped way, was steaming. He advised the White House of the political futility of further battle, but did not publicly retreat until word came from the president. When Dole made a commitment, he could be counted on.

At the same time there were issues where the calculations of presidential politics interceded and Dole set his own course. He fought the administration vigorously, for example, over its nomination for ambassador to Mozambique; the nominee was an innocent caught in the middle, but the vote was a convenient way to protest U.S. policy toward that country, a matter of concern to conservative colleagues whom Dole actively courted. Similarly he battled to extend subsidized commodity sales to the Soviet Union despite furious objections from Secretary of State George Shultz that he was tampering with sensitive foreign-policy positions for transparent political gain; Dole's determination to boost farm exports, everyone knew, had to do not only with his natural agrarian sympathies as senator from Kansas but also his acute knowledge that the first presidential caucus would be held in grain-rich Iowa.

That these matters fell outside my area of international trade did not mean I was wholly detached. The leadership staff was a tight-knit group. Sheila held frequent staff meetings at the long conference table in her office, at which time we would each contribute a précis of what was happening in our respective sphere and were invited to comment on office activities generally; the unstated objective, naturally enough, was how to advance Dole's legislative and political agendas. Later in the day the same table would often be occupied by representatives of other Senate staffs, or even senators themselves, stitching together "unanimous consent" agreements that governed floor debate, or amendments, or the many clever compromises that Dole's leadership produced.

Life in the Leader's office gave old experiences a new twist. Years before, as an ordinary LA, I was free at most times to walk onto the Senate floor, but I needed first to sign in opposite the Senate reception room and then clip a large badge onto the breast pocket of my suit coat. For all the status of mingling in the company of senators, displaying such a thing made me feel like a prisoner wearing striped clothes in polite society. Of leadership staff, however, no badges were required; we could use the entrance nearest our office, where the plain-clothed officers who guarded it would recognize and wave us through.

I missed another peculiar ritual. When bells rang for a vote, LAs often rushed to position themselves near the bank of elevators on the second story of the Capitol, opposite the Senate floor. As the door of the "Senators Only" elevator opened, their bosses would pour out, having come up from the tram in the basement that carried them from their offices. If they did not know what they were voting on (votes occurred frequently throughout the day, and it was hard to keep track), and if an aide had not already intercepted them en route, they would glance to the side to see if someone were waiting. A staffer might wave and run up for a huddled conference behind a pillar; or if the senator were in a hurry to make the fifteen-minute deadline for voting, he might simply expect a quick thumbs-up or thumbs-down gesture.

In compressing their advice so crudely, of course, aides were not merely expressing their own arbitrary notions as to a "correct" vote; more often they were translating what they knew to be their bosses' positions. A senator might know, for example, that an impending vote concerned Social Security cost-of-living increases; but he might not know that it was phrased as a Hollings motion to table a Mitchell substitute to an Inouye amendment. In addition an aide might be able to provide critical last-minute information, such as the fact that an important constituency group had just phoned pleading for support or that Senator So-and-so (whom the aide's boss particularly respected on the issue) was recommending a particular position. In the aide's absence other cues were available. A senator could expect to be greeted on the floor by colleagues proselytizing pro and con; he could walk to the well of the chamber and examine the tally sheets to see how other senators had already voted; or he could find Howard Green, or one of the other Republican or Democratic cloakroom attendants, to ask for either basic factual information or candid political advice. Now that I worked for the Leader, I didn't have to run over to the Capitol anymore and idle next to the elevators. I was already in the area, and I knew exactly where my boss would be: on the floor himself and supremely knowledgeable about the vote taking place.

The hallowed custom of editing transcripts of floor debate was also greatly simplified. Many Senate LAs routinely go into the clerk's office minutes after their bosses speak to emend their remarks. Stenographers walk the Senate floor taking shorthand on quaint machines that they carry strapped from their necks like ice-cream vendors at the ballpark; afterward, their notes are quickly transcribed for inspection by aides before going to the Government Printing Office to be incorporated into the *Congressional Record*, which will appear on every office's doorstep the next morning. In theory aides are supposed to review the transcripts only for grammatical or factual errors, but the fact that in practice even wholesale changes can be made is suggested by the presence of scissors and tape on the table in the middle of the clerk's room where the aides do their work.

Indeed it is not uncommon simply for a senator to say what he

264 / IN THE SHADOW OF THE DOME

wants, hand in a prepared text that he does not actually use, and expect the aide to go in and reconcile everything afterward. The *Record*
is so notoriously inaccurate that, in one macabre instance, a speech
by the late House majority leader Hale Boggs appeared as part of a
debate that was stated to have taken place two days after he had per-
ished in an airplane accident over Alaska. In 1989, when Speaker Jim
Wright was criticized for touting his wife's employer in a piece inserted
into the *Record*, his defense was that everyone does such things and
that they shouldn't be taken seriously—even though each page costs
hundreds of dollars to print. In this matter there were now two differences in Dole's office. First, owing to the Leader's status, transcripts
of debate were walked over to us, making a visit to the clerk's office
unnecessary; and, more importantly, Dole spoke so frequently and was
so unconcerned about appearances in the *Record* that we simply let
most of his remarks stand as they were actually uttered, for the Congress nearly an unheard-of thing.

26

SOUND BITES

When the Iran-Contra scandal came to light in late 1986, Republican presidential candidates found themselves in a quandary. They could hardly defend such bizarre activities, but neither could they desert a beleaguered president of their own party. Dole was scheduled to appear on a Sunday morning news show shortly after, and I flipped it on, curious to know how he would navigate among the shoals. His proposal was bold: Bring Congress back from its Christmas adjournment to address the crisis. To me the idea seemed out of proportion to a story that was still unfolding and, in any case, of questionable usefulness. What could Congress do in a couple of days, other than resolving to investigate further? It did not surprise me to learn the next day that, characteristically, Dole had consulted no staff member on the idea and simply floated it for the first time on live TV.

As usual, however, he proved to be two steps ahead; at a time when Ronald Reagan was about to suffer his first real loss of public confidence, it was a brilliant political stroke, bridging seemingly inconsistent positions. On the one hand, the press hailed it (both at the time and for months afterward) as evidence of Dole's serious concern about the scandal—and therefore his independence of the White House; and yet the White House also could claim to be pleased, saying it would help exonerate the president and restore his strength. No such session was ever held, but it was enough simply to have proposed it.

Both the Congress and the modern presidential campaign have become, in large measure, a contest for visibility: quotes in the morning paper, "sound bites" on the evening news. Often it is a quicker and simpler means of influencing policy than the gradual and laborious process of legislating; and because it may also be more entertaining, the press is a willing accomplice. Does a congressman think nuclear power plants need greater safeguards, or that the minimum wage is too low? If so, he can take action that day: issue a press release, give a speech on the floor, arrange to be interviewed by newsmen, make a pointed remark in committee. Aides thus spend much of their time crafting positions and statements with an eye to "getting press," usually in their districts, where it does the most electoral good, or nationally, if their bosses have larger ambitions. Even when congressmen take the trouble to devise bills and amendments, it may be not because they want them passed but because they want to advertise the fact that they are "out front" on an issue. In 1987 of over 6,500 bills introduced, fewer than 200 were enacted; congressmen knew the probabilities when they dropped their ideas in the hopper.

The approach is not as cynical as it may seem. Because procedural wrangling has become more common, legislation has jammed up, and the Congress may go for long stretches without accomplishing much. Many of its votes now concern noncontroversial matters, such as commemorative resolutions; at the same time it has frequently failed to approve individual appropriations bills. For the first several months of 1989 the most important vote taken on the House floor concerned the proposed congressional pay raise. Avoiding the legislative quagmire and simply sending a message through the press may stir the public and precipitate far more immediate administrative action than Congress could hope to force by law.

Admittedly there is a tendency, as a result, to focus only on "hot" topics, issues of the month that make the headlines; there is also an element of "negative campaigning," such as proved so effective in recent election battles. Just as the 1988 presidential campaign seemed at times to turn on such issues as Joe Biden's plagiarism and Gary Hart's extramarital activities—not to mention Mike Dukakis's associations with Willie Horton, the Pledge of Allegiance, and the ACLU—the Congress now spends much of its energy debating highly personal (but titillating) matters, such as the drinking habits of cabinet nominee John Tower and the ethical practices of Speaker Jim Wright. Perhaps Ronald Reagan's success at presidential choreography inspired the Congress to think along new lines. Many Democratic senators privately expressed dissatisfaction that Majority Leader Byrd and other candidates who vied to succeed him were not "telegenic" enough; by the same token Congressman Newt Gingrich, in his campaign for house minority whip, was trumpeted as the natural leader of the C-SPAN generation.

One of Dole's privileges was a reserved period every morning to pronounce on national events. This "Leader time" was an opportunity to gain useful press attention; it was left to the staff to scour the newspapers for timely ideas and draft daily statements. There were only so many subjects to address and so many slants: I told Dole one day that I had heard him denounce Nicaraguan junta leader Daniel Ortega so many times that I was beginning to feel sympathy for the villain of these set pieces. Al Lehn, the foreign-policy adviser, was a one-man assembly line for such statements; more than anyone else he had learned the simple, jabbing style that Dole liked. Still, the right statement at the right time could command front-page or even—and this was the jackpot—TV news coverage. Did Dole think the Federal Reserve should lower the discount rate, or that Gorbachev's position on removing troops from Eastern Europe should be treated skeptically? The microphones and cameras were right there, ready for him to say so. Perhaps no single story would catapult him to front-runner status, but the unstated principle in presidential campaigns, especially with free resources available, is that every little bit helps.

Although a school of thought existed that the way to run for president was to be unemployed (e.g., Carter in 1976, Reagan and Bush in 1980) so as to be free to spend full time campaigning in barbershops and Kiwanis clubs, serving in Congress seemed to offer at least as many useful opportunities. Indeed if I wanted to give visitors to the Capitol an authentic feel for daily life there, nothing impressed them so much as a tour through the catacomblike newsrooms surrounding both the House and the Senate. In one large area a dozen "print" reporters would be banging out stories at their typewriters; around the corner, others busily phoning in to editors; and everywhere the *click-clack*ing of wire-service tapes and the chatter of journalists transmitting and discussing the day's events. The main lounge featured a large display rack showing the latest press releases from every office. DODD BLASTS ADMINISTRATION ACTION ON NICARAGUA, one senator's release might scream; WIRTH SAYS GLOBAL WARMING A DANGER, another might announce, more sedately. Suddenly a voice would come over the public address system: "Senator Rudman will be available at three P.M. at the conference table to answer questions on his budget proposal." Upstairs several senators might at that moment be crowding around a lectern in the TV gallery, ready to announce a new bill or react to a news event. And if these locations were not convenient, interviews could be conducted in individual members' offices or, more scenically, on the east Capitol lawn. Should legitimate media be insufficient, canned news feeds could be produced in the extensive House and Senate recording studios and beamed by satellite to the district.

Walt Riker was Dole's capable press secretary, helping to guide him through these precincts, but in a real sense Dole was his own. If the senator went to the White House, he often did so alone; unlike many press secretaries who never leave their boss's side, Walt would have to rely for his information on cable TV news or Dole's own elliptical reports phoned in from his limousine en route back. In addition Dole kept his own counsel about his plans and strategies and resisted briefings and coachings of staff. Yet although sparing in granting press access, his interviews were models of candor and intelligence, and he was a favorite of reporters; it was forgivable if he thought he could handle himself adeptly without the protective assistance of others.

Moreover Dole had superb press instincts, as the position he devised on the Iran-Contra affair suggested. I never doubted Dole's political judgment after November 1986. On the day of congressional elections, many observers said the overall contest was too close to call. Dole came into the office early that morning and walked by my desk, where several of us were making last-minute bets. Some thought the elections would be a draw between the parties; the more pessimistic wagered that two or three GOP seats could be lost. We looked to Dole to settle our dispute. Categorically he stated that eight Republican senators would be defeated. Although he had been traveling widely on behalf of GOP candidates and obviously had his ear to the ground, it was a prediction so contrary to conventional wisdom that we assumed for much of the day he had been joking; he was, after all, very good at keeping a straight face. Unfortunately it turned out that he had hit it on the nose.

Still, a problem in the press area arose because Dole could not be everywhere at once. It was not that he didn't try. Even more than other workaholic senators, he was simply not content unless in motion. Often on weekdays he would put in a full legislative day only to board a chartered plane in the evening for a function in New Hampshire or Iowa, then return after midnight. On perhaps the most extreme occasion he spoke on the Senate floor one afternoon, went for the evening to Los Angeles, and was in the office again early the next morning for a breakfast meeting. (The motivation for the trip was compelling: a bash of Hollywood entertainment moguls, netting over $1 million for his campaign.) Fortunately for Dole, his wife Elizabeth was a horse of the same stripe, and neither seemed to complain if their crazy schedules allowed them to cross paths only occasionally on the road or on a rare Sunday of rest at their Watergate apartment.

But I personally received numerous calls from reporters frustrated that they could not get through to Dole nor obtain the scoops they wanted from his press office; it did not relieve their annoyance that I was of little help either. Good relations between journalists and public officials are neither trivial nor accidental. Secretaries of state James Baker and Henry Kissinger are legendary examples of Washingtonians who earned the admiration of the city's press corps—and spent several hours a day doing so. If Dole did not have the time or inclination, then it may be he needed staff all the more. A candidate is expected to have surrogates available to speak for him, confidants to explain his purposes, advisers to describe his strategy. Overall they build impressions of his character and his chances. Reporters aim to be objective, but they are human and have their favorites; these prejudices are daily played out in newspaper columns and on TV. In Dole's case the press seemed to feel an ambivalence between its obligation to scrutinize front-runners (the category in which Dole had honorary status despite Bush's actual lead) and a personal feeling that he would make a good president. It was important to give them attention, and reporters told me (even if their view on the subject was self-serving) that Dole would have been better off investing his press staff with greater authority.

Dole was also, like many politicians, his own speechwriter. Early on I saw him address a crowd of several thousand in the ballroom of the Washington Hilton. He was a big hit, witty and entertaining, and established immediate rapport with his audience; as I stood in the back of the hall, I found myself laughing in anticipation of jokes I had heard before. Yet he all but ignored the announced topic—small business—despite vast preparations by staff. It was hard to blame him. In the week before, a half dozen of us had contributed components for a formal speech, then edited the whole amalgam into polished prose, then (when word came back that Dole wanted something more informal) transformed them into fragmentary "talking points." Not knowing what exactly he wanted to say, we finally presented him with forty-two pages of material, which he had a chance to look at only as he was heading to his car. He lugged this compendium to the podium, but ultimately had the good judgment not to stand before the huge audience trying to turn all the pages.

The next day I composed a memo diplomatically suggesting that in the future he give us clearer and earlier guidance on what he wanted so that we could provide him with more usable material. He was equally diplomatic, calling me into his office along with Sheila and Walt, saying the idea was well taken, and suggesting that we work on improving our procedures. I was elated for a moment to imagine that I had exerted influence on a situation so widely lamented, until I announced my feat to Dale Tate, one of Dole's veteran assistants, who informed me that half of the office had made similar recommendations in the past when they too were new on the job.

It is probably inevitable that, working for intelligent and self-confident politicians, staff perform some superfluous functions. In compiling background materials for one of Dole's debate appearances, for example, our job was to prepare him for virtually any question he might be asked. As a result, he was inundated with issue briefs and position papers that he might well have used to deliver lengthy academic discourses. In fact he would be asked only two or three questions and allotted all of forty-five seconds each to answer. Moreover, in such a short span anything highly specific would be too dry to keep the audience's attention; and if general comments were in order, Dole's best material was extemporaneous.

Everyone recognized the disadvantages of drafting-by-committee, but the search for a single person or formula to guide the effort was challenging. Dole, proud of his humble roots, resisted fancy oratory, yet was frequently urged by campaign advisers to offer loftier themes; for a while intrastaff debates raged over whether he needed what some called "vision." (By now we had collected an impressive set of political strategists—former Reagan campaign manager John Sears and former Bush adviser David Keene among them—but if anything, this assured only frequently divided opinion.) Ultimately a compromise was reached: Dole would speak more about his personal background and early experiences in the hope that this might demonstrate a heartland sense of values that could substitute for soaring rhetoric.

It had always seemed to me that Dole's *actions* told his vision of governance: that of someone with a knack for practical rather than ideological solutions, a battler who could also bridge—factions, parties, branches. The testament to this was his startling ability to draw support from across the political spectrum. As in my days with Anderson, I heard repeatedly from Democrats and Independents that he was the one Republican candidate they could consider supporting. I might have feared this as the kiss of death in the context of Republican primaries, but it so happened that he also maintained good relations with Jesse Helms and many others of the party's right wing. This feat was hard to explain, except perhaps in terms of Dole's ability to give each group valuable support on certain issues even as he took exception with them on others. He did not promise everything to everybody but was able to give *most* groups *something*.

Dole had won favor among liberals, for example, for his longtime support on issues related to food stamps, voting rights, and the handicapped. He had become a darling of moderates in the early 1980s for his outspoken skepticism toward prevailing supply-side economics. ("The good news," he said, "is that a bus carrying supply-siders went off a cliff. The bad news is a couple of the seats were empty.") And conservatives in his party, such as Helms and Jeane Kirkpatrick, applauded his foreign-policy positions, which were almost strident in their anticommunism. Moreover, his reputation for pragmatism meant that he was often forgiven for positions thought to be motivated by electoral necessity. (It has been said in this regard that Washington sooner excuses insincerity than sincerity.) Thus liberals accepted his pro-life and pro-Contra stands because they believed them to be essential in courting conservative Republicans during the primaries; and conservatives averted their eyes to Dole's progressive civil-rights record because they appreciated the needs of a general election.

But whatever his themes and positions, humor remained Dole's fallback. Fortunately not everyone was as familiar with his repertoire as his staff. Often he opened with a story about the time he had been driving through Kansas en route to a campaign speech and over the radio heard an announcer describing the event. The announcer said it would feature Senator "Doyle," who, he would explain, had sustained a *head* injury in the war and then gone on—this would be stated in a tone implying there was a connection—to run for Congress. As if the radio announcement had not been discouraging enough, he had finally arrived at the speech to find a group of farmers sitting in the front row wearing "Dump Dole" caps. The story had no real punchline, but such a series of folksy self-put-downs would be enough to have the audience laughing. Still, as much as we usually enjoyed Dole's jokes, this one was pretty well worn, and we groaned to hear it repeated.

One weekend Dole was scheduled to join his fellow candidates in making five-minute speeches to a large audience in New Hampshire. Given the importance of the occasion, he asked several of us to prepare separate sets of remarks from which he might choose, and of course we all vied to produce the most elegant and insightful material we could, eager for the distinction of having him use our work. He took the batch of our efforts with him in the afternoon as he left for the airport, and we waited breathlessly to see newspaper coverage the next morning, wondering whose version he had selected. The event did indeed receive coverage, and the *Washington Post* summarized each speech, noting, for example, that Kemp had used his turn to call for a restoration of the gold standard. Dole, it said, had built his remarks around a humorous anecdote involving a group of farmers wearing "Dump Dole" caps. We needed to read no further. We loved him anyway.

27

SETTING THE TERMS: THE ROLE OF LEGISLATORS

As much as they have come to depend on large staffs, congressmen are far from automatons. Most have strong opinions about most issues or they would not be in their line of business. If their aides are active and powerful, it is not necessarily that they work for weak bosses who have abdicated their role in making decisions. Certainly there is some of that: subcommittee chairmen, for example, who are uncomfortable with subject matter under their responsibility but want to project an aura of knowing authority all the same and are therefore willing to sign off on virtually any letter, hearing, or amendment their trusted aides suggest. A very different breed, however, are members who are themselves opinionated and activist and instruct staff quite specifically.

Bob Dole was an example of the latter. I learned this one Saturday afternoon early on, as I was floating drowsily on a raft in the soothing waters of a backyard swimming pool. Jim Whittinghill called from the cloakroom to say I was needed urgently on the Senate floor, where the chamber was in rare weekend session trying to catch up on business. "But Whit," I protested, certain I had checked the Senate calendar, "nothing's happening on trade today . . . right?" He laughed: "Not until Dole brought it up." Under the loose "germaneness" rules of the Senate, our boss had spontaneously decided to offer an amendment (to an unrelated bill) to allow subsidized wheat sales to the Soviet Union. I had qualms myself about the merits, but the matter at this point was not open to debate, and my obvious role as a loyal aide was simply to help my boss draft and pass his amendment.

I rushed to the Capitol and ran up the outside steps toward the Senate chamber on the second floor. Dole was busy corralling his colleagues and could hardly be expected to sit down and explain things to me. Friends from other offices observing floor action from the couches in the rear brought me up-to-date on the procedural situation. For substance I ducked into a phone booth in the cloakroom and reached John Gordley, Dole's former aide on agricultural matters who had been the one to write such proposals in the past. As the office subdivided subjects, farm exports were more "agriculture" than "trade," and I knew little of it. I drafted skeletal language, and Dole handed it in. Then I circulated among aides and senators milling in the back and sought their intelligence about whom we would need to satisfy to assure swift action. Conservative Senator Helms, for example, had obvious concerns about an action that would aid the Soviet economy. Dole took my information and masterfully placated each prospective adversary, agreeing to minor modifications in the amendment (in Helms's case, for example, limiting its period of operation) or asking what he could do in another area by way of recompense. The Senate passed it handily, and the administration, recognizing Dole's steely resolve and strategic position, soon extended the program voluntarily.

The only other problem was mopping up the foreign consequences. The Australian government complained vigorously that U.S. subsidies would displace it in the competition for the Soviet wheat market. Dole was hardly oblivious of global sensibilities, but sometimes felt they were exaggerated for negotiating purposes and in the end would accommodate to strong-willed U.S. positions. In addition he had his priorities and knew that in getting elected president it was probably more important to spend time pleasing American farmers than foreign diplomats. As a result it was to my desk that imprecations from embassies often came, and in this case my job was, alternately, to calm the tempest with a careful explanation of Dole's views and in return to communicate to Dole the intense level of the concern.

My job was made simpler when the Australians decided to dispatch a cabinet-level delegation to press their case. I urged Dole to face the critics himself, showing doubting U.S. editorialists that he valued friendly foreign relations. He agreed to a brief meeting and invited half a dozen other senators to join him. With an equal number of guests they crowded into his personal office, and as I escorted them to their places, I could tell that Dole's hospitality had already lent him a statesmanlike aura, burnished presently by his practiced diplomatic ability to express the highest regard for his visitors' views. No minds were changed, but tensions abated quickly. In 1989 I visited Australia and found that members of Parliament still had vivid memories of the farm-export controversy; matters that seem modest in the U.S. Congress can loom quite large elsewhere. Fortunately they also recalled Dole's graciousness and I was not deported on the spot.

Many of a Leader's daily positions are determined by the favors he must bestow, in almost feudalistic fashion, on his followers; "Chafee needs this, Domenici needs that," we would report fresh from our soundings of other senators' staffs. Neither as a party official nor a presidential candidate could Dole ignore the interests of members whose intramural support sustained him in office or promised to further his other quests. Although he had almost single-handedly drubbed the administration on farm exports, for example, he showered public credit on other senators, such as James Abdnor of South Dakota, who needed aid in their election campaigns—and who were in a position to help Dole in his. Did western Republicans want cosponsors for an amendment to restrict lamb imports? Did southern colleagues need help on textiles? The Leader had little choice.

Even in good relations with the other side of the aisle there could be advantage, although lurking dangers as well. One day Dole came to my desk to inform me that he had agreed to a personal request of House Speaker Jim Wright to cosponsor a semiofficial congressional conference on "competitiveness"; it seemed an innocent enough idea, and Dole was glad when he could promote comity between chambers and parties. I scrambled to find out more, and soon discerned a more ambiguous motive: It looked to be a public-relations gambit to assert legislative claims on the issue before the White House could appropriate it. President Reagan was scheduled shortly to deliver his State of the Union address and had long been expected to make competitiveness a centerpiece; Wright's event seemed intended to steal Republican thunder. It would take some doing to persuade Dole to modify a commitment to the Speaker of the House, and I alone could not do it. I asked my White House contacts for advice, and the next day it arrived in the form of requests to Dole from Treasury Secretary Baker and Trade Representative Clayton Yeutter to limit GOP participation. Dole obliged, asking Wright for a postponement and then conveniently discovering competing obligations when the Democrats failed to budge. I was just as happy to protect my boss's interests circuitously as directly.

Dole also expected us to exercise our own initiative, subject to his broad approval. Because the environment of Congress is naturally somewhat freewheeling—no one "fact-checks" speeches as they might a legal document, since political advocacy is *supposed* to be zealous and emotional—staffers tend to be given wide latitude for action. This could be apparent even in the most minor matters. When the governing Liberal Democratic party triumphed in Japanese elections, I proposed calling upon Prime Minister Yasuhiro Nakasone, armed now with a fresh mandate, to make long-promised reforms in trade policy. A speech seemed too ordinary to have impact, but why not a letter from the entire U.S. Senate (which Dole could get credit for orchestrating)? "Fine," Dole said, but, man of action that he was, added that it ought to go out that same day. So I scaled my project back, seeking instead the signatures of the twenty members of the Senate Finance Committee. This, I rationalized, would have nearly equal dramatic impact (the committee was, in Japan's eyes, Congress's most important subgroup) and greater likelihood of unanimity.

The letter, of course, was left entirely to me to draft, circulate, and send; my boss would want to hear about it again only if it prompted Japanese reaction. Such group missives are common, but my means of processing this one were not. Normally they make their way around the Hill through "inside mail," directed to appropriate LAs who, enlightened by accompanying Dear Colleague letters and reminded by phone calls, obtain required approvals, perhaps from senators themselves, perhaps only from AAs. Owing to the time-sensitive nature of the appeal, I decided to walk the letter around personally. Between a committee meeting and floor activity, I calculated, I could encounter every senator directly within an hour. My task turned out to take an entire day.

At the Finance Committee hearing room I found just a handful of senators, but even to reach them, there were obstacles. First I had to show the letter to cognizant staff members, who, rightly guarding their bosses' time and interests, examined the content with a critical eye and asked detailed questions about it. In the etiquette of the situation it was then up to them to pass the letter on to the senators seated at the dais. A couple walked right up, handed it to them with a hurried explanation, and in a moment had returned it to me with signatures. Others looked for just the right opening when their bosses seemed undistracted by other paperwork or debate; meanwhile I waited. On receiving the letter, one senator put it aside until he had finished everything else in front of him, then motioned to his aide, who stepped forward and leaned into the dais for private conversation. He returned to me still hunched over as if to symbolize continuing confidentiality. "Can't we have something on . . ." he began to say, mentioning an interest or two of his senator's home state. I explained that we needed to get the letter out quickly and didn't want to tamper with the wording. I could see the senator nod when his aide repeated this; both had done their duty. Finally I got my letter. On the floor I went through much of the same. "Great idea," everyone said, signing.

Some senators were not to be found in the obvious places. Senator Bradley was occupied much of the day at a tax conference in the House Ways and Means Committee room on the other side of the Capitol. Naturally when I arrived, he was speaking and I had to wait. Alone among the committee members, he asked me several questions about the purpose of the letter. At first this perplexed me, since I thought it was apparent from its few straightforward paragraphs, and I had imagined that everyone would jump at the opportunity to admonish the unpopular Japanese. Even now I don't know whether his questions reflected excessive caution or impressive intellectual curiosity, but the fact that he did finally sign made his support seem all the more valuable. Senator Chafee was on his way into the senators' dining room for lunch when I found him. Just as he was about to sign, he paused and, having borrowed a Cross pen, asked, "Do you know where this is made?" I thought quickly. "Rhode Island?" I supposed I might be wrong but was confident he would be pleased by mention of his home state. "Exactly," he said, signing with a flourish.

By early evening I had come for my last signature to a corner of the Hart Office Building, where a senator was preparing to leave town. I was told he had just walked out the door, but when his LA saw that his was the only blank signature line among those for all twenty committee members, he decided to take executive action. "I'll be right back," he said, and went looking for a secretary. A few minutes later he returned my letter with a wink. "I'm sure the senator would approve," he said, reassuring himself as much as me. It was, in the end, the only forged signature, and more than one colleague advised me to keep the original as a collector's item, so unusual was this pastiche of authentic autographs.

I ran into Dole in the subterranean concourse leading from the office buildings to the Capitol (the Senate had recessed, meaning that subway cars had stopped running for the day) and we walked back. "Last time I try to be helpful," I sighed. He was consoling. "It's a hard job to get these guys together on something. Next time I'll have you circulate an amendment that way." I sent the original the following day to the Japanese embassy. Press stories reported it seriously, as though it might have consequences. But if we ever received a reply, I didn't see it.

I had not invented the letter to Prime Minister Nakasone in isolation. Its whole purpose had been to give concrete expression to my boss's strong view that Japan needed to open its markets to U.S. products. I simply chose the time and manner of doing so, as I would on a daily basis in all matters under my supervision. The same was true of fellow staffers in all the other offices. It was Congress, in the form of members themselves, who dictated our broad values and objectives. The drafting, battling, dealmaking, and enactment of a trade bill, a central focus of my efforts, was a classic instance of this fundamental congressional synergy: legislators setting the terms of the debate and their staffers filling in the blanks.

The experience of my colleague Leonard Santos, a knowledgeable former Treasury official serving as international trade counsel to the Senate Finance Committee, showed how the system worked. In January 1985, Len arranged a series of informational hearings on issues in his field; he expected that a few members might attend—senators such as Jack Danforth of Missouri, who chaired the trade subcommittee—but that the topic would not excite general interest. One session, however, scheduled for March, concerned Japanese trade barriers to U.S. exports and turned out to be a perfect stroke of timing. President Reagan, in a goodwill gesture to visiting Prime Minister Nakasone, declined to press for an extension of "voluntary" quotas on automobile exports to the United States. The prospect of Japanese cars flooding the market jolted many in Congress to a new recognition both of America's precarious trade balance and what critics considered the administration's laissez-faire attitude about correcting it.

Interest in Len's impending hearing began to mushroom. A staffer from a different committee, Bill Triplett of Senate Foreign Relations, himself roused by the issue, volunteered background material. He took a batch of trade data to the Dirksen basement, enlisted the aid of the Senate graphics department, and returned with colorful charts showing Japanese exports in red towering over American. Len located Senator Danforth at a Budget Committee meeting and unveiled the artwork in an anteroom. "You've *got* to bring those to the hearing," Danforth said, adding, "and I want *you* to describe them." When the morning arrived, camera crews lined the side of the room, and a remarkable fifteen members (out of twenty on the committee) had taken their places on the dais. Opening statements scolded Japan with startling virulence. Len gave his presentation to a riveted audience, and committee members grilled witness Michael Smith, the deputy U.S. trade representative. As they left the room at the end, Danforth congratulated Len and commented, "This hearing could have been about canned tuna from Norway, and these feelings about Japan would have come out. It was a volcano waiting to erupt." Within days Len had drafted a Senate resolution criticizing Japanese trading practices as unfair. The committee had not yet considered it before Clyde Farnsworth of *The New York Times* reached him and transformed the resolution into a major news story; shortly the committee, then the whole Senate, passed it unanimously.

Like a great love affair congressional involvement in major national issues can be as tempestuous as it is transitory. Reflecting changing public attitudes as capably as it does, Congress is subject to wide swings of mood; its members pour great emotion into their political affairs, and issues long dormant can suddenly arise to become preoccupations. During the Reagan years this happened, for example, with respect to Central America, drugs, and trade. New interest in these issues was not precipitated by new underlying developments. Cross-border subversion was occurring in Central America long before Secretary Haig focused attention on it in early 1981. Large quantities of cocaine were being sold on the streets of America before sports-hero tragedies in the mid-1980s caused a public outcry for government action. And the U.S. trade posture had been in steady decline before Congress at last became concerned about Japanese trade barriers. But when matters do rise to the surface, Congress can set itself dramatically in motion. Now this would happen in the trade area.

Senator Danforth—an ordained minister, heir to the Purina dog food fortune, and Missouri attorney general before entering the Senate in

1977—had grasped the political potency of the issue earlier than most of his colleagues. Aging shoe factories in his state provided many jobs, and a firestorm of constituent protest greeted President Reagan's refusal in 1984 to limit briskly selling footwear imports. The International Trade Commission, an independent agency of the U.S. government, had argued the need for quotas and tariffs, but Reagan, citing economists' claims that each job thus saved might cost consumers as much as $200,000 in higher prices, exercised his right under the law not to accept its recommendation. Danforth vowed to overcome the president's inaction and began his offensive by asking his trade staff—Len, fellow committee counsel Ted Kassinger, and LA Sue Schwab—to a series of luncheon tutorials in the Senate dining room, where they would systematically discuss possible legislative initiatives. When the rest of Congress came around, they would be ready.

An intelligent and well-liked senator, Danforth commanded particular attention in the trade area; his deep, gravelly voice, a slow and philosophic manner of speech, and a patch of premature white in an otherwise dignified coiffure would have made him a distinctive presence in any case. But he wielded influence because he had methodically gained relevant expertise as chairman of the Senate Trade Subcommittee. (Clout did not necessarily follow position; Hawaii's Spark Matsunaga would succeed Danforth in the position in 1987, but colleagues never considered his competence to match his amiability, and his actions as a result carried much less weight.) He also had a crack staff to back him up. Len and Ted technically reported to the Finance Committee, but Sue, the LA, toiled full-time for Danforth.

I disagreed with a number of Sue's positions—I tended to be more "free trade" in disposition and less inclined to erect barriers to imports even in retaliation for foreign practices—but it was difficult not to admire her. She was a former Foreign Service Officer who had been stationed in Tokyo and, although only in her early thirties, was already a veteran of several years on Danforth's staff. Sue was no technocrat; like many staffers she combined equal interest in politics and substance. Supremely self-confident, resourceful, and persuasive, she had been known to say that her ambition was to become the "Richard Perle of trade," a reference to the onetime foreign-policy adviser to Senator Henry Jackson (and later a Pentagon official under Reagan) who had attained legendary influence in the Senate, instilling awe, and not a little fear, among his colleagues. In time Sue would nearly achieve that goal; the Japanese, her particular *bête noire*, saw her as a wily and determined foe and were astonished at the influence of such a young person in setting American trade policy. But Danforth had cause to be thankful. She was very good.

In the spring of 1985 Danforth convinced Dole that Democrats would inevitably take the lead on trade issues unless the Republicans beat them to it. Dole gave the go-ahead, and in countless meetings in the majority leader's office among selected GOP staff, the beginnings of a Senate trade bill came to life. No senator attended these sessions; drafting the details of a bill was a matter for aides, each of whom carved out issues of special interest. Sue, reflecting Danforth's objectives, sought to make presidential implementation of "Section 201" ITC recommendations more automatic; Bill Reinsch, representing Senator Heinz and the interests of the declining Frost Belt industries of Pennsylvania, wanted to relax standards and procedures for proving unfair trading practices of foreign countries; Len felt that the role of a strong dollar in discouraging U.S. exports had been overlooked and wanted to introduce language dealing with exchange rates.

By mid-1985 this rump group of Republicans was at the point of producing a GOP bill, but Senator Packwood, chairman of the Finance Committee, which would have to take it up, demurred; much of his energy at the time was directed toward tax reform, and he was, in any case, skeptical that an interventionist new trade law, as congressional action promised, would be an improvement. Dole, the last Finance chairman, had enjoyed better relations with Danforth, partly because it was Dole's pragmatic nature to defer to other members' specialized interests; Packwood had a more assertive ideology about many issues. His resistance, as a result, spurred Danforth toward a bipartisan approach, and together with Democrat Pat Moynihan of New York he moved to create a larger and more consensual trade bill. For weeks half the staff of the Senate seemed to be engaged in drafting sessions, tossing in such provisions as necessary to build support. Out of this process emerged S. 1860, the centerpiece of Senate trade debate until the beginning of 1987, when a new Congress produced a variation renumbered S. 460. Over time the bill would be extensively modified in committee, on the floor, and in House-Senate conference, but there would still be many recognizable similarities between its original incarnation and the Omnibus Trade Act of 1988 signed into law three years later.

My boss was already a cosponsor of Danforth's original bill when I arrived in mid-1986, but by the standards of "cosponsorship" this committed him more to the principle of a bill than to its particular provisions. Senators often lend their names to legislation without close inspection and largely as a gesture to persistent colleagues or constituents. Danforth believed that trade laws needed to be strengthened, and in light of the worsening U.S. trade balance it was not difficult to convince other senators of this view; supporting a bill was a token that one wanted to "do something" about the situation. Not surprisingly nearly fifty senators joined the effort. My mission as Dole's aide in this area was to learn as much detail as possible about the bill so as to advise my boss which of its many provisions to support, oppose, or attempt to change.

My viewpoint on trade issues had, beyond the most general philosophy, never been asked; it is often assumed that aides will simply apply their powers of rational analysis to suggest courses of action that they believe to benefit their employer's interests. The opinions I happened to possess about these issues came mainly from textbook instruction years before, the editorials I had regularly read over morning coffee, and a casual acquaintance with international trade litigation during my days in a law firm. When I first read S. 1860, I was fairly astonished; it seemed largely to be a collection of procedural changes that would make it easier for U.S. companies to seek legal relief against foreign competition. I had no doubt that many countries had unfair trading practices and that action needed to be taken against them, but the bill seemed to put its entire stock in this approach. Not only did I have questions about this on its own terms—blocking imports can have the effect of raising consumer prices and complicating foreign relations—but it seemed inconsistent with claims that such legislation would solve the U.S. trade crisis. Personally I believed the major causes of the problem to be larger and more economic in nature: such factors as exchange rates, differing economic growth rates among countries, and the U.S. budget deficit. But within the Congress, the identification of precise causes took a distinctly secondary position to the search for immediate palliatives that could help stanch declining sales and employment in affected domestic industries. (Since farm exports were the one bright spot in the U.S. trade picture, we did not hear from Kansas voters quite so much as other offices heard from theirs, and this may have given me more latitude to weigh the merits of the issue.)

It is not difficult to see why Congress would approach matters narrowly. Wherever a powerful industry lost ground to foreign imports, offices could expect to hear from managers, unions, and lobbyists urging solutions, most of which, no matter how disguised, had as their obvious object the curtailment of foreign imports. The trade in automobiles was a classic example. In the early 1980s Chrysler and others were reeling. Critics said this was due to the outdated designs of their products (cars remained too big for newly energy-conscious consumers) and a reputation for poor workmanship. Others said the problem was low wage rates and government assistance in foreign countries. It hardly mattered. Senators Danforth and Bentsen mounted an effort to limit Japanese imports, the upshot of which was a preemptive agreement by the Japanese to arrange so-called voluntary restraints. Similar pressure was brought in numerous other areas, such as steel, machine tools, and clothing. Congressmen now boasted of being fair-traders rather than free-traders, although that most were not wholly against imports was suggested by the fact that Danforth and Bentsen themselves, in reference to their own automotive preferences, were known as the "Mercedes twins."

Congress, of course, is oriented not to academic theory but to constituencies—whose voices, financial contributions, and votes carry decisive weight in elections. In trade matters, as a result, it tends to listen to well-organized groups that have a clear focus of concern, strong local support, and a situation susceptible to ready emotional understanding: the loss of jobs of autoworkers in Detroit or steelworkers in Pennsylvania or garment and apparel workers in North Carolina. Who cannot be moved by their plight as foreign imports so visibly threaten their livelihood? Who cannot visualize the relationship between foreign imports and idle American factories? Who cannot grieve about the loss of America's traditional position in heavy industry and manufacturing? And who especially, when one's financial and political patrons are making the case? (The executive branch is not immune to these sensitivities either, and even the Reagan administration in practice compromised its free-trade ideology more than its rhetoric suggested.) "Losers" in the trade competition are often more motivated than "winners," since their very jobs are on the line.

In contrast, economics professors or consumer advocates, who might be counted on to expound the virtues of free trade or at least to counsel patience, are not renowned for their ability either to raise campaign funds or to get out the vote for their friends. They tend to be heard from only if quoted in the newspaper or if an aide goes to the trouble of reading a publication that crosses his desk from a scholarly institution. Again, Dole's office was unusual because his presidential frame of mind gave us an incentive to consider larger perspectives; I went out of my way to consult well-known economists such as Mike Evans and Larry Kudlow, former trade officials such as Bob Hormats, trade scholars like Mac Destler, and trade lawyers like Gary Horlick. All of them tended to take a broader view of the trade problem than did Congress. Politicians can be forgiven if they are not particularly receptive to the argument that painful economic adjustment—the rise and fall of different industries, possibly in their states—is the natural and desirable result of shifting advantages among nations in technology, capital, and human resources. Congress knows that if the causes of a problem are "economic," it can do little and therefore it often prefers diagnoses for which it can write prescriptions. It wants to see problems as amenable to new laws.

Corporate executives, although many think they exert great influence because of their financial contributions, had (at least in the trade area) much less impact than I expected. For one thing their interests diverged: Low-priced imports alarmed the steel and semiconductor industries, for example, but pleased others who relied on inexpensive component parts. Occasionally I invited prominent business representatives to talk with Dole about trade issues. Typically half a dozen CEOs (such as Colby Chandler of Kodak, David Scott of Allis-Chalmers, or T.A. Wilson of Boeing) would assemble for an 8:00 A.M. breakfast meeting at a long table in our formal conference room. If Dole had not yet arrived, I would outline his positions and suggest points that he might like to hear more about. Soon he would walk in, shake hands, and take his place at the head of the table. Despite all their employees, fiefdoms, and large incomes, it was clear that these titans of the private sector held the majority leader in awe: He was a recognizable celebrity, and he helped to run an entire country. They were delighted to give advice, but it was often too general to translate into concrete legislation.

Pressure for trade legislation heated up through 1986, and the Reagan administration continued to resist. Democrats, as Danforth had anticipated, saw in this recalcitrance a major election-year issue, believing it would further their portrayal of Republicans as blind apostles of discredited policies, indifferent to the plight of workers. Particularly outspoken on the subject was Congressman Richard Gephardt of Missouri who, doubtless hoping to jump start his lagging presidential campaign, proposed severe limits on imports. In mid-August Democratic senators Bentsen, Glenn, Baucus, and Dixon gathered in the Senate press gallery to urge passage of a trade bill before the end of the session and accused the White House of orchestrating Republican opposition. Their aides winked at me as I sat in the back of the room taking notes; they knew I would shortly be preparing Dole's response to the speeches they had just written for their bosses. In fact we were having our disagreements with the White House. GOP congressmen were not as devoutly observant of their party's economic orthodoxy as their president, and by now many had clambered aboard the trade-bill bandwagon, urging Dole, as leader, to help pull it. The industries of their constituents, too, were under siege: steel in the Northeast, textiles in the South, computer chips in California. Some of them, like Jim Broyhill of North Carolina and Mack Mattingly of Georgia, were up for election and faced close contests. (In November both would lose, placing partial blame on unpopular administration trade policies.)

I wrote so many speeches for Dole in this period reiterating his intention to bring a bill to the floor that I finally stored the appropriate paragraphs in my word processor rather than compose them anew each time. The word *intention*, of course, was used advisedly; it meant something along the lines of "hope" rather than "promise." While Dole had influence when matters reached the floor, Senator Packwood controlled the Finance Committee agenda, where consideration of a bill would begin. He had chosen this year to try to reform the tax system, and that pursuit occupied the committee's attention all summer long. The House overcame initial jurisdictional conflicts among its committees and speedily reported a bill, although this simply may have reflected the fact that it was not intended to become law but only to document convenient positions for impending election campaigns. Packwood took the bill seriously, found much of it anathema, and was afraid also of "killer" amendments that would prolong committee debate, further provoke presidential veto, and ultimately render the exercise both intense and pointless.

Packwood was an Oregon Republican, liberal and feisty enough to have traveled to New Hampshire in the early 1980s, allowing rumors to fly that he was thinking of challenging President Reagan's bid for a second term. His manner was casual, as if to symbolize his western roots: rumpled jacket, shirt perpetually coming untucked, a slow and friendly gait around the Senate floor or down the halls that invited others to come up and chat. But his usually gentle voice and patient pace of lucid, professorial explanation could rise to great oratorical heights when the subject touched on issues he held dear; and one of them was free trade, which, nearly alone, he eloquently defended. He had terrifically competent aides in these matters—Len Santos and then Josh Bolten—but Packwood, like Dole, was a boss who made up his own mind and then looked to his staff to plow accordingly. Without prompting, he had decided he didn't like the trade bill and that there would be no hearing.

While rumors persisted in the fall of 1986 that Packwood planned committee action, others knew better. He went through the motions of holding a brief markup at the end of the session, perhaps to deflect claims that Republicans were obstructionist, but allowed the effort to be smothered to death in procedure, perhaps a poetic fate for such a large and lumbering bill. Committee consideration proceeded at a snail's pace as staff laboriously outlined the provisions of S. 1860 with which many members, despite their endorsements, were unfamiliar. For this purpose each senator had been given a sheaf of papers known as a "side-by-side," a helpful array of columns comparing current law, the House bill, the Senate bill, and a compromise proposal prepared by Packwood's staff. Notably absent was an indication of administration positions (which Congress, proud of its independence, did not like to acknowledge too explicitly), but in almost every case the staff compromise (reflecting Packwood's own pro-administration bias) narrowed the distance. Each issue provoked prolonged discussion, and senators talked of offering as many as seventy-five amendments. Danforth proposed accepting the staff blueprint as the baseline for markup, but Senator Baucus, who regarded it as a weakening step, insisted on maintaining S. 1860 as the basic document, thus placing the burden of proof on those who would want to conciliate with the White House.

Dole made a rare appearance to help spur the committee on. He was often sidetracked on the floor during the day, but, as an ex-chairman of the committee, even a cameo visit commanded great attention. Committee proceedings are notorious for starting late as members straggle in; almost everyone likes to give a flowery opening statement, but no one, it seems, wants to hear the others. Dole arrived before Packwood had gaveled the meeting to order, and the room was still noisy and crowded as though expecting dramatic events to unfold. Dole had a keener eye: "There's nothing going on here," he said, surveying the commotion around him. I had taken it to signify productive activity, but he realized that it meant potential conflict. He took his seat, memorized the notes I had prepared for him, and, when it came time, quickly said his piece—which was to urge restraint on time-consuming amendments, offering to set an example by compromising on some of his own special issues. Everyone listened closely, but when he left, which was almost immediately, reality set in just as he had predicted: One by one his colleagues announced myriad matters they were determined to pursue.

At the end of a second day of meetings Packwood announced that resumption of markup would be difficult given conflicting House-Senate conferences on budget reconciliation, the debt ceiling, and the "superfund." It was hard to see how time remained for action, especially if no effort were made to expedite it. Congress would be adjourning within weeks, and this was only the committee phase. On the floor a trade bill could quickly become a magnet for extravagant election-eve amendments. Dole talked about the "uncontrollability" of such a situation and its self-fulfilling character. If members thought a bill would become so laden with amendments as to prevent enactment, they would treat it all the more lightly and seek to add even more decorations. Under the circumstances many lost motivation. Democrats were just as happy to go without a bill, so they could blame the GOP for failing to pass it. Republicans were glad to be spared the embarrassment of battling their president. And for those who genuinely wanted legislation, the staff could begin repackaging it immediately after the election.

28

FILLING IN THE BLANKS: THE ROLE OF STAFF

In December 1986, fresh from victory at the polls, Senate Democrats began planning for their return to power. Senator Lloyd Bentsen of Texas, the ranking Finance Committee Democrat, who could expect to become the new chairman, directed his staff to begin drafting another trade bill. It was clear that such legislation would top his agenda; the Democrats had campaigned in part on this platform, and whether it really had anything to do with the election results, they were by now publicly committed. Besides, with any luck they could sustain the issue through the next election cycle; the trade deficit wouldn't be getting much better. As for Bentsen himself, here was an apparent last chance for glory; who could foresee that eighteen months later he would be picked to run on his party's national ticket? Committee chairmen make their mark by reporting legislation, and Packwood, who could claim stewardship during the much-vaunted tax reform of the previous session, had set a high standard.

For several weeks during this electoral interregnum, aides representing each of the twenty committee members assembled at a long conference table in Dirksen 211, where Jeff Lang, the Democratic trade counsel on the committee, methodically supervised the formulation of a new bill; of course much was imported from the trade proposals of the previous Congress. Jeff was the perfect metaphor for the process. A former attorney at the International Trade Commission, he was deeply knowledgeable and infinitely patient, speaking slowly and precisely and glad to parse the smallest details to be sure he understood exactly what others in the room wanted; he knew it was Bentsen's disposition to give every senator *something* so as to induce the broadest possible support. Some of the solutions devised for the bill tended, as a result, toward the mechanistic: differing appeal possibilities from ITC decisions, for example, depending on whether its commissioners might vote 4 to 1, or 5 to 0, on an issue.

Bill Reinsch, representing Heinz, was the graybeard among us, having battled many of the same issues during the entire previous decade; almost alone, he had a sense of how arcane provisions might actually work in practice. Sue Schwab, reflecting Danforth's inclinations, reserved her focus for the largest issues, and while the rest of us tended to consider them on the terms Jeff presented, one could almost see a glimmer in Sue's eye as her mind leaped ahead to imagine fundamentally different approaches. Bob Kyle and David Apgar, although not previously trade experts, were creative whizzes quick to devise new ideas and to see the inconsistencies in those of others; their opinions carried special weight because they represented senators—Max Baucus of Montana and Bill Bradley of New Jersey—who took intense interest in trade matters. Josh Bolten, now Packwood's shrewd representative on the committee staff, faded somewhat into the background, in part a recognition of how starkly out of place his boss's free-trade positions would seem under the committee's new Democratic regime. A number of staffers, especially those younger and less experienced, tended to listen passively, taking notes to summarize the drift for a senator or AA or simply wondering to themselves when this laborious exercise would end.

In general it was hard to tell what senators themselves actually wanted, what aides thought they *might* want or hoped to convince them of, or what were simply the musings of those of us who wanted to be heard in the process much as a few years before we might have contributed to a discussion in a college honors seminar. I knew that Dole had no personal interest in such fine level of detail, yet I could hardly remain silent: To do so might betoken lack of interest in the process, and I knew that Dole, above all else, liked to see things worked out. Besides, I grew to have strong views about many of the items under discussion.

Oddly the proceedings were divorced from direct contact with ex-

290 / IN THE SHADOW OF THE DOME

ecutive-branch experts who, unlike legislative aides, had actual experience in administering the laws under discussion. Seasoned trade officials, such as USTR general counsel Alan Holmer and his deputy Judy Bello, talked occasionally with Jeff and his assistants, but while they were welcomed to suggest modifications to make individual provisions more workable, they were hardly invited to collaborate on the underlying principles of a bill. All they could do much of the time was to rely on GOP offices for intelligence or intervention; owing to my boss's leadership position and my own sympathies, I tried to be helpful. Most often they kept in touch with Josh, who, as aide to the committee's ranking Republican, attempted to negotiate improvements with Jeff in private meetings, but the fact that the "majority" and "minority" staff offices of the committee were, at one point, located on different floors of the Dirksen Building symbolized the distance that divided them. Occasionally Josh was able to enlist Packwood or Danforth in taking a matter directly to Bentsen for decision, but on many items he was simply thanked for his suggestions and kept only skeletally informed until a final product was unveiled. Bentsen and his staff were, understandably, caught between a chivalrous sense of obligation to hear the administration out and their knowledge that it was emphatically opposed to their bill. An attitude of "us versus them" often exists as Congress looks down Pennsylvania Avenue, but it seemed especially so in the trade debate.

Inevitably the process tended to be driven by those who had the strongest interest. Although in theory a "generic" bill that established abstract rules and procedures, it was often very specific industries and companies that sought those changes because of their own expected benefits. If an agricultural group contacted a staffer about its special need for "fast-track relief for perishable commodities," the aide was much likelier to know about it than anyone else in our group and to make a persuasive argument; moreover, since others needed to preserve goodwill for their own initiatives, there was little incentive to challenge a would-be ally. Still others deferred on the thought that there would always be time to change objectionable provisions. If I expressed reservations about a provision to colleagues who were promoting it, I might well be told, "Don't worry, it won't get through markup," or "it'll be thrown out on the floor," or "it won't survive conference," referring to the many further stages prior to final enactment. And my colleagues were right. For all the hours we spent at it, the original act of drafting a piece of legislation is only the barest, and most reversible, of beginnings.

There were occasional limits to what we accepted. Senator Arlen Specter of Pennsylvania, at the behest of his steelmaking constituency, pushed hard for a law allowing domestic parties to seek civil damages against foreign exporters who violated U.S. trade laws. That he was not a member of the committee made his task harder, but the rest of us heard regularly from his office. The idea had a plausible appeal, but many trade staffers, and Senator Danforth himself, recognized its extremely controversial implications. It would blatantly violate agreed-upon international rules of trade, clog the courts with complex new cases of an unusually punitive character, and threaten as a result to chill overall foreign imports even if fairly traded. In the end, the Specter "private right of action" measure attained such notoriety that many of us felt its inclusion could make the Bentsen bill seem frivolous. It was left out.

If other questionable provisions remained (many did), it was commonplace for sponsors of the trade bill to say it was merely a "discussion piece," not a final document. Privately some had strong misgivings and confronted a legislator's classic philosophical quandary: whether to give precedence to constituent preferences or national interest. This could be resolved by sponsoring the bill and hoping it would never actually pass, at least in anything like its present form. Indeed as much as the administration was derided for its conservative trade posture, I sensed a relief that, if added provisions of the bill truly went beyond the pale, it was there to draw the line. Obviously some senators genuinely supported the bill, but they, too, had the comfort of knowing that they could change their minds at any point, asserting that modifications were not made as they desired. Meanwhile it was an inexpensive way of demonstrating concern about an issue and "sending a message."

Dole's calculus in coming to a position illustrates the complex considerations that daily face politicians. He could support the Bentsen bill, making him a "player" in the process and giving him more influence to modify its questionable aspects. His very embrace could make it seem bipartisan, helping to deny Democrats a claim in the next election that Republicans had favored inaction. On the other hand, this could make it harder to alter; Dole would be expected to use his leadership position to help advance the bill through the Senate, raising the possibility of direct confrontation with a Republican administration expected to oppose it strongly. If the president tagged it as protectionist, Dole would be tarred with the same brush.

Still another possibility presented itself. The administration had decided to change course from the previous year, when it had rejected a trade bill altogether, and to propose one itself now, although a breed apart from Bentsen's. "Competitiveness" had become a fashionable rallying cry, notwithstanding that few knew what the term meant, but at least it offered the advantage of letting the administration oppose a congressional bill without appearing to stand for nothing itself. These were days of activist government, when one was expected, Republican or Democrat, always to have a plan of action. Now the administration could do Congress one better and say that the real answer to trade problems lay in a broader and more fundamental approach: restoring America's ability to compete in world markets through long-term reforms in education and employment programs, improvements in the regulatory and financial environment, and so forth. Thus the administration scrambled to find every proposal it could to create sheer bulk in a bill of its own, obscuring the fact that it was offering no conventional trade remedies parallel to Bentsen's.

The "competitiveness" package may well have been superior on its merits, but the prospect concerned us that it could go nowhere: Dole might look obstructive for supporting it against the wishes of the Finance Committee chairman and a broad bipartisan group in Congress. Moreover while Dole considered himself obliged to provide support to a Republican president, his own White House bid required him to begin establishing a separate identity. The one option clearly not available was to remain above the fray, for then he would stand accused of the worst sin: doing nothing. The option he finally chose was to back *both* the Bentsen and the administration bills, and accordingly my job was to explain the seeming inconsistency. Thus I drafted speeches and press releases arguing that the two were complementary rather than competing pieces of legislation, and making a point of stating significant reservations about several aspects of the Bentsen bill—actually constituting the guts of the legislation—and expressing Dole's determination to modify relevant provisions in committee or on the floor.

As long as Dole was supporting the president's bill, I thought it would be a nice touch for him actually to introduce it (bills could be considered only if legislators placed them in the hopper), but he was not enthusiastic. With help I enlisted from the White House legislative office, he was persuaded to do so. The bill was assigned to seven major committees (in the House it was ten) owing to the multiple jurisdictions involved in its subject matter. The division was not scientific: Sheila and Whit negotiated with staff directors, Senator Byrd's office, and the parliamentarian to assign those portions where more than a single committee had claim or where the ego of senior members was involved. The competitiveness legislation was given highest priority by both parties, and committees reviewed it within several months; this was considered extraordinary speed. By the end of the process, however, little of the original package remained. Much of it never had a chance, since the administration's proposals frequently departed from the consensus of the committees that would consider them; indeed the White House submitted numerous provisions in this knowledge, presumably with the purpose of placing its positions on the record as much as in the law.

The Finance Committee received the right to review the skeletal trade provisions of the president's bill and considered them in conjunction with the Bentsen bill. In early 1987 expert witnesses (present and former trade officials, CEOs, economists) presented their views on the trade crisis, but their contributions were largely cosmetic, since the preliminary legislation had by now been drafted. Testimony was helpful in establishing a record of investigation and concern; the committee report following markup made a point of citing relevant remarks as the ostensible basis for action. Yet this was after-the-fact rationalization, much as a judge might order his law clerk to find convenient precedents that support his instinctive opinions. Indeed much of the testimony was in fundamental contradiction to central aspects of the contemplated bill. And it was not as though many minds would be changed. Few members attended the hearings, and those who did often contented themselves with general questions and little attention to detail. Senators who agreed with what they heard were reinforced in their attitudes, and those who didn't simply viewed the hearings as an opportunity to spar with opponents; it is hard to remember anyone's acknowledging a change of heart. Taking testimony at times seemed a public-relations function of the committee, separate from its legislative duties.

By late April the committee could proceed to markup. It began slowly with a "walk-through" of the major issues; again, only a handful of members attended, although the seats behind the dais were crowded with staff there to observe for their absentee bosses. Chairman Bentsen was very much in charge. Centrist and mild-mannered, he was a lanky and wizened Texan who never seemed to be in much of a hurry; the way he pursed his lips and measured his words bespoke a refinement, even an elitism, that seemed almost out of place on Capitol Hill. I could not help thinking of his short-lived 1976 presidential campaign as I watched him, and I understood why it had been so distinctly unsuccessful: Bentsen seemed to lack the driving ambition, the animal instincts of other politicians. He was deferential to his colleagues and religious about building consensus; he even treated staff pleasantly, not always a senatorial attribute. One day I was in the committee room early when a senator walked in anxiously. "Has anyone seen Chairman Bentsen?" he asked. The two secretaries nearby, whom he seemed to be addressing, were on the phone. Trying to assist, I whispered to them, "Have you seen Bentsen?" The senator heard me and scowled. "*Chairman* Bentsen," he corrected me, appearing to consider my omission a slur. The irony, of course, was that Senator Bentsen himself, although a man of formality, would never have minded.

Yet for all his gentlemanly ways, Bentsen was a practiced politician. He was a persuasive advocate of his positions but did not seem reluctant to admit that he relied greatly on staff guidance, nor to engage in gambits of public relations. Everyone knew that even the best trade bill would hardly make a dent in the country's massive trade imbalance—many of the problems were macroeconomic and not regulatory in nature—but Bentsen never lost an opportunity to declare that passage of his recommended program would be of historic consequence. Everyone knew that many of its provisions were mere sops to special interests, but he hailed them all as models of responsibility. And he claimed, too, that just about everything was vital to enact, although the world knew that pragmatic Lloyd Bentsen would be among the first to compromise.

Already the House Ways and Means Committee, our counterpart in the other chamber, had passed its version of a trade bill. Chairman Dan Rostenkowski was a dealmaker who, like Bentsen, seemed determined most of all to get something through; the content was almost secondary. He knew it needed to be moderate to win administration support. On the bulk of the bill he won a magnificent compromise in support of his "chairman's mark," but a glaring exception was passage of the Gephardt amendment, which was essentially the price of his accomplishment: This Draconian provision—threatening massive retaliation against countries that sold us too much more than we sold them—was a salve to the conscience of those who feared they would otherwise stand accused of selling out to the forces of moderation. But it was a cheap price, because it was not expected to survive House-Senate conference.

The House success encouraged Bentsen to think more in terms of legislation that might actually be enacted into law. Until now he and his staff had seemed determined to develop a stark congressional alternative to administration policy, acting as though negotiation with the other branch would dilute the purity of the effort. Some senators seemed to feel almost bitterly that the president would not take forceful action against imports unless Congress pointed a gun. But now Bentsen sought to move his bill beyond political manifesto. He became more accommodating of administration opinion, allowing USTR general counsel Alan Holmer, for example, to come to the witness table during markup to appraise prospective committee action. (It may have helped that Alan was well known to the committee as Senator Packwood's former AA and that it was often Packwood himself, never mentioning the relationship, who called forward "the administration's representative" for comment.)

Sometimes when markup became bogged down by senators struggling to understand technical issues, Bentsen would suggest reconvening in the committee's anteroom after dinner to "work out" compromises that would accelerate the proceedings the next day. Soon this became a noun, as staffers—who scrambled while senators dined—presented "workouts" between interested senators' offices and administration trade experts. Only a handful of senators would show up at this late hour, and Jeff Lang would outline a proposed agreement; the more legalistic the issue, the likelier they were to acquiesce in staff recommendations. The conference table at which principals sat would be ringed by the rest of us, crowded together and balancing on our knees our various notebooks and worksheets. Among us for the first time were administration counterparts, and although when given the opportunity they made lucid contributions, they, like others in the staff tier, did not speak unless spoken to. At a much later phase, when report language was written, they would be given the privilege of reading it in advance of the public—but again treated no better than an aide to the most junior committee member. I always imagined that, behind the scenes, more communication occurred, but these sorts of cursory encounters turned out to be as much as they got.

Of course no provision was too "technical" if an important constituency group backed it, and during public markup members displayed an impressive grasp of the most unlikely issues. Senator Moynihan argued eloquently for a rebate of duty on imported sugar for U.S. refiners, some of whom happened to be located in his state and, according to administration estimates, would receive benefits worth scores of millions of dollars. Senators David Boren and Bennett Johnston sought to extend eligibility for trade-adjustment assistance to oil and gas workers, well represented in their states of Oklahoma and Louisiana. Baucus of Montana tried to expand coverage of the Meat Import Act to include lamb products. And Chairman Bentsen himself, concerned about plummeting crude oil prices back home in Texas, successfully tacked on a "peril point" energy program designed to force government action if oil imports climbed above certain levels. Their staffs did superb jobs preparing fact sheets and talking points, while the opposition tended to be armed only if a conflicting constituency interest arose or if the administration stood up and pointed out the fallacies.

Committee members as a whole (at least the eight or so stalwarts out of twenty who regularly attended) exhibited most interest in the large and highly publicized issues that symbolized a new, more aggressive congressional attitude on trade. The "Section 201" debate, for example, raised the question of whether the president would be required to implement International Trade Commission decisions rather than considering them as mere advisory opinions. The idea had a logic—didn't the ITC know most about trade questions?—but in fact the agency was explicitly instructed by statute to consider only narrow industry issues, without regard to broader questions such as cost to consumers or consequences for foreign policy. The points were easy to understand, and senators applied their philosophies accordingly. Some said it was time to bring trade policy to the forefront and end its role as mere "handmaiden" to foreign policy; others saw in this change an infringement on traditional presidential prerogative. Staffers did not have to prompt their bosses in such big-picture debate, although their passions often ran as high; their primary use in these circumstances was to help negotiate a middle ground. Thus committee staff (in consultation with personal staff) proposed a softer option on 201; the administration still pronounced it abhorrent, but Bentsen embraced it as a symbolic expression of congressional will. Everyone spoke in terms of high principle, but they knew that much negotiation lay ahead.

Dole had little hesitation siding with the administration on an issue such as this having to do with executive discretion; increasingly he was in a presidential frame of mind. Other matters were of lesser interest, which was a good thing because his floor duties often made personal participation impossible. Many amendments were moved by acclamation or quick voice vote; several each day were recorded, and absent members had until 5:00 P.M. to cast a proxy. If I was certain of Dole's position, I would vote him on the spot. Usually this took the form of a word to Packwood or his staff, but if I was seated inextricably in the audience facing them, I might simply give a prearranged hand signal, making me feel momentarily like an anonymous rich person bidding on a Rembrandt at auction. Otherwise I would return to the Capitol and either poke my head into Dole's office to give him a briefing or, if he was away or distracted, type out a summary at the word processor on my desk. Dole, of course, would be interested in not only the merits of the issue but the administration's stand and the votes of other senators. Almost always he took my recommendations, although obviously they were made with his anticipated reactions in mind.

The committee staff repeatedly asked me whether Dole wanted to pursue his "GSP" amendment. This was a reference to a proposal he had once made to modify the "graduated system of preferences," which assessed lower duties on imports from developing countries. Sometime before I arrived, Dole had participated in a congressional trip to Asia, where proud hosts unwittingly showed him their most prosperous areas, making him wonder why such countries qualified for concessional tariffs. On returning to Washington, he called for a "graduation party" to end such treatment, and appropriate language had been placed in the original Senate trade bill. In the meantime the administration had, largely with Dole's views in mind, reviewed the program and made substantial, if not fundamental, revisions. Did they, I was asked, go far enough to satisfy my boss?

My own view, expressed to Dole early, was that something involving an acronym—GSP—that not one in a hundred thousand voters recognized was not well suited as an issue in a presidential campaign. But even on the merits I had qualms. Holding out the GSP carrot offered useful leverage in negotiations on other issues. Newly imposed standards promised to eliminate one-fourth of the $12 billion in annual benefits. Markets lost by developing countries stood to be gained in some cases not by the U.S. but by Canada and Japan. Dole accepted these points and we dropped the effort.

Here I must digress to mention again the role of lobbyists. Many of these arguments did not come to me on my own. Ex-administration trade officials now serving as lawyers for the "GSP coalition" brought them to my attention. Why did I listen? Because I listened to almost anyone who called or wrote me. (Foreigners did not always appreciate the easy access of most aides, reportedly paying PR intermediaries hefty fees on occasion to make unnecessary introductions.) The GSP pleaders were well informed, pleasant, and cogent, and they happened to represent important U.S. firms that benefited from low-priced imports. They were also clever: Knowing the crowded schedule of a Hill aide, they suggested lunch, and a couple of times we met at 209-½, one of the Hill's best restaurants. The food was good, but I found the greater attraction to be the opportunity to learn something in a convenient and relaxing way. Invitations to lunch with lobbyists came almost daily, but I could manage them only once or twice a week. Even so, I felt like a café-society habitué: It would be rare to walk through such popular Capitol Hill haunts as the Monocle, La Colline, or La Brasserie at noontime and not see numerous of my fellow aides similarly engaged.

In the international trade area our benefactors were a mixed group: representatives of the American steel or textile industries, agricultural or banking associations, the governments of Australia, Korea, and even Bangladesh. Their purpose, of course, was not always to impart information but often to gather it. I might be expected to sit back and discourse on the congressional process, providing tidbits of insight into the potential fate of legislation they found of interest. Sometimes the underlying purpose seemed simply to get acquainted for possible use on future occasions: I might return a call more quickly from someone I knew. (Or I might not, if I knew their purpose. I did make it a point, eventually, to phone everyone back, perhaps not a universal principle among Hill aides to judge from the embarrassingly profuse thanks I sometimes received for doing so.) Occasionally an attempted persuasion backfired: A newly acquired interest in the subject would motivate me to go to other sources to learn more and I would discover another side to the issue that had not been originally disclosed.

The Bentsen bill passed the Finance Committee on a vote of 19–1. It was still not acceptable to the president, although the improvements made in markup permitted the administration to say that it formed a basis for further negotiation. Even Senator Packwood, who had offered free-trade objections at every turn, pronounced himself pleased by the progress, although he said he would support a presidential veto if the bill were not changed further during floor consideration or House-Senate conference. The last contribution during the committee phase would be an official report purporting to explain the intentions of members in approving the bill's provisions, an important source of "legislative history" as regulatory agencies and courts sought to interpret the meaning and enforce the operation of new trade laws in later years. Although report language liberally invokes "committee" sentiments, typically it is clear from its esoteric quality that the content is staff-conceived. One section, for example, tried to limit the holding of a controversial court decision that established the principle of "de facto specificity" in determining the countervailability of subsidies. The administration was at loggerheads on the issue with the ammonia-fertilizer industry, and I heard regularly from both sides pleading with me to convey (preferably in Senator Dole's name) that I either supported or opposed the "Cabot" decision. Had I actually taken the time to explain the matter to Senator Dole, he would very likely have questioned my sanity.

Now a strange sequence of events ensued. On the last day of markup, Senator Riegle of Michigan had begun to propose a Senate counterpart to the Gephardt amendment; auto unions, upset by Japanese imports, were a major political factor in his state. Bentsen had quickly dissuaded him out of concern that committee meetings that had gone so smoothly might be disrupted by such a large new controversy, even though it was considered unlikely that Riegle would prevail; by now the Gephardt amendment had been so roundly denounced in the intellectual community that it was losing steam even among more populist politicians. After brief debate Riegle withdrew, vowing to bring the matter to the floor instead. Relieved, members took turns praising his intentions but criticizing the amendment itself. Nonetheless Riegle maintained afterward that the committee had implied its support of efforts to construct a Gephardt-like amendment for the floor. Whether this was strictly true—a public colloquy between Riegle and Bentsen on the point had been somewhat ambiguous—was beside the point. Riegle had now enlisted the potent support of Senator Danforth.

Why Senator Danforth chose to become involved in such an incendiary effort remained obscure. Whenever Sue Schwab tried to inspire my enthusiasm for it, she said Danforth wanted to go to conference armed with an *alternative* to Gephardt lest the Senate be forced to accept Gephardt itself. My own instinct was different: that we would have more negotiating room going in completely opposed than with something similar. Others had a more political interpretation of motives: Danforth came from the same state as Gephardt. Gephardt was a dark-horse Democratic candidate for president, but there was speculation that, should he raise his visibility during the campaign and ultimately fail to achieve his goal, he might set his sights on Danforth's

Senate seat. Surely Gephardt would make much of his well-known amendment, and Danforth would need evidence of prominent involvement in the issue. A broad-based Senate proposal supported by Gephardt's fellow Democrats would at once demonstrate Danforth's effectiveness and discredit Gephardt's most visible legislative achievement.

Bentsen set the Riegle/Danforth process in motion by authorizing formal discussions among the staff of all Finance Committee members in the same manner as we had met to draft the original Bentsen bill. In seven laborious two-hour sessions twenty of us met around our familiar conference table debating the fine details of proposals for retaliatory schemes against Japanese imports. (The formulas we discussed would apply theoretically to any country, but it was clear which offender most aides had in mind.) All of us shared the frustration of our bosses that had brought us to this point: Administration efforts to pry open Japanese markets had been excruciatingly slow and of limited success; concessions won in one area were quickly offset by new problems in another. Beyond this our group divided sharply. Some wanted a sort of nuclear response. Riegle's aides, for example, proposed estimating the dollar value of U.S. imports foregone as a result of foreign barriers, and closing off our markets in equal amount. How these estimates would be made, by whom, and how America's own numerous trade barriers would be treated in the calculation, was not clear; what was evident was that Riegle's Detroit auto-industry constituents would not shed many tears over prohibiting (according to one number on the table) $20 billion a year of Japanese imports.

Others of us listened in alternating amusement and disbelief at the utterly mechanical and unrealistic nature of the ideas. A fellow aide told me he did not know which was worse: an incredibly convoluted proposal we discussed at one point or the fact that he actually had understood it! But few found it in our interests to complain. We were ultimately representing not ourselves but our bosses, public officials who hardly wanted to be thought soft on Japan, a country held in wide disfavor at the time for its trading practices. Never mind that the proposals might have aggravated rather than solved the problem; the premise that some action was necessary tempted us to suspend critical judgment. Indeed the intellectual integrity of our deliberations relied on circular assumptions: We were comforted in knowing that Chairman Bentsen had placed his imprimatur upon them; but of course he had done so in the belief that we would produce a responsible result. Still, our differences were great. Senators sitting in a room together might have been able to bridge them, but in fact most were only vaguely aware of our discussions and few of us felt pressure to reach agreement. If anything, Bentsen had promised only "best efforts." The discussions (for the time being) collapsed.

When the bill came to the Senate floor that summer, improvements continued to be made, although not always in highly deliberative fashion. On Section 201, Senator Packwood offered an amendment to restore the president's power to overturn an ITC decision if warranted by the "national economic interest." To critics this was code for discretionary reversals by the president, and they were determined to tie his hands; the proposal was solidly defeated, although not before staffers to committee Republicans had rounded up their bosses to offer Packwood grandiloquent speeches in support. Senator Bradley, a Democrat who agreed with Packwood on the substance, recognized that his political affiliation might give him better auspices to address the issue and proposed his own version of the amendment: that the president could reject an ITC decision if it would disproportionately harm the interests of the poor.

This was extraordinarily loose and loaded language, which had actually originated as a staff joke; it had been laughed about in discussions as a way of smoking out the hypocrisy of the 201 debate. Liberals, sensitive to union interests, tended to be the ones who supported limitations on presidential discretion, but who could allow himself to be recorded as opposing poor people? Incredibly Senator Bradley put it on the table, and the fact that he was a Democrat in good standing made others take it seriously; the amendment passed handily. The iron hot, conservative Senator Phil Gramm immediately offered a tongue-in-cheek variation: an exception for the interests of farmers. Bentsen, anxious to avoid another embarrassing vote, exercised his prerogative of accepting the change quietly on behalf of the committee. Thus were exceptions purposely created to swallow the rule. Packwood's side had won after all by clever indirection. And the staff, scurrying back and forth to the desk with new amendments and imagining endless variations on the gag, had been treated to a wonderful time.

Aside from these larger political issues, amendments as in markup focused on matters of constituent interest. Senator Baucus sought new "anticircumvention" standards that would impose duties equally on raw and processed products. Otherwise, he pointed out, duty due on Canadian hogs could be avoided by processing them first into ham and bacon before shipping them across the border. Baucus was known among staff as "the Boy Scout" for his fresh scrubbed appearance and sometimes breathlessly earnest manner; he also really seemed to know the subject himself. Senator Charles Grassley, who joined him in proposing the change, drew on examples from his own Iowa agricultural background, pointing out that fresh raspberries subject to duty could be brought in as frozen raspberries without duty, but his citations to sections of the Federal Register and "three-pronged" tests of the Commerce Department suggested a heavy reliance on staff and possibly, in turn, a staff reliance on the lawyerly prose of interested parties.

One of staff's important functions was to flag for their bosses opportunities that the trade bill presented to fight for local groups. Thus with obvious staff guidance Boren of Oklahoma sought to extend the voluntary-restraint agreement on steel to cover steel-wire fabric and welded wire-mesh products, and Congressman Thomas Daschle of South Dakota proposed an increase in duty on casein, a competitor of his state's milk producers. Minnesota senators were concerned about the importation of furs from Russia. California senators wanted to equalize customs duties on tuna packed in water and tuna packed in oil and to have the ITC treat certain grape growers as part of the wine industry for purposes of bringing unfair trade cases against France and Italy. Domenici of New Mexico, protective of his state's copper and aluminum interests, talked of rules having to do with "expanded plant capacity to produce nonagricultural fungible commodities in times of world oversupply." And Senator Hollings, representing an important roller-bearing firm in his state of South Carolina, spoke passionately about the need to eliminate an ITC standard known as the "exporter's sales price offset." In a "Dear Colleague" letter sent around at the time, he explained that the existing statute "provides that in an antidumping investigation, when the foreign producer has sold the product in this country through a related party, the Department of Commerce shall deduct from the price at which the product is sold to the first nonrelated customer in the United States all commissions and other expenses incurred by the related party importer in selling the merchandise." Although in theory a personal communication from one senator to his ninety-nine fellow members, the document was sufficiently opaque to know it could have been written, and read, only by staff.

In the midst of floor action the Riegle effort again reared its head. Many of us had thought it moribund and assumed Danforth and Bentsen's continuing support to be perfunctory. Apparently not, for Danforth approached Dole on the floor one day and, all my previous arguments to the contrary, convinced him that Republicans "needed" an alternative to Gephardt—whereupon Dole agreed to "work something out." A few minutes later Dole told me of his conversation and suggested I get together with Danforth's staff. I phoned Sue Schwab, who confirmed that her boss was willing to press Riegle for changes if my boss would come on board. Dick D'Amato of Senator Byrd's staff then contacted me to say his boss would be interested in joining Dole in an unspecified "leadership amendment," although he cautioned that Riegle might not budge much further. I assumed this to be a mere opening, but much coordinated, position; Dick and Sue were good friends, and I could tell the bargaining was about to begin.

I worked on language for a proposal, soliciting ideas from USTR lawyer Judy Bello and former Dole aide Claud Gingrich (whom I used as a sounding board on occasion because he had also been a Reagan trade official). Hastily we devised an alternative to the original Riegle/ Danforth proposal: unpleasant still but, in our opinion, infinitely more workable. Over lunch in the staff dining room of the Capitol, Claud and I presented it to Sue, and to our surprise she readily agreed to consider it. Evidently we had more negotiating leverage than we realized; the proposal was so far from her starting point that we assumed she might well reject it out of hand. I had several further conversations with her, but within a day she had made only minor changes and pronounced it acceptable.

Sue's acquiescence, it turned out, did not seal the matter. She volunteered to take our informal outline to legislative counsel for translation into statutory language. En route, attempting to be helpful, she fleshed out the wording a little more herself. When it reached me later, I realized that a key word was different from what I had agreed to; I saw no choice but to object categorically since in the meantime I had recommended acceptance to Dole based on the original understanding, and he would be counting on me to defend our position forcefully. Moreover I was convinced of the genuine virtue of our wording from a trade-policy point of view, and as a practical matter based on Judy's reactions it seemed the only possible way of avoiding virulent White House opposition. I considered it in Dole's interest to take account of USTR views, since they could well influence senators' votes. If I seemed overly solicitous, my actions were nothing compared with Senator Riegle's, who at one point had reportedly assembled union lawyers in a room near the Leader's office to help the Danforth team inspect our potential agreement. At the beginning of this book I described the denouement of our late-night negotiations during which our forces ultimately conceded the other their position.

The bright side was that at least this decided the matter, allowed us to go home for the night, and the next day caused the politics to fall almost effortlessly into place. Byrd now swung his forces behind Riegle, seeing general Democratic advantage in the outcome; he joined Dole in offering a bipartisan leadership amendment, which passed overwhelmingly. "Super 301" became a centerpiece of the trade bill, and everyone was happy: Riegle and Danforth had something to show for their efforts, Bentsen and Byrd had earned their gratitude for helping, Dole could boast of having made a major contribution to the bill, and the administration could be thankful that the Senate had not passed something worse.

The floor statement I handed Dole as he rose to pronounce victory took a moderate tone, suggesting that Super 301 was not the "son of Gephardt," as critics had charged, nor "a cousin or stepchild, but an alternative." A sympathetic view of the entire bill seemed appropriate for that matter, since Dole had cosponsored all its various versions and continually urged their passage. A conciliatory approach might have been expected even of the administration; although originally opposed, it had for the previous several months advertised a new willingness to cooperate. The final Senate legislation had been greatly modified during its journey, and in almost all respects was far more modest than in its initial incarnations. Conditions seemed propitious for a grand congressional-executive compromise.

At the eleventh hour, however, Treasury Secretary Baker requested that Senate Republicans stand fast against it. His expressed rationale was that sizable opposition would demonstrate the Senate's ability to sustain a presidential veto and strengthen the hand of those who would seek in conference to bring the bill still closer to administration objectives. Unfortunately little preparatory work had been done, and only twenty-eight negative votes could be corralled, short of the thirty-four needed to sustain a veto. At Dole's request I now drafted an explanatory statement enumerating as many questionable elements of the bill as possible, even though they had not in truth influenced his decision. For all the fanfare of the Byrd/Dole amendment, in the end we tried to defeat the very piece of legislation that contained it.

The Senate went to conference with the House in the fall of 1987, where the bill remained the better part of a year. It was a mammoth production; two hundred House members and thirty-four senators were assigned as conferees. (By comparison, the milestone trade bills of 1962 and 1974 were ironed out by seven members from each body.) When I walked into the first conference session in one of the Capitol's largest caucus rooms, so many participants stood around that I wondered for a moment if it was to be a reception rather than a formal business meeting. Subsequently it divided into seventeen subconferences, but bureaucracy was not the only thing that stalled the proceedings. The crash of the stock market in October made congressmen think twice about enacting legislation that Wall Street continually denounced as "protectionist." (Congressmen rejected that characterization, even if they strove more to avoid the label than the deed.) By mid-February it was rolling again, as the two chambers exchanged offers and counter-offers.

Dole declined to be a conferee; he was preparing to take his leave to Iowa and New Hampshire, and he wanted in any case to give his place to Senator Chafee, who seemed to think the actions he could take as a conferee might be useful in his pending Rhode Island reelection campaign. As a result I had little involvement and, as I shall describe, moved on to other things. Staff have a particularly important role in conference, where the details of final compromises are everything; those who have followed the bill from beginning to end are invaluable in crafting the trade-offs that resolve impasse. Meanwhile members are often involved only in the occasional meetings that approve staff efforts, making their decisions as much on the basis of political deals and calculations as on intensely debated intellectual merit.

The administration was included somewhat more in the conference phase than before. At one interagency meeting where he reported initial success in moderating congressional positions, USTR official Alan Holmer turned to Tom Moore, a member of the Council of Economic Advisers, who saw virtually no redeeming qualities in the legislation. "How well did we do, Tom?" Alan asked. "Too well, I think," Tom replied, meaning that, despite his own sentiments, the bill might now pass presidential muster. Even so, on the last day of the conference, March 31, everything boiled down to four people sitting in Room H-106 of the Capitol: Ways and Means Chairman Rostenkowski and his aide Rufus Yerxa, and Lloyd Bentsen and aide Jeff Lang. "Rosty" was inclined to include administration representatives, but not Bentsen. It was, perhaps, the entire universe they needed: Rosty and Bentsen knew the politics better than anyone else in Congress, and Rufus and Jeff knew every line of their bills. Final decisions were made, and subsequent approvals of conference committees and chambers were virtually pro forma.

So much of the bill was technical that, when the president was forced to explain his continuing opposition, he cited a provision added on in the broader "competitiveness" debate mandating advance notice of factory closings, an issue that was easy to grasp. When Congress later removed the offending section, Reagan had little choice; Vice President Bush did not wish unnecessary controversies to dog him in the approaching election. Reagan signed the bill into law in August 1988, a considerable political success for all sides. Whether it would do any good was another question.

29

REFLECTIONS AND AFTERLIFE

Some years back, one of Senator Dole's aides had occasion to deliver remarks before a group while the senator sat nearby on the dais. After the aide had spoken a few minutes, the senator passed him a note in his rather illegible handwriting, which the aide, glancing quickly, had trouble reading. Looking again, he decided that it said, "More detail." With his boss just a few feet away, he had no choice but to comply. He reached back into his memory and began to recall anecdote after anecdote about the issues under discussion. Much later he concluded his presentation and returned to his seat, passing a frowning Senator Dole. The aide sat down and pulled the note from his pocket to examine it again. He stared and stared, trying to make it out. Finally it dawned on him: The note said not "more detail" but "move faster."

Rod DeArment, a former Dole aide and now deputy secretary of labor, swears this happened, and I don't doubt it. It is precisely the job of aides to guess what their bosses want, but it would be surprising if they always got it right. Senators are busy people and give them only quick and skeletal direction; yet their aides' actions have consequences all the same. It has become commonplace to question whether congressional aides have become too powerful. I am not sure that is the real issue. It implies an abuse of authority, as if their bosses have not delegated them the power they exercise. Yet I think their bosses know well their power and generally *want* them to use it, even if they don't control it very closely. The real question that large staffs raise is how powerful Congress itself should be.

A modest example of the issue? Of all the lobbyists who plied Capitol Hill, my favorite were the chocolate manufacturers, who sought help in reducing excessive Japanese tariffs that inhibited the export of their candies. It was a virtuous and easy position to support, especially since they sent Hill offices unending supplies of one-pound bags of M & M's to sweeten our consideration. I personally wrote letter after letter in my boss's name making polite demands of the Japanese; Dole would hardly have taken the initiative himself, but he had no problem approving mine. One day Prime Minister Nakasone, on a state visit to Washington, arrived on Capitol Hill for a private meeting with the two Senate leaders; around a small table with him sat Senators Byrd and Dole and U.S. ambassador to Japan Mike Mansfield; a couple of staff aides sat discreetly on the side. Trade relations with Japan were tense, and we nervously awaited Nakasone's words. What momentous issues would he address: Steel? Autos? Electronics? The yen-dollar exchange rate? After diplomatic pleasantries he came to his point; he had an olive branch to offer. We leaned forward to hear more. What could it be? Knowing both senators' acute interest in the issue, he said, he had ordered a reduction in the . . . chocolate tariff.

Inevitably the consequence of large staffs is that they empower Congress to take a broader and more detailed role in policymaking, often reflecting the interest of aides as much as that of members. Traditionally the legislative branch is referred to as a deliberative body, but now it has become a sort of alternate administration. It has more employees than work in the Pentagon, the world's largest office building. Question the need for so many and you will be reminded of a presidential policy you don't like and how the Hill is nobly fighting against it. Of course Congress should stand up to executive abuses and unpopular policies, but how routine should its other battles be? It is as if some are saying if you didn't like the results of the last presidential election and wish now to reverse administration policy in a particular area, all you need do is come to the Hill and find a sympathetic congressman or staffer to hear your appeal. Some defend the size of congressional staff by pointing to the growth in the executive branch, as if there should be a ratio because the Congress is a *miniature* executive branch.

How is it we wish to govern? I suspect most people would say they want Congress to debate and decide the big issues; yet members are now pulled in so many different directions that they have surprisingly little time left to engage in thoughtful deliberation. There are few dramatic floor debates anymore where a chamber full of legislators actually sit listening to speeches, weighing issues, and deciding how to vote. Do congressmen need so many aides because they're so busy? Yes, of course. But why are they so busy? Could it be because their aides are giving them so much to do? Maybe it is no coincidence that at the same time there are complaints about the small things congressmen have become involved in—"micromanagement" of executive-branch policy, daily intervention with agencies in the name of "constituent service," constant newsletters, bills, and press releases geared toward reelection, staff-ghosted speeches to interest groups and honoraria givers—there are also increasing complaints that they do not take time to deal with big issues like the budget. Nor are they under much pressure to do so from constituents who enjoy all these same small things pouring out of their offices.

Shortly after I left Dole, I wrote a couple of articles about staff, perhaps too provocatively, arguing a version of "smaller is better": Congress might be more efficient with leaner staffs. (Not to mention the issue of unfair incumbent advantages: There is a reason that congressmen are reelected at a rate greater than members of the Supreme Soviet before Gorbachev.) Friends in the House said, "That's true in the Senate." In the Senate they said, "That's true in the House." Friends on personal staffs said, "That's true on committee staffs"—and, again, vice versa. At least one member of Congress objected. Congresswoman Patricia Schroeder (D-Col.), chairman of the House subcommittee that reviewed legislative appropriations, actually took to the House floor to rebut my contentions. I regarded her as an able representative and was gratified that, whatever her viewpoint, she was at least elevating the issue to greater attention. I called her office to leave an appreciative message. Her press secretary said, "Oh, you don't want Mrs. Schroeder. You want Andy Feinstein of the Civil Service Subcommittee, who wrote her speech." I groaned, and smiled.

The leadership offices were a crossroads of Congress, but they remained obscure to the rest of humanity. Guided tours of the Capitol would pause every fifteen minutes in the corridor outside, and as I entered our suite through a side door, the snippets of lectures I heard always struck me as incongruous. Visitors would be told the number of light bulbs in the largest chandelier, how much it weighed, and how long it took to clean, when only a few feet inside our door, unknown to tourists, the true workings of the Capitol were on display.

It was easy to have smug feelings of power knowing this, but they were as illusory as the Capitol tours. One of the ironies of the Hill is that congressmen and their staffs—elected and unelected representatives of "the people"—are in fact so exalted. They are used to summoning others and having them hop, dealing with issues that affect the lives of many people, involve large amounts of money (or at least excite the interest of expensive lawyers), and are reported in the newspapers. You imagine Washington to be the center of the world and the Hill to be the center of Washington. It is hard at times to empathize with ordinary citizens. But after a while, for these very reasons, the Hill begins to seem unreal and you find yourself thinking maybe it would be nice, certainly a little more relaxing, to be back on the outside looking in.

I was getting older—thirty-five by the end of my term with Dole in late 1987—and these thoughts were growing keener. Moreover we were on the verge of the presidential primaries and the office was shifting into high campaign gear. As much as I supported Senator Dole's quest, this was not the existence I had come back to the Hill to lead. I would be writing political speeches, perhaps even conscripted to help in New Hampshire hauling voters to the polls; I would certainly not be needed at this point for trade legislation.

Once again I thought about alternatives. The most obvious was the administration, but no doubt the White House personnel office would still have qualms about me. I had joked on coming to work for Dole that at last I might rise above my Anderson background. One is remembered in Washington for his last notable association with a public figure, no matter how many other experiences have intervened. For years—and even still—acquaintances will ask, "So how's John Anderson?" expecting that we are still in as much contact as before. (I see him perhaps once or twice a year.) It was hard to imagine that Dave Stockman, who had worked for Anderson twice as long as I did, would ever be asked. The solution? Go work for someone more famous. In fact the Dole experience did seem to divert attention and cleanse me briefly of my dubious background as an independent. But I had traded one liability for another. The personnel vigilantes in Reagan's White House were supporting Bush over Dole, I learned, and it was now the *Dole* entry on my record that raised eyebrows. Well, that was progress.

Alan Holmer at USTR talked to me about succeeding Judy Bello as deputy general counsel. Both were scheduled to move up a notch in the hierarchy, and I would have been pleased to join them. Unfortunately Judy, immensely talented and in tune with President Reagan's trade philosophy though she was, lacked proper political credentials and would be kept waiting nearly a year for her new post. I did not have equal patience, especially when an old friend, Alan Woods, became administrator of the Agency for International Development and asked me to be his general counsel. The White House nixed this, again on political grounds, but then Alan asked whether I would like to come aboard briefly as "special counsel" (a position he could appoint without personnel-office clearance) to organize a task force to review the financial management of the $6 billion U.S. foreign-aid program. I was delighted to, at last learning the halls of the State Department which for so many years had intrigued me. Months later, when the task force completed its work, I left by prearrangement to become assistant to the chairman of a large Washington-based corporation; still adventurous in my job inclinations, I had become eager to see how private enterprise worked. Even later, I would establish my own legal practice.

I tried to help Dole, then Bush, in small, extracurricular ways, but being absorbed in work outside of government made it difficult. In January 1989 my wife and I, with half of Washington, trooped down the Mall toward the West Front of the Capitol to witness the inauguration of a new president. Although we had tickets to a reserved section, so did thousands of others, and from where we stood, the participants in the ceremony were only faint specks. I was relying now on the clout of my wife, an administration official, for seating privileges rather than bothering my old colleagues at the Capitol; I had forgotten that if something takes place at the Congress, it is of course congressional offices that have the real influence.

The moment was not only historic but, for an unsated political junkie, exciting. A new era in Washington was about to begin, and the president was setting out fresh plans and hopes in the shadow of the huge Capitol dome, where I had spent so much of my adult life. Off to the left was the Robert Taft carillon, whose chimes at fifteen-minute intervals I had heard so often in warmer weather when I lunched on the spacious lawns around the Senate office buildings. To the right I saw the Department of Health and Human Services building, which I remembered years before being dedicated to Hubert Humphrey, and above it the Rayburn House Office Building, the complex internal geography of which it had taken so long to learn. Did it still have a Library of Congress outlet next to the carryout, I found myself wondering, thinking of the next time I might visit there? The whole area seemed like an ancestral home.

I thought back to the previous inaugurations I had attended of presidents Carter and Reagan. In a few days the papers would be filled with ambitious new proposals, gossip about political infighting, and the predictions and commentary that I used to debate so vigorously with my co-workers. I thought of the late-nighters they would soon be facing, but also of the exhilaration and satisfaction. And now I squinted again to make out the dais; I knew the leaders of Congress would all be up there, including Senator Dole, who had just been reelected Republican Leader. The great imposing presence of the moment was not that of any individual—for from this distance I could not identify a single one—but that of the mammoth, stately, majestic Capitol dome, symbol of a country and, to me, of much else. I thought of all the time I had spent on the Hill, and of my decision to leave. My head told me I had done the right thing—but my heart, I confess, remained behind.

INDEX